SUPERMARINE
FIGHTER AIRCRAFT

VICTOR F. BINGHAM
I. Eng (CEI), AMRAeS, AFSLAET

Illustrations by Lyndon Jones MCSD

The Crowood Press

First published in 2004 by
The Crowood Press Ltd
Ramsbury, Marlborough
Wiltshire SN8 2HR

www.crowood.com

British Library Cataloguing-in-Publication Data
A catalogue record for this book is available from the British Library.

ISBN 1 86126 649 9

Typeset by D & N Publishing
Lowesden Business Park, Hungerford, Berkshire.

Printed and bound in Great Britain by CPI Bath.

Contents

Acknowledgements

As with most books of an aviation technical nature, the author is dependent on the perusal of technical reports as well as the expertise of personnel at technical establishments. That the A&AEE and RAE Farnborough over the years, pre- and post-war, have been in the forefront of aviation research and knowledge is well known, and I am indebted to the personnel of those establishments. This book is based on the author's own records, with help from personnel involved within the aviation industry, the above establishments and the RAF. I would like to thank all who contributed, no matter how small their help.

Special thanks go to the following, not in alphabetical or preferential order: Denis Goode and staff at main library archives at RAE Farnborough; Brian Kervell, Curator of the RAE Farnborough Museum; the staff of the RAF Museum archives; the staff of the Public Record Office, Kew; David Birch and the Rolls-Royce Heritage Trust; the late Ken Fozard of Rolls-Royce; John Wood, ex-RAF and civil pilot; A.W. Paterson and B. Buckley, ex-RAF Spitfire pilots; W.G. Molyneux of RAE Farnborough; the late Robert Page, ex-Westland and Folland. P.W. 'Paddy' Porter ex-RAF, and Group Captain J. Wray DFC RAF Retd; Group Captain G. Storey, Group Captain N. Walpole, Geoff Marlow, Phil Crawshaw and Peter Adair, all ex-2nd TAF Swift pilots.

Many thanks also to Mike J. Corner, ex-RAF pilot, for his most extensive and professional write-up on the Swift and its performance/handling parameters based on his piloting experience. Also to Brian Buss for a comprehensive set of notes and information on Tiltman Langley Laboratories' design involvement with Supermarine on the Type 535/Swift airframe.

I would also like to thank John Wood for reviewing and correcting the manuscript where applicable to the Spitfire, and to thank my friend and illustrator, Lyndon Jones, for his continual support and for supplying fine drawings at my request, often at short notice. Photographic contributions are credited under the photographs concerned. Opinions expressed in this book, unless otherwise attributed to some other person or document, are the author's, so compliments or brickbats should be heaped on my head alone.

Victor F. Bingham

Introduction

This book describes the period in Supermarine's history from the birth of the Spitfire to the demise of the Swift, with a short résumé of the Supermarine's last design, the Scimitar. It is a critical assessment of the company's designs from that period, its main aim being to correct a number of misconceptions about the Supermarine fighter aircraft and instead to spell out the true facts. Most books on the Spitfire celebrate its superb flying capabilities, and some foster various myths that have grown up around it. However, few authors delve into the Spitfire's full technical and flying history to describe the large amount of development work that Joseph Smith and his design team did in modifying the airframe designed by R.J. Mitchell. Nor do many say much of the problems encountered in making it a satisfactory flying machine and fighter over a number of years. This results in the layman being under the impression that the Spitfire was perfect from the start. The same things apply to the adverse statements about the Supermarine aircraft that followed the Spitfire.

The following chapters describe the technical development at Supermarine, from the Spitfire to the final version of the Swift. It is not, however, the intention of the author to go into all the testing of the Spitfire series, as Jeffrey Quill has done this more than adequately in his book *Spitfire – A Test Pilot's Story*.

Supermarine was formed in June 1914 by Noel Pemberton-Billing as a limited company at Woolston, Southampton. Experimenting with various landplane designs, as well as the PB.7 single-seat flying boat, the firm became established in the aviation scene during the First World War.

The name Supermarine has become synonymous with high-speed performance, mainly because of the Schneider Trophy racing seaplanes of the 1930s and the Spitfire fighter. The fact that the bulk of its designs between the two World Wars were mundane flying boats of stately appearance is usually forgotten. Likewise, the Spitfire is synonymous with RAF Fighter Command in the Second World War, but few remember that it evolved from the mediocre Type 224 monoplane, an aircraft that was beaten in the Specification F.7/30 competition by a biplane, the Gloster Gladiator. Nevertheless, since 1939 the name Supermarine Spitfire has been associated with high-speed performance and good handling for the period.

Supermarine had been absorbed into the Vickers-Armstrongs' empire during 1928, and renamed Vickers-Armstrongs (Supermarine Works). Unfortunately for British aircraft designers during the late 1920s and the early 1930s, Great Britain's political leaders desired entrenchment, not advancement, with the result that new aircraft designs were but slight variations on past designs. Furthermore, as there was a large amount of First World War-surplus equipment in stock, such as bombs, bombsights, gunsights, machine guns and so on, these had to be used whether the aircraft designer liked it or not.

Therefore, the prospects for new or advanced aircraft were few, and until Hitler came to power in 1933 no design of any importance appeared. By this time the monoplane was being viewed more favourably in the fighter role than before, but there was still no suitably powerful engine, and no viable variable-pitch propeller, in production in Great Britain. The latter issue was only resolved in 1937, when de Havilland bought the production rights of the Hamilton Standard variable-pitch propeller and Rotol was formed by the engine manufacturers Rolls-Royce and Bristol.

Supermarine's designer during this period was R.J. Mitchell. His final design was the Spitfire, the result of which he saw fly in prototype form shortly before his early death. His position as Chief Designer was taken over by Joseph Smith who, with his design team, was then responsible for the development of the basic Rolls-Royce Merlin-engined Spitfire airframe into a variety of fighter marks far beyond the original design as envisaged by Mitchell. A further development was the Seafire, built to a naval requirement, and Spitfire versions powered by the Rolls-Royce Griffon engine.

With the Spitfire series, Supermarine reached their pinnacle of piston-engined aircraft performance. The company followed the Griffon-engined Spitfire with the Spiteful and Seafang near the end of the Second World War. However, their low-drag, laminar-flow wings produced handling problems, and they appeared at a time when the changeover from the piston engine to the gas turbine was taking place, and interest was lost in new piston-engined fighter designs. This was also a period of change from war to peace, and the perusal of reports from captured German research establishments was upsetting the design parameters of research and design teams in Great Britain, causing the new Labour Government to go into a panic in decision-making about where best to spend money.

This was followed by a period when the government appeared on the one hand to be more intent on creating a socialist utopia than the defence of the nation, yet on the other hand developed the British atom bomb as a prestige project – without a modern bomber to carry it. The post-war Air Staffs appeared to be intent on equipping the RAF with a never-ending series of dated Vampire and Meteor fighters, whether to the diktats of their political masters or for economic reasons it is not known.

LEFT: *The Supermarine Seagull II amphibian, powered by a Napier Lion engine.* R.E. SMITH

BELOW: *The Supermarine Stranraer flying boat, powered by two Bristol Pegasus Mk X engines.*

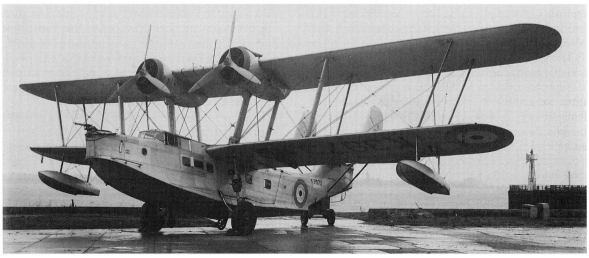

This book is mainly intended as an appraisal of the company's history from Spitfire to Swift, where in the end the company's fighter aircraft following the Spitfire did not measure up to it in gaining government orders of any great size. It is also an appreciation of the problems facing Supermarine's Joseph Smith: at the start of the Second World War from a shortage of skilled workers; and post-war from the Air Staff, the new Labour Government's defence spending restrictions and the changing aviation scene. Smith had the unenviable task of taking over the design reins of Supermarine on the death of R.J. Mitchell, the creator of the Spitfire, and so has remained in Mitchell's shadow, even though it was Joe Smith and his team who developed the basic Spitfire airframe into a production fighter and followed it with developments and marks never envisaged by Mitchell.

The Spitfire and its great rival during the Battle of Britain, the Messerschmitt Bf 109, have become legends in their respective countries. Each was an excellent aeroplane, the result of their design teams' knowledge, based on the information and structural designs of the period; likewise, both had their faults. Over the years facts and myths have become so entwined that the post-war British generations have come to regard the Spitfire as the ultimate piston-engined fighter. It is to be hoped that the following chapters will destroy the myths, for the Spitfire can stand on its own merits as a classic fighter aircraft of the period.

Post-1945, the Supermarine flight-test establishment was based at Chilbolton airfield in Hampshire, approximately 10 miles north-west of Winchester. This flight-test section was relatively small and at the start included four test pilots: Mike Lithgow (Chief Test Pilot), Les Colquhoun, Guy Morgan and Peter Roberts.

There have certainly been criticisms of the Spiteful, and of the Attacker and Swift jet fighters that followed it from Supermarine, yet at this time other aviation firms were also struggling with aerodynamic problems, or hanging back from embarking on advanced designs. As a result of the lack of orders and the dated aircraft in RAF service, when the confrontation occurred between the Western Allies and the USSR over Berlin in 1948, followed by the Berlin Airlift, Great Britain had no viable or modern fighter in service. It was only with the return of a Conservative Government in 1951 that 'super-priority' orders were placed for new fighter aircraft designs. The failure to put an advanced fighter design into production

earlier in the post-war period eventually resulted in the expensive purchase of the North American Aviation F-86 Sabre as an operational necessity.

In 1945 Specification E.10/44 was issued for an experimental jet fighter that could possibly replace the Vampire and Meteor, yet it only seemed to be the catalyst to spawn even more versions of those two aircraft. Supermarine's proposal to E.10/44 was a project that matched the Spiteful's low-drag wing to a circular-section fuselage of quite clean lines. This was originally known as the 'Jet-Spiteful' and was relatively simple, strong and conventional, even having a tailwheel undercarriage. It failed to interest the RAF but was developed into the Attacker and accepted by the Royal Navy as their first carrier-borne jet fighter; it was also bought by the Pakistan Air Force.

The trouble with most post-war British single-seat fighter aircraft was that they were cast in the mould of pre-Second World War interceptors and carried little fuel internally, so to achieve the range of the equivalent US fighters of the period it was necessary to attach overload fuel tanks. The Attacker, Hunter, Swift and Lightning were no different in this respect, all requiring the addition of overload fuel tanks for operations away from the interceptor role. It would appear that with the Attacker no thought was given during its development to the possibility of increasing the range by internal wing tankage or by pinion tanks. Instead, the palliative of a 250-gallon drop tank was added under the fuselage, which would be repeated by English Electric on the Lightning.

The Attacker was used by Supermarine as the basis for a research vehicle with swept wings, the Type 510, which led to the swept-wing Type 535 with a tricycle undercarriage. As the Type 535, during development, seemed to offer the basis for a high-speed, swept-wing fighter in the F-86 Sabre category, it was tendered against specification F.3/48, and was ordered mainly as a back-up in case of failure of the Hawker Hunter design, which at one point seemed a possibility.

Contractor's trials showed up a number of deficiencies in the flight performance of both the Hunter and the Swift. However, it was decided to go ahead with development of both types, due to the Royal Australian Air Force's experiences operating outdated Gloster Meteors against MiG-15 fighters in the Korean War in 1950. The potential of the Swift F.1 was spoilt by the fact that it mounted only two 30mm Aden cannon, against the Hunter's four, although some experts argued that four 30mm cannon was

The Supermarine Works at Woolston 1922, with an early Seagull on slipway.
R.E. SMITH

over-gunning an aircraft. The Swift's fixed tailplane was dated as it reduced the elevator's effectiveness when the aircraft went supersonic. The Swift did, however, using reheat, achieve the fastest time to 40,000ft (12,200m) of any British aircraft of the time.

Whether Supermarine's position post-war as part of the large Vickers-Armstrongs' empire had anything to do with the dated layout and slow development of the E.10/44, or whether it was inhibited by Vickers-Armstrongs' interest in the civil aviation market, which siphoned off finance from fighter development, is hard to judge as little has been made public about the demise of the major aeroplane manufacturers and their incorporation into British Aerospace. It has been suggested that many British senior design people 'burnt out' during the war years while developing and producing leading fighter aircraft, but so far as Joe Smith is concerned it would appear that this was not the case. The problem lay with the government's financial restraints and the Air Ministry's changing requirements, not too mention lack of research into high-speed flight over three years of the post-war Labour Government.

These factors were felt by many aircraft manufacturers, and many well-known firms worldwide would be absorbed into larger conglomerates or go bankrupt. The fact remains that Supermarine, in spite of disappointment in the interceptor field, rebuilt the Swift for the RAF's low-level photo-reconnaissance role and, like the Hawker Typhoon in the Second

World War, it was superb for these low-level tasks. It was followed by the Scimitar for the Fleet Air Arm, which on acceptance was demoted from fleet fighter to a 'jack of all trades and master of none'. Although the Scimitar is briefly included in the text, this is solely because it was Supermarine's last production aircraft, as it was in no way in the theme of fighter aircraft, and was even described in one instance as 'an over-powered flying brick'!

Along with the Supermarine story also goes Rolls-Royce's engine achievements, for they supplied the superb engines that powered Supermarine's aircraft from the Spitfire to the Swift. Having overcome early problems with the Merlin, Rolls-Royce improved its performance to the point of extracting a 'quart from a pint pot', so that in late 1941 the two-stage, two-speed Merlin had a performance at altitude greater than the larger and newer Griffon, with neither standard engine having to resort to various means of power boosting, as did the enemy's engines. Due to the design features of both the Merlin and Griffon they were adapted to tasks both at low level and at high altitude. Then, came the Nene and Avon turbojets, which also became great engines once the pangs of birth had been eliminated.

Data figures quoted are from RAE Farnborough and A&AEE Boscombe Down test reports, and Air Ministry or manufacturer's information. Opinions quoted are the author's, unless otherwise stated.

1
Origins of the Spitfire

The Type 224

The origins of the Spitfire lie in the issue of Specification F.7/30 in 1931, although some argue that they lie further back, with Supermarine's range of Schneider Trophy seaplanes. Certainly the aerodynamic information obtained from testing and racing these seaplanes, as well as the development of the Rolls-Royce engines that powered them, added to both Supermarine's and Rolls-Royce's knowledge. However, the seaplanes were racing aircraft and by no stretch of imagination could they have been converted into fighters from what they were.

There is no doubt that R.J. Mitchell was attempting at the time to apply the knowledge gained in designing and building the Schneider Trophy seaplanes to the design of a high-speed landplane fighter, which was a totally different proposition. Specification F.7/30, though it did not require a specific aircraft shape, set out requirements of engine, performance and armament as follows:

- the Rolls-Royce Goshawk engine;
- exceptional manoeuvrability;
- low landing speed and short landing run;
- maximum speed of more than 250mph (400km/h);
- higher performance than contemporary fighters;
- long endurance;
- steep climb-out on take-off; and
- four machine guns.

Among the companies tendering to F.7/30 were Hawker and Supermarine. Hawker's offered a monoplane version of the Hawker Fury fighter, which by October 1933 had progressed to a general design based on the prototype of the Fury II fighter, with a thick cantilever mainplane, a fixed, spatted undercarriage and four machine guns. Supermarine's project to the specification – the Type 224 – was a cranked

low-wing monoplane of not unpleasant appearance for the period, although a bit angular. It was initially based on a thin wing, unlike the Hawker design, yet emerged in practice with a relatively thick wing. The Type 224 has been described by some as a 'pedestrian' design, for it had a trousered fixed undercarriage, an open cockpit and four fixed Vickers 0.303in machine guns, two located in the fuselage synchronized to fire through the propeller and one on the inside of each undercarriage fairing.

The Rolls-Royce Goshawk engine was an 'evaporative', or steam-cooled, type, which in theory reduced the weight of coolant carried by letting it boil and then condensing the steam. It was hoped that this system would weigh less than the coolant and radiator of a normal system. In the Type 224, the leading edge of the mainplanes contained the condensers, reaching back to the main spar, with chord-wide corrugations to improve the condenser efficiency. Aft of the main spar, the mainplanes were fabric-covered.

The Type 224's fuselage was of semi-monocoque construction with formers, frames and longitudinal stringers covered by a stressed skin. Mitchell worked on various modifications to the design, including thinner and differently shaped mainplanes; he also toyed with changes to the wing fillets, and considered increasing the wing loading to 18lb/sq ft (87.86kg/sq m) and increasing the wing area. Most of these ideas got no further than the drawing board, although the cranked-wing design went through a series of modifications to the wing centre-section to improve lateral stability and the fin and rudder areas were increased to improve directional stability.

Having designed an aircraft he was not satisfied with, Mitchell then began to commit to paper a further development of the Type 224, still powered by the Goshawk engine. The revised design had mainplanes of smaller span that tapered towards the wingtip, both on the leading and trailing edges. Split trailing-edge landing flaps and a retractable undercarriage were also envisaged as part of the final design.

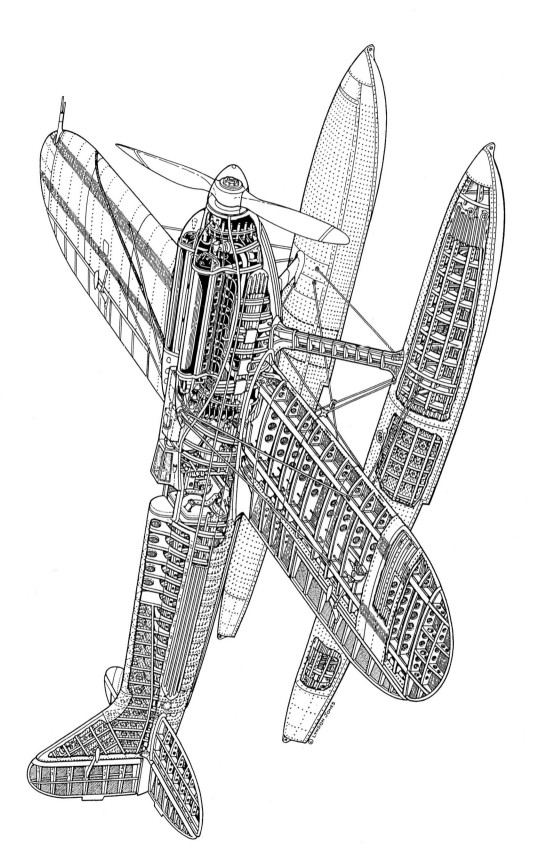

Supermarine S6B.

Twenty months elapsed between the arrival of 'Instructions to Proceed' from the Air Ministry and the Type 224's maiden flight on 19 February 1934. The general specifications of the Type 224 in its final form, and the performance it achieved, as determined by the A&AEE are summarized in the box (*below*).

The Type 224 was not successful in the F.7/30 competition, but neither were the other official contenders – this showed how right Mitchell was to start work on further developments. The contest was won by the private venture Gloster SS37, which became the Gladiator; even though it was a biplane and not powered by the Goshawk engine, it was awarded the contract. The Gladiator was 4mph (6km/h) faster than the Type 224 in level flight and took 1½ minutes less to climb to 15,000ft. After further tests at both RAE and A&AEE Martlesham Heath, the Type 224 served out its time as a 'hack' at Martlesham from 1937 until struck off charge.

Specification – Supermarine Type 224 (final form)

Engine	600bhp Rolls-Royce Goshawk
Weight	Empty 3,442lb (1,560kg); all-up 4,743lb (2,151kg)
Dimensions	Span 45ft 10in (13.97m); wing area 295sq ft (27.41sq m); wing loading 15lb/sq ft (73.22kg/sq m); length (tail up) 29ft 5¼in (8.97m); height (tail up) 11ft 11in (3.63m)
Performance	Maximum speed 228mph at 15,000ft (367km/h at 4,500m); climb to 15,000ft 9½min; absolute ceiling 38,800ft (11,600m); landing speed 60mph (100km/h)

A Supermarine S5 Schneider Trophy racing seaplane at Calshot. R.E. SMITH

The Supermarine Type 224, built to Specification F.7/30 and powered by the Rolls-Royce Goshawk engine. R.E. SMITH

Improved Armament

Sqn Ldr (later Air Marshal) Ralph Sorley of the Operational Requirements Department of the Air Ministry had, in the early 1930s, come to the conclusion that to destroy a modern, fast aircraft in a realistic engagement time it would be necessary to inflict fatal damage with a burst of gunfire lasting no more than two seconds. Working with Sqn Ldr Spreckley he demonstrated that, to achieve the necessary concentration of bullets, a minimum of eight machine guns in the wings of a fighter aircraft would be required. This was confirmed by experiments, which indicated that eight machine guns at a firing range of 400yd (370m) would do the necessary damage. In fact, during the Battle of France and the Battle of Britain it was found necessary for the Spitfire's machine guns to be re-harmonized for a range of just 250yd (230m) to achieve the maximum effect.

It had already been realized that the then-standard Vickers 0.303in fixed machine gun was not ideal for fitting in an aircraft's mainplane, as it was relatively unreliable: it needed to be within reach of the pilot so he could deal with any stoppages. It was also decided that a weapon with a greater rate of fire

would be necessary for the fighter aircraft of the future. Therefore a competition of various weapons, including foreign ones such as the Colt 0.5in and the Colt 0.3in, was arranged. The Colt 0.5in had a low rate of fire and suffered from high wear (its barrel life was reputed to be 7–8,000 rounds at that time), which militated against its use. While other makes from Europe were considered, none offered any improvement on the Vickers, although the Hispano-Suiza 20mm cannon was of future interest.

Therefore the choice was the Colt 0.30in machine gun, which was re-chambered for use with the British 0.303in rimmed cartridge and accepted into the RAF as the Browning. After trials its firing action had to be changed, so that when firing ceased the bolt was clear of the chamber. This was because in the original design, after firing ceased the bolt came forward and fed a round into the chamber; the heat of the barrel sometimes then 'cooked' the round and fired it off.

The Type 300 is Born

When the Bristol Type 142 prototype appeared (which was developed into the Blenheim light bomber), its high speed compared with the RAF fighters then in service clearly showed that it was essential to provide a fighter aircraft with greater speed to carry out an interception; the armament development referred to above was part of this re-appraisal of the situation. For by then the German Luftwaffe was introducing its own high-speed bomber prototypes such as the Dornier Do 17 and Heinkel He 70 and He 111. Also, during 1934 there was a controversy within the Air Ministry over fighter design, armament and tactics, and on 19 July 1934 an important conference was called at Air Ministry to discuss these questions. This conference included a number of senior officers as well as Sqn Ldr Sorley, who put forward the case for an eight-gun fighter. This was confirmed by Captain F.W. Hill, Senior Technical Officer (Ballistics) at A&AEE, with the results of extensive firing tests at A&AEE.

During this period, Specification F.5/34 had been issued, the first paragraph making clear the Air Ministry's awareness that there was now very little margin in speed between the modern high-speed bomber of the Blenheim/He 111 type and fighter aircraft of the RAF. It went on to say:

> This specification is issued, therefore, to govern the production of a day fighter in which speed in over-taking an enemy at 15,000ft, combined with rapid climb to this height, is of primary importance.

The specification also called for an armament of at least six, and preferably eight, machine guns. Although Supermarine did not tender to this specification, like other aircraft manufacturers they recognized that the armament requirements would be repeated in other fighter specifications – or even heavier weapons demanded.

In November 1934 Mitchell was refining his fighter design, with the approval of the Vickers (Supermarine) Board to build it as a private venture (PV). At the same time Rolls-Royce were developing their PV.12 engine, which promised an output of 1,000bhp in the future. The Air Ministry then issued, on 1 December 1934, Specification F.37/34 and a contract for the Supermarine PV fighter. (A separate Specification, F.36/34, covered a PV design by Hawker's, which became the Hurricane.)

Specification F.37/34 still required the use of the Goshawk engine; yet it was obvious that its evaporative cooling system, with its large area of condensers spread across the mainplane, was more vulnerable to enemy action than a normal liquid-cooled system.

However, the emergence of the Rolls-Royce PV.12 engine gave both Mitchell of Supermarine and Camm of Hawker the extra horsepower required. The evaporative cooling system was out, but dissipating the large amount of heat generated by the 1,000bhp of the new engine would require a new radiator design. This had already been solved by a scientist at RAE Farnborough named F.W. Meredith, who had headed the development of the ducted radiator. In this design the cooling air was expelled, giving a small amount of thrust; at the same time, by restricting the duct's exit area and so maintaining the dynamic pressure of air behind the radiator at high speed, the design reduced the drag.

Although Supermarine's design staff no doubt took notice of Meredith's report (R&M 1683), they failed to implement it fully. In the Spitfire's design, while positioning the radiator matrix partly buried in the wings, they only allowed two positions for the exit duct flap: either closed or fully open. In the fully open position the flap created considerable drag and overcooled the engine, thus failing to ensure a high-velocity exit. In short the Spitfire's duct exit, being only slightly smaller in area than the inlet, was too large. In later years Rolls-Royce Hucknall did modify one of their trial Spitfires with a variable radiator flap system that gave six positions between open and closed and, post-war, hand 'inching' controls were installed on a number of Merlin-powered aircraft.

With the issue to Supermarine on 1 December 1934 of a contract for the prototype (serial number K5054), the design was allocated the type number 300 to Specification F.37/34, which included the following requirements:

- the Rolls-Royce PV.12 engine;
- an airscrew of wooden construction;
- service load as specified in Specification F.7/30;
- all four guns could be installed outside propeller diameter; and
- tailwheel to be fitted if practicable.

The Rolls-Royce PV.12 (Merlin) Engine

During the early 1930s Rolls-Royce had begun the design of the PV.12 engine. The design studies were prompted by features introduced on the 'R' racing engine, which in turn had been developed from the Buzzard engine. The PV.12 engine was similar to the Buzzard in that it was a scaled-up Kestrel engine; it would require considerable development work to eradicate its defects, but would also have considerable development potential.

The PV.12 was originally intended by Rolls-Royce to be built as an inverted 'Vee' to allow a lower sight line over the cowling, but after the mock-up was demonstrated in 1932 there was apparently considerable opposition to this from the airframe manufacturers, causing Rolls-Royce to build the engine as an upright 'Vee' instead. Design work proper began in early 1933 as a private venture and the Air Ministry was kept fully informed of its development, although at that time no official development funds had been made available.

Early development work included redesign of the reduction gear and the strengthening of the block casting, and by July 1934 the PV.12 had passed its first type test with a rating of 790bhp at 12,000ft (3,700m) at a dry weight of 1,777lb (806kg). A new cylinder head was then introduced, known as the 'ramp head' as it had a shaped combustion chamber with two ramps of unequal width and inclination. This was intended to give a shortened flame travel and a high degree of turbulence of the charge in the combustion chamber. The ramp head was completed in October and introduced on two Merlin Bs that were built and tested in February 1935; on test, these engines delivered 950bhp. (PV.12 does not seem to have been named Merlin until the appearance of the B models.)

The next development concerned the monobloc casting of the crankcase cylinder block, which had proved unsatisfactory. It was decided to produce two separate castings, both to improve the casting process and to simplify the manufacture. This feature was incorporated on the Merlin C, which was tested in April 1935. Problems were by now being experienced both with the cooling system and the ramp head, the latter suffering from local detonation, cracks and exhaust valve fractures. Following this, the Merlin C failed its civil 50-hour type test and then a Merlin E failed its 100-hour military type test. Emergency measures were now taken to get the Merlin into service, so it was decided to scale up the standard Kestrel cylinder head to the Merlin size (creating the Merlin G) and an improved Merlin E, designated Merlin F, went into production with the type-test requirements relaxed. The first Merlin F (later designated Merlin I) failed

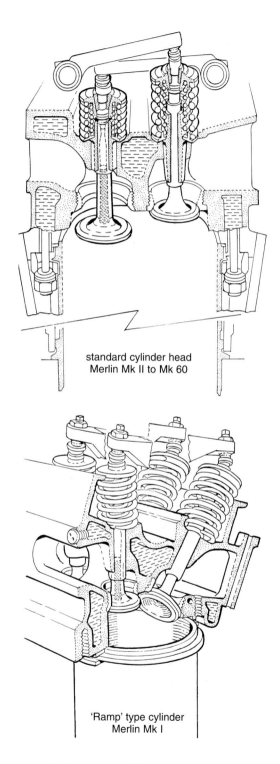

standard cylinder head
Merlin Mk II to Mk 60

'Ramp' type cylinder
Merlin Mk I

Merlin, sectioned different cylinder heads.

Specification – Rolls-Royce Merlin II

Bore and stroke	5.4 × 6.0in (137 × 152mm)
Cubic capacity	1,649cu in (27,022cc)
Compression ratio	6:1
Reduction gear ratio	0.477:1
Nett dry weight	1,335lb (605kg)
Fuel octane rating	87
International power rating	990bhp at 2,600rpm, +6¼psi boost at l2,500ft (3,800m)
Maximum power rating	1,030bhp at 3,000rpm, +6¼psi boost at 16,250ft (4,950m)

its relaxed type test in July 1936, but the Merlin G passed its type test with flying colours. Therefore the Merlin G went into production as the Merlin II and production of the Merlin I engines was restricted to 180 units, which were fitted to Fairey Battle light bombers.

The first production Merlin II was delivered in August 1937; it produced 1,030bhp at 16,250ft (4,950m) with a dry weight of 1,335lb (605kg). With the engine in service, coolant leaks from between the liner and coolant chamber were experienced, so work began in March 1938 on a new cylinder block with a separate head casting. However, with the need for mass production of the Merlin for the Hurricane and Spitfire fighters, the two-piece head was not introduced until the Merlin 60 series, although Packard-built Merlins incorporated it from the start of their production.

The Type 300, F.37/34 Aircraft

The prototype aircraft that was to be named Spitfire – a name apparently disliked by Mitchell – was under construction at Woolston. Even at this early stage it was undergoing a series of modifications. The final mock-up conference was held on 26 March 1935 at Woolston and by early January 1936 the prototype, which had been allocated the serial number K5054, was completed. The first test flight took place on 5 March 1936 from Eastleigh airfield with test pilot Joseph 'Mutt' Summers at the controls. For this flight the aircraft was powered by a Merlin C driving an Airscrew Company two-bladed, wooden propeller, and the undercarriage was locked down. Due to the propeller torque there was a tendency to swing on take-off, but Summers easily held it. Much has been made of the fact that on landing he requested that no adjustments should be made, but this was nothing extraordinary after a short test flight; the aircraft's handling would be quantified on subsequent early tests and then, if necessary, adjustments would be made. What came as a disappointment to Mitchell and his design team during following flights was that the aircraft failed to achieve the hoped-for 350mph (563km/h) – the best it could manage was 335mph (539km/h). A tight review was then undertaken of every part of the structure that might affect the airspeed, and a number of small alterations were incorporated, but it was only with the installation of a finer-pitch propeller that a major improvement came about: on the next test flight the aircraft reached 349.5mph (562.3km/h).

At first K5054 wore an all-silver colour scheme, but then was sprayed a light grey. Then, when exhibited at RAF Hendon in the New Types Park, a black number '2' was painted beneath the cockpit. At this stage it had a fixed tailskid.

Maximum speeds of Spitfire K5054

Height	True Air Speed (TAS)	Engine speed	Boost
10,000ft	330mph	2,785rpm	+6psi
16,800ft	349mph	3,025rpm	+6psi FTH
20,000ft	345mph	3,015rpm	+3psi
25,000ft	337mph	2,915rpm	0
30,000ft	324mph	2,760rpm	0

Supermarine test pilots carried out a programme of development testing, during which it was determined that K5054 with a Merlin C had a take-off run to clear a 50ft (15m) barrier of 480yd (440m), a service ceiling of 35,400ft (10,800m) and a landing run of 525yd (480m).

The aircraft was then sent at the request of the Air Staff to the Aircraft and Armament Experimental Establishment (A&AEE) at Martlesham Heath for a quick check as to the aircraft's suitability for use by average fighter pilots, although there was still considerable work to be done to the aircraft before it was acceptable to the Service as a fighter. At this stage it was still only a prototype airframe, not a fighter, and the engine was still a development Merlin; in 1937 the Merlin C was replaced by a Merlin F, though this was still not the production engine. Full handling trials were carried out at Martlesham Heath from 23 February 1937, when the height and speed figures in the table on the previous page were logged. The rate of climb at sea level was 2,400ft (730m) per minute, which was in excess of the specification figures.

Following further modifications and the addition of its eight 0.303in Browning machine guns, a gunsight and tailwheel, K5054 returned to Martlesham Heath on 23 October for production trials and was taken on RAF charge, Supermarine having been awarded an initial production order for 310 aircraft on 3 June 1936. By early 1937 it had been realized at the Air Ministry that if the Luftwaffe continued to expand at its present rate, then the provisions of Scheme F of the Expansion Scheme, which called for a front-line force of 1,736 aircraft by 1939, would not be achieved, and so parity with Germany would also not be achieved. Then, having rejected Scheme H due to the use of obsolescent aircraft in front-line units, Schemes J and K both became panic measures that were eventually replaced by Scheme L. This again was almost sheer panic, as it envisaged a front-line strength of 12,000 aircraft over a period of two years – providing a war occurred. Scheme L, for a change, placed the emphasis on fighter production, the immediate result being an order for 200 more Spitfires to complement the initial order of 310.

The Supermarine Chief Designer, R.J. Mitchell, succumbed to cancer on 11 June 1937 at just forty-two years of age, having seen his F.37/34 fighter design take to the air. Mitchell's position as Chief Designer was eventually taken over by Joseph Smith, who had previously been Chief of the Drawing Office. Smith was a thoroughly practical engineer,

Spitfire prototype K5054 with Jeffrey Quill; note the fixed-pitch propeller.

16

A 66 Squadron Spitfire I at Duxford in 1940 with Fg Off F. Rimmer. P.W. PORTER

and in his position had a deep understanding of the Spitfire concept, detail design and development – the ideal person to bring Mitchell's concept to practical fruition. As such, and thus in Mitchell's shadow, Smith was to develop the Spitfire into an operational fighter aircraft, to further develop and extend the airframe, and to redesign it to accept all manner of equipment and more powerful engines. His achievements with the Spitfire show that Joseph Smith was a brilliant designer in his own right, for which he has never really been given credit.

The Spitfire design was an aircraft of its time, without any doubt representing the end of one era and the start of another. Leaving behind the period of fabric-covered metal and/or wood airframes, the Spitfire was of all-metal, stressed-skin monocoque construction, yet its detail construction was still of the 1930s, with overlapping skin panels, dimple riveting and cowlings held on by metal fasteners that did not improve aerodynamics. Notwithstanding the latter, the Spitfire was aerodynamically an excellent design. However, the huge amount of curvature on the design of the wings, tail unit and fuselage made both manufacture of panels and assembly a nightmare, and in practice the build quality did not compare favourably with that of the much later North American P-51 Mustang. This was due partly to the haste with which aircraft had to be produced prior to and during the early war years, and

partly to the extensive use of unskilled labour drafted in from other industries.

A few points might be worth relating in regard to the early Spitfire I. To start with, the early Merlin engines were far from reliable. Also, because the flaps only had a 'down' position of 60 degrees and a two-point selection of 'down' or 'up', the approach to land was made with the – already quite long – nose high in the air. Later on the flap 'down' position was altered to 90 degrees, which improved vision on a landing approach. The ailerons were initially fabric-covered, and at speeds over 300mph (500km/h) they became almost immovable, with the aircraft tending to yaw to the right. The other problem concerned longitudinal stability, which was marginal and caused problems when the centre of gravity was at its aft limit. As a result of these problems, a number of bent wings occurred during testing, and some structural failures in service.

Early marks of Spitfire had hand-operated undercarriage retraction, which during the climb-away after take-off meant moving the left hand from the throttle lever to the control column and the right hand from the control column to operate the hand pump. The result of the pumping action with inexperienced pilots could be seen in the undulating climb-away flight!

As well as the problem of manufacturing a mainplane with elliptical – rather than straight or tapered

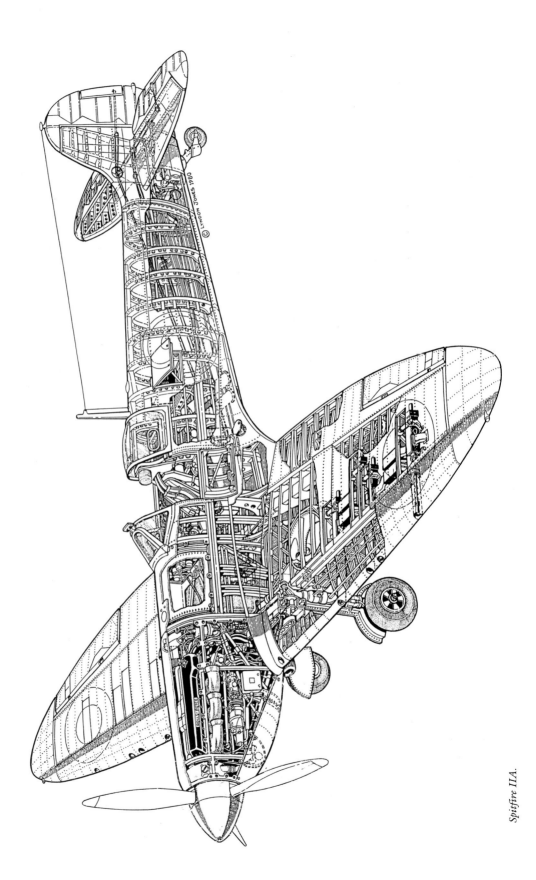

Spitfire IIA.

– leading and trailing edges, there was the problem of subcontracting to small firms and a shortage of machinery for bending and forming. The latter problem was due to the small orders issued to firms between the wars, which had forced them to operate on shoestring budgets and left them financially incapable of buying new or more sophisticated tooling.

Further Airframe Development

Further flight testing of K5054 followed at a loaded weight of 5,332lb (2,418kg). Ground handling was considered satisfactory at this weight, but flight handling was a different story:

- the elevator was too light and too powerful, and it was recommended that the elevator control could be improved by reducing the gear ratio in the control circuit;
- the aircraft was unstable in the glide with undercarriage and flaps down;
- the moulded Perspex windscreen distorted the vision;
- the diving speed was limited to 380mph (610km/h); and
- the guns refused to fire at altitude due to temperature.

Production problems at Supermarine and with its contractors delayed the first flight of the first production Spitfire (K9787) to 15 May 1938. In July K9787 went to A&AEE for its type test and the second production aircraft (K9788) flew on the twelfth of that month. The prototype airframe was far from satisfactory for production and considerable structural

modifications had to be introduced under the guidance of Joe Smith, to make for easier production. With these incorporated the maximum diving speed would then be increased to 450mph (720km/h).

In production form the Spitfire I had an all-up-weight (AUW) of 6,400lb (2,900kg) and was powered by a Merlin III with a fixed-pitch propeller. It took off at 2,850rpm with +6¼psi boost, needing 720yd (660m) to clear a 50ft (15m) barrier. The Merlin's maximum power was 1,030bhp at 3,000rpm with +6¼psi boost at 16,250ft (4,950m). K9787, when tested at A&AEE with the Merlin III and a de Havilland two-pitch propeller, gave the fuel consumption figures shown in the table (*below*) at 20,000ft (6,000m).

To return to Spitfire development, tests were carried out at A&AEE on a Spitfire II P7280, fitted with a Merlin XII engine driving a Rotol constant-speed propeller. The engine's maximum power was 1,140bhp at 14,750ft (4,500m) and the rated power was 1,090bhp at a rated altitude of 13,600ft (4,150m); the AUW at take-off was 6,172lb (2,800kg). The maximum speeds achieved during the test are shown in the table (*see* p.21). (*see* p.21)

With the introduction of the Spitfire II powered by the Merlin XII operating on 100/130 octane fuel and driving a Rotol RXS/1 CS constant-speed propeller, an increase in altitude of 2,000ft (600m) was attained, with the engine delivering 1,150bhp at 14,500ft (4,400m). This model entered service in 1940, during which year the Spitfire V went into production (*see* p.21).

Amongst a number of comparison trials carried out was one between three different Spitfires, each with a different engine and propeller, concerning

Fuel consumption figures for the Merlin III

TAS (mph)	RPM	Boost control (psi)	Mixture	Fuel consumption (gal/hr)
210.5	1950	-5.7	auto-weak	25.2
222.5	2010	-5.4	auto-weak	27.0
235	2085	-5.0	auto-weak	29.5
247.5	2160	-4.6	auto-weak	32.2
260	2250	-4.0	auto-weak	35.3
271	2350	-3.1	auto-weak	38.4

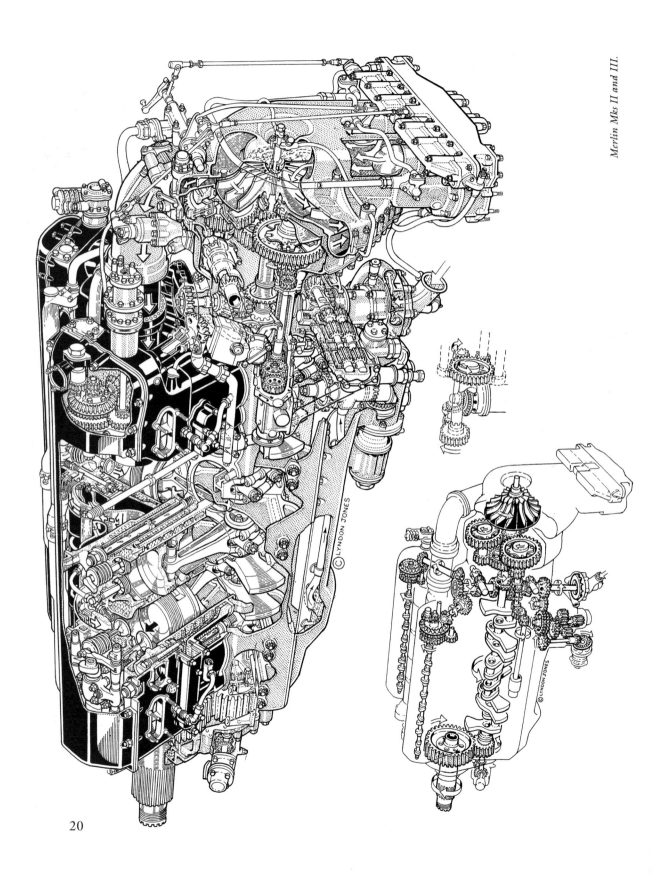

©LYNDON JONES

©LYNDON JONES

A&AEE-recorded maximum speeds of P7280

Height (feet)	TAS (mph)	Propeller speed (rpm)	Boost (psi)
5,000	306	3,000	+8.8
10,000	325	3,000	+8.8
15,000	344	3,000	+8.8
20,000	350	3,000	+6.2
26,000	335	3,000	+1.5
30,000	321	3,000	-0.9

Sqn Ldr Boussa of 350 Belgian Squadron RAF with his Spitfire Mark Vc.

Specification – Supermarine Spitfire IIa

Weights	Load at take-off 6,275lb (2,846kg)
Dimensions	Wingspan 29ft 10in (9.09m); wing area (gross) 242sq ft (22.96sq m); length (aircraft horizontal) 29ft 11in (9.12m)
Engine	1,175bhp Rolls-Royce Merlin XII
Performance	Maximum speed 370mph (600km/h); rate of climb 2,500ft/min (760m/min); combat range 395 miles (635km); ceiling 32,800ft (10,000m)
Armament	Eight 0.303in Browning machine guns

the time to height. The results are shown in the table (*see* p.22).

Further development had started with the fitting of a Merlin XX engine minus the supercharger MS gear (the engine being designated Mark 45) into a Mark I airframe to obtain higher altitude performance. This, in production form, became the Spitfire V, using a Mark II airframe fitted with a Merlin 45 engine. The standard Spitfire Vb with the 'B' wing (*see* p.49) had an armament of two 20mm Hispano-Suiza cannon and four 0.303in Browning machine guns, though due to a shortage of Hispano-Suiza 20mm cannon the early Mark Vs were fitted with eight 0.303in Brownings and no cannon, and as such were designated Mark Va aircraft. In the development of the Spitfire V, 90,000

A&AEE comparison trials on three Spitfire types

Aircraft, engine, propeller, all-up-weight	Height (feet)	Time to height (minutes)
K9787. Merlin I, wooden propeller, AUW 5,819lb	10,000	4.4
	20,000	9.4
	25,000	13.8
	30,000	22.4
K3171. Merlin III, Rotol constant-speed propeller, AUW 6,050lb	10,000	3.5
	20,000	7.7
	25,000	11.0
	30,000	16.4
P7280. Merlin XII, Rotol constant-speed propeller, AUW 6,172lb	10,000	3.3
	20,000	7.0
	25,000	9.6
	30,000	13.7
	35,000	21.3

design hours and 105,000 jigging and tooling hours were expended.

Frequent stoppages occurred in the original cannon installation in the Spitfire's wing. This was partly due to the fact that the cannon was designed for use as a *moteur-canon* (engine cannon), where the cannon body and breech are mounted in the 'V' of the engine cylinders and the barrel fires through the hollow propeller shaft, so the engine formed a stiff mounting (*see* the photograph on p.23 of the Dewoitine 510 that was bought by the Air Ministry to study its engine-cannon installation). The Spitfire's wing was far too flexible, compared with the engine installation, and Supermarine contributed to the stoppages by mounting the cannon on its side, so as to accommodate the cannon within the depth of the wing, along with the feed chutes and cartridge ejection chutes. Spitfire L1007 was the development aircraft for the installation.

The first RAF success with the cannon-armed Spitfire occurred on 13 January 1940, when an A&AEE pilot, Flt Lt Proudman, joined up with some Auxiliary Air Force Spitfires to intercept an enemy attack.

Specification – The Merlin 45 engine

Reduction gear	0.477 to 1
Supercharger gear ratio	9.089 to 1
Supercharger disk diameter	10¼in (260.35mm)
Nett dry weight	1,385lb 628kg)
Take-off power	1,185bhp at 3,000rpm, +16psi boost
Combat power	1,515bhp at 3,000rpm and 11,000ft (3,350m)
Maximum climb power	2,850rpm, +9psi boost
Maximum cruise power	2,670rpm, +7psi boost

He came across a He 111 trying to make its escape, and though his starboard cannon jammed after firing one round, he pressed on and saw the port cannon shells hit the aircraft: a large part of the Heinkel detached itself before the port cannon also stopped.

ABOVE:
The Dewoitine D510 purchased by the Air Ministry to carry out trials of the Hispano-Suiza 20mm moteur-canon.

RIGHT:
The Hispano-Suiza 12Y engine, power unit of the Dewoitine D510.
AMR Vraux

Shortly afterwards the He 111 came down in the sea about 20 miles off the coast.

A number of cannon-armed Spitfires were operated by 602 Squadron during the Battle of Britain period to gain operational experience, but due to the number of cannon stoppages they were considered unsatisfactory and were withdrawn.

The Hispano-Suiza 20mm cannon produced for the RAF aircraft were licensed produced from Hispano-Suiza France and manufactured in the UK by

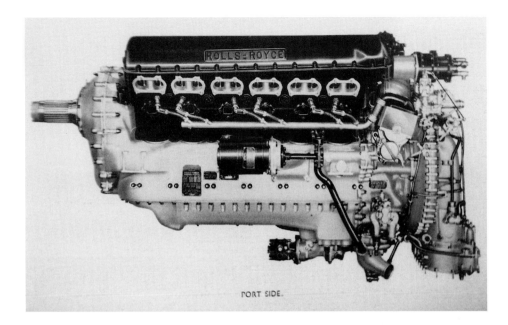

*The Rolls-Royce
Merlin III.*

the British Manufacturing and Research Co. (BMAR-Co). As opposed to the then-current Luftwaffe 20mm cannon, the MG/FF, the Hispano-Suiza had a higher muzzle velocity and a higher rate of fire. The original cannon produced and used by the RAF were magazine-fed, the magazines on the Spitfire necessitating a raised blister cowling on each wing, but a belt-feed was later produced. The ammunition could be ball, high-explosive or armour-piercing.

During the development of the Merlin, Rolls-Royce introduced a two-speed drive for the supercharger, but as it did not satisfy Rolls-Royce's standards they obtained a licence to produce the established Farman drive. A Merlin with this modification was first flown in September 1937 and the engine went into production in 1938 as the Mark X. The next important step in Merlin development was carried out after S.G. Hooker (later Sir Stanley Hooker) joined Rolls-Royce as an assistant to J. Ellor (Chief Development Engineer) and an investigation into improving supercharger efficiency and the Merlin's power output was embarked on under Hooker. This was achieved by an increase in the cross-sectional area of the intake at the impeller eye and a reduction of approximately one third of the rotor vane's width. This engine then went into production as the Merlin XX, and gave an increase in FTH of approximately 3,000ft (900m) over the Merlin III. The Mark XX supercharger efficiency

Specification – Hispano-Suiza 20mm cannon	
Calibre	20mm (0.787in)
Length of barrel	5ft 7¼in (1.71m)
Overall length	8ft 2½in (2.50m)
Number of grooves	9
Rifling twist	1 in 53, right-hand
Weight	109lb (49kg)
Muzzle velocity	2,880ft/sec (880m/sec)
Effective range	2,000ft (600m)
Rate of fire	*Mark I* 650rpm
	Mark II 720rpm

was raised to 65–70 per cent, compared with the 60–65 per cent of the Merlin III.

Alternative Airframe Material

After the fall of France in 1940, a shortage of aluminium alloys was anticipated and at least two investigations into substitute materials were carried out by the RAE Aero Structures Department. One of these concerned the manufacture of Spitfire tail

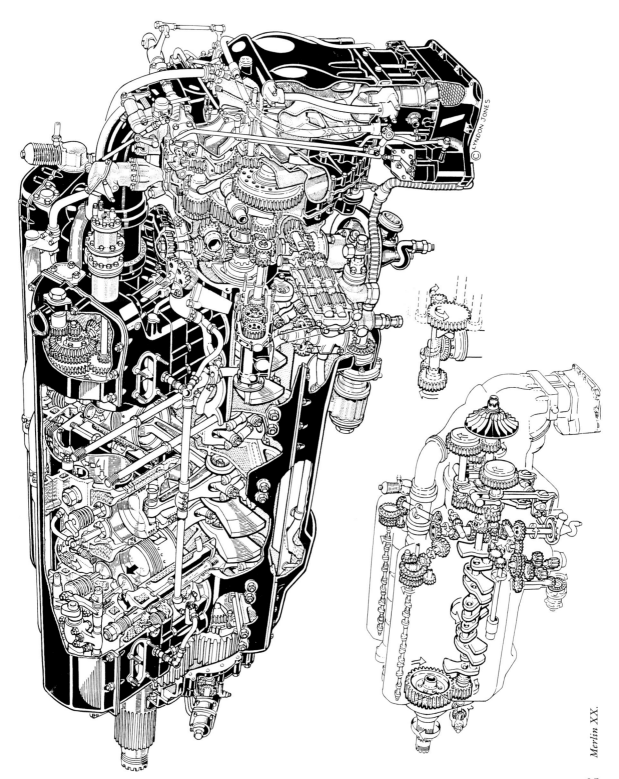

©LYNDON JONES

Merlin XX.

25

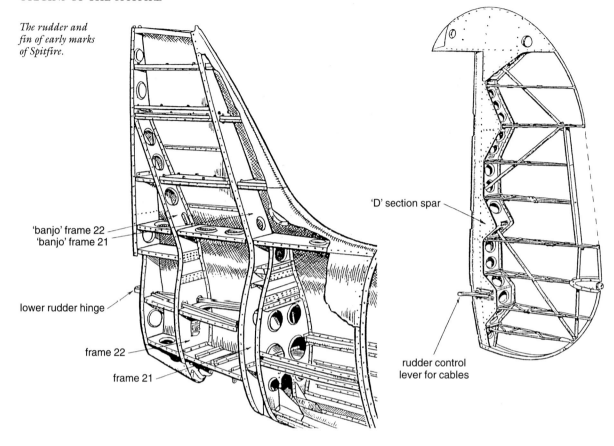

The rudder and fin of early marks of Spitfire.

'banjo' frame 22
'banjo' frame 21

lower rudder hinge

frame 22

frame 21

'D' section spar

rudder control lever for cables

building Spitfire Vs under contract to the Ministry. As the Westland flight-test section had experienced different longitudinal handling, Chief Test Pilot Harald Penrose had been flight-recording some longitudinal data and trim curves of the Spitfire for Petter. As a result, and at Petter's instigation, an experimental plywood-covered elevator with a modified aerodynamic section was fitted to a Westland-built Spitfire. Flight tests of what was called the 'Westland elevator' proved there was an increase in longitudinal stability worth several inches of CG travel. This was followed up by Supermarine aerodynamicists enlarging the horn balance of the standard elevator by stages, which gave flexibility in CG movements and cured the longitudinal instability problem.

Spitfire III, V, VI and VII Airframes

The introduction of the Mark III was expected to be the first major change in the Spitfire, as it was

envisaged that the Mark III would replace the earlier marks in production, but in the end only one was built, N3297. The Mark III was intended to be powered by the Merlin XX, which was a single-stage, two-speed, supercharged engine delivering 1,390bhp at take-off at 3,000rpm and +14psi boost. The differences on the Mark III were as follows:

- wingspan shortened to 30½ft (9.39m);
- wing area reduced to 220sq ft (20.44sq m);
- aircraft overall length 30ft 4in (9.25m);
- bullet-proof glass panel inside the windscreen;
- retractable tailwheel; and
- strengthened main undercarriage and undercarriage location points.

The problem of the Mark III lay with the engine. Being more complicated, the Merlin XX was proving more difficult to produce than the previous single-stage, single-speed units. Furthermore, the Merlin XX had been allocated to the Hurricane to improve

28

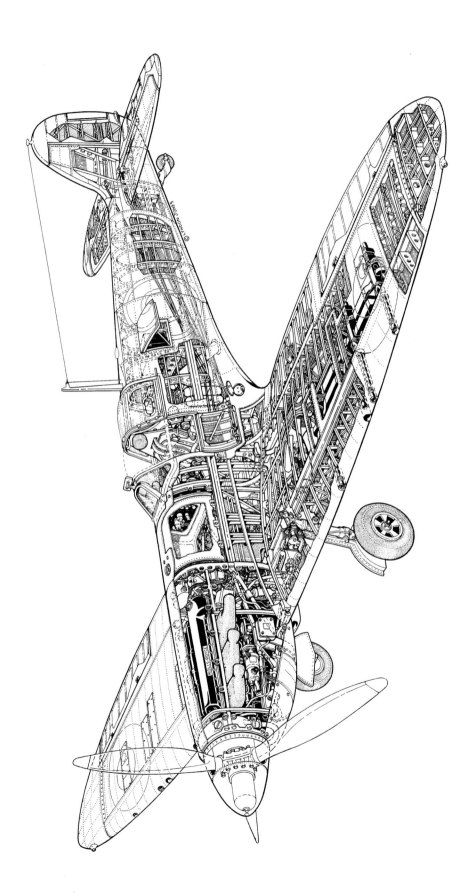

Spitfire I.

29

A 66 Squadron Spitfire I at Duxford in 1940 with Plt Off L. Collingridge. P.W. PORTER

Specification – Merlin XX

Cubic capacity	1,649cu in (10,639cc)
Reduction gear ratio	0.42 to 1
Compression ratio	6.0 to 1
Supercharger type	single-stage, two-speed
Supercharger ratios	MS 8.15 to 1
	FS 9.49 to 1
Supercharger impellor diameter	10¼in (260.35mm)
Carburation	SU AVT.40
Nett dry weight	1,450lb (660kg)
Fuel grade	100/130 octane
Take-off rating	1,280bhp at 3,000rpm and +12psi boost
Maximum power rating	MS 1,470bhp at 3,000rpm at 6,250ft (1,900m)
	FS 1,435hp at 3,000rpm at 11,250ft (3,430m)
International rating	MS 1,240bhp at 2850rpm at 10,000ft (3,000m)
	FS 1,130hp at 2850rpm at 16,500ft (5,000m)

its performance, and was also required for the Halifax and Lancaster bombers of Bomber Command.

As Rolls-Royce was unable to cope with demand for the Merlin engine and the latest Bf 109 was proving a problem to Fighter Command, a meeting was held at A&AEE Boscombe Down on 24 December 1940 to analyse the situation. The view was expressed that the Spitfire and Hurricane were losing the tactical advantage to the Luftwaffe at altitude, neither of the two RAF fighters being as fast as the latest Bf 109 above 25,000ft (7,500m).

Thus was sounded the death knell of the Spitfire III, for what was now required quickly was an answer to the new Bf 109s, a Spitfire that had a better performance at altitude and a better ceiling. Thus was born the Spitfire V and the Merlin 45 engine,

the latter basically a Mark XX engine less its MS gear and with a more efficient supercharger. This engine had been on the test beds at Rolls-Royce under the guidance of Ellor and Hooker, and raised the Spitfire's ceiling by 2,000ft (600m).

Returning to the production run and marks of Spitfire, the Mark V was basically a derivative of the Mark II airframe fitted with the Merlin 45 engine, and was considered to be just a stopgap pending further engine development. In the event, the Spitfire V was the mark that equipped many squadrons at home and overseas. As previously mentioned the Spitfire Vb was armed with two 20mm cannon and four 0.303in Browning machine guns, and at an AUW of 6,500lb (2,950kg) it had time to height and rate of climb performance as shown in the table (*below*).

The engine installation of Spitfire F.Mk IX. MH434 at Duxford.

Climb performance of the Spitfire V

Height	*Time to height*	*Rate of climb*
10,000ft (3,000m)	3min 6sec	3,250ft/sec (990m/sec)
20,000ft (6,000m)	6min 25sec	2,440ft/sec (740m/sec)
30,000ft (9,000m)	12min 12sec	1,170ft/sec (360m/sec)

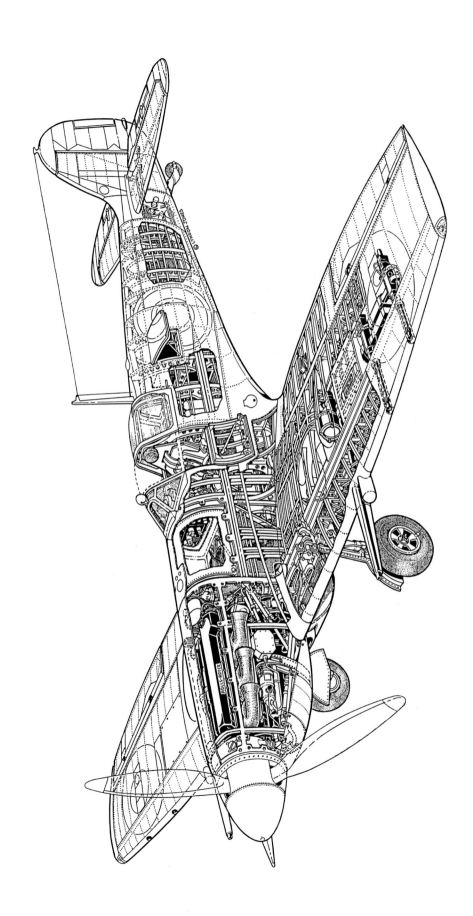

Spitfire Vc.

A&AEE trials data on Spitfire VI AB200

Wingspan	40ft 2in (12.24m)
Wing area	248½sq ft (23.09sq m)
Length	29ft 11in (9.12m)
Engine type	Merlin 47
Take-off power at sea level	1,100bhp at 3,000rpm, +12psi boost
Combat power	1,415bhp at 3,000rpm, +16psi boost
Maximum climb rating	2,850rpm, +9psi boost
Engine nett dry weight	1,400lb (635kg)
Aircraft loaded weight	6,740lb (3,060kg)
Wing loading	27lb/sq ft (133kg/sq m)
Maximum speed at	
21,800ft (6,640m)	356mph (573km/h)
38,000ft (11,600m)	264mph (425km/h)
Maximum test height	38,000ft (11,600m)
Time to	
20,000ft	7min 50sec
38,000ft	27min 54sec
Service ceiling	39,200ftm (12,000m)

Technology never stands still during a war, as one is always trying to stay ahead of the enemy, and in mid-1941 the Air Ministry suddenly requested production of the Spitfire VI. This was a panic response to the appearance of the Junkers Ju 86P high-altitude reconnaissance aircraft, which the Air Ministry feared was the forerunner of a fleet of high-altitude bombers – which in the event it turned out not to be. The Spitfire VI was intended to have a pressurized cockpit, and as such the prototype, X4942, made its maiden flight on 5 July 1941. Neither X4942 nor a pressurized-cockpit Mark V that had been hurriedly modified at RAE Farnborough were totally successful – lash-ups very rarely are – so in the end the best features of both were amalgamated in the production Mark VI.

The worst part of the early pressurization systems was always the compressor, for it nearly always seemed to pump oily smells and mist into the cockpit along with the compressed air. However, such was the urgency of the requirement that such built-in problems had to be accepted! The Mark VI was powered by a Merlin 47 engine that drove a four-bladed propeller of 10ft 9in (3.28m) diameter, and its mainplane had extended wingtips that increased the span to 40ft 2in (12.24m), and added to the type's lateral stability. The production run of the Mark VI was only 100 aircraft, as other more competitive types of Spitfires were now urgently required to combat the Fw 190 and Bf 109F and -G fighters at lower altitudes. The second production Mark VI was AB200, and this featured in an A&AEE Boscombe Down report, which is summarized in the table (*left*).

The Mark VII that followed on also had a pressurized cabin, but differed in that its airframe was considerably strengthened and it had a Merlin 61 engine. This airframe type had a 14gal (64ltr) fuel tank in each mainplane leading edge to increase the fuel capacity, a retractable tailwheel and the wingspan increased to 40ft 2in (12.24m), similar to the Mark VI's. A further adaptation of the Mark VII was the Mark VIII, but in this mark the pressure cabin was deleted. Early deliveries of the Mark VIII had the extended wingtips of the Mark VII, but the majority had the normal wingspan of 36ft 10in (11.23m). (The Mark VIII is described in more detail in Chapter 2.)

The Spitfire and its Competitors

There was, without any doubt, a world of difference between the handling of the RAF's earlier biplane fighters and that of the Spitfire. With the Spitfire came retractable flaps and undercarriage, and an enclosed cockpit with the view ahead restricted by the long nose housing the Merlin. The Spitfire was both thoroughbred and beast, depending on the pilot's experience and the circumstances. To most young fighter pilots of the RAF it seemed the ultimate 'dream' fighting machine, but there were times during the Second World War when the Luftwaffe had superior aircraft, and the only defence left was the Spitfire's tight turning circle – a manoeuvre that was both time- and fuel-consuming. Yet time and time again during those years Joe Smith and his team at Supermarine modified or produced new types of Spitfires that could compete or beat the best of the German fighters, be it at low level or high altitude. It is, however true that the major improvements in

A Spitfire of the Battle of Britain Memorial Flight on engine run in 1983. P.W. PORTER

aircraft speeds over the first couple of years of the war were mainly due to increases in engine performance alone.

The Spitfire's airframe construction was itself a break-away from previous practice: the initial order for 310 Spitfires in 1936 came at a time of policy change at the Air Ministry, who now insisted on the breakdown of the airframe into sub-components for subcontracting. With this system some bottlenecks inevitably occurred, aggravating an already tenuous situation: the prototype being hand-built, it required redesigning for quantity production, a job that Joe Smith had already embarked on. Many of the subcontracting firms were initially unable to cope with the mass production methods of the motorcar industry, who were themselves now being introduced into aircraft manufacture. The result of this was that there were only six complete Spitfires at the end of 1937, due to a hold-up in the production of mainplanes.

In its construction and handling the Spitfire had its credits and debits, as has been covered previously. The Spitfire and the Bf 109E were not only contemporaries, but had a very similar overall performance and shared a common weakness – the undercarriage. The Spitfire's cockpit appeared narrow, but on the Bf 109E the cockpit canopy (which hinged to one side) made it seem the most claustrophobic. The airframe structure of the Bf 109E was far easier to construct than the Spitfire's, and the Bf 109E's cannon armament was more effective against armoured aircraft than the original 0.303in armament of the Spitfire. Both aircraft suffered poor lateral control at high speed, but the Bf 109E was the worst of the two, with the Spitfire I's aileron control becoming very heavy above 350mph (560km/h) and the Bf 109E's becoming almost solid. The aileron control of the Spitfire was vastly improved with the fitment of the metal-covered ailerons that were introduced on later marks. The early Spitfires with two-bladed wooden propellers or the de Havilland two-pitch propellers were at a disadvantage to the Bf 109E and its VDM variable-pitch propeller, this position only being rectified with the fitting of de Havilland or Rotol controllable variable-pitch propellers.

A&AEE comparison trials between Bf 109E and Spitfire I

	Bf 109E	*Spitfire I*
Wingspan	32ft 5in (9.88m)	36ft 10in (11.23m)
Wing area	172.84sq ft (16.06sq m)	242sq ft (22.48sq m)
Wing loading	32lb/sq ft (156kg/sq m)	22.8lb/sq ft (111kg/sq m)
Power loading	5.07lb/bhp (2.3kg/bhp)	6.0lb/bhp (2.7kg/bhp)
Mean chord	5ft 4⅛in (1.63m)	6ft 2⅜in (1.89m)
Aspect ratio	6.0 to 1	5.68 to 1
Aircraft height	8ft 5½in (2.59m)	8ft 10in (2.69m)
Aircraft length	28ft 10½in (8.8m)	29ft 11in (9.12m)
Weight gross	5,667–5,747lb (2,570–2,606kg)	6,200–6,275lb (2,800–2,846kg)
Armament	2 × 7.9mm MG + 2 × 20mm cannon	8 × 0.303in MG
Engine type	DB601	Merlin III
Power at take-off	1,175bhp	1,030bhp
Power at full throttle height	950bhp	990bhp
Propeller type	VDM variable pitch	Rotol 3 blade C.S
Maximum speed at sea level	283mph (455km/h)	282mph (454km/h)
at 15,000ft	338mph (544km/h)	348mph (560km/h)
at 20,000ft	343mph (552km/h)	354mph (570km/h)
at 25,000ft	328mph (528km/h)	341mph (549km/h)
Maximum speed at FTH	348mph at 17,500ft) (560km/h at 5,300m	346mph at 18,900ft (557km/h at 5,760m)
Service ceiling	35,200ft (10,700m)	34,700ft (10,600m)
Time to		
15,000ft (4,600m)	5.9min	6.5min
25,000ft (7,600m)	11min 39sec	11min 33sec
30,000ft (9,100m)	17min 12sec	15min 42sec
Rate of climb at		
15,000ft (4,600m)	2,542ft/min (775m/min)	2,307ft/min (703m/min)
25,000ft (7,600m)	1,340ft/min (408m/min)	1,660ft/min (506m/min)
30,000ft (9,100m)	740ft/min (226m/min)	1,020ft/min (311m/min)

The Spitfire's stressed-skin construction – as with the Bf 109E – meant that combat damage was harder and more time-consuming to repair than with the Hawker Hurricane, which in its Mark I version had fabric-covered wings and a fabric-covered Warren girder fuselage. However, as aircraft speeds increased the Hurricane's shape and construction made it an also-ran as far as speed was concerned, and left the field to the stressed-skin newcomers.

In the ordnance field the Luftwaffe had considered heavier armament at a fairly early stage – far earlier than the RAF, if one ignores the early trials of the 37mm Coventry Ordnance Works gun. On the Continent there were a number 20–23mm cannon that were manufactured by Madsen, Mauser, Oerlikon, Solothurn and others; the Luftwaffe opted for the Oerlikon 20mm cannon and produced it as the MG/FF. This was a 'blow-back' design with a muzzle velocity of 2,296ft/sec (700m/sec) and a rate of fire of 540rpm. The MG/FF was obsolete in the Luftwaffe by around late 1940–41, though still used in *Schräge Musik* upward-slanting installations, and replaced by the MG 151/20. This was a far superior weapon, with a muzzle velocity of 2,590ft/sec (790m/sec) and a rate of fire of 800rpm.

The RAF, meanwhile, remained wedded to the Vickers 0.303in machine gun for far too long, which inhibited the acquisition and/or development of more reliable and more modern weapons, as well as ones of a heavier calibre. As related earlier, it was the mid-1930s before alternatives to the Vickers were looked into, leading to the adoption of the Colt 0.30in. At the same time, representatives of the Air Staff and Air Ministry Gun Section visited Hispano-Suiza in Paris to view their 20–23mm cannon, leading to the purchase of a licence to produce the Type 404 20mm cannon in Britain. As opposed to the 'blow-back' system of the MG/FF, the Type 404 was gas operated. Therefore, by 1941–2 the Luftwaffe and RAF were more or less on equal terms as regards aircraft and aircraft weapon capability.

During the Battle of France (although Spitfires were not based there) and during the Battle of Britain, the Merlin-powered aircraft were at a distinct disadvantage to the Bf 109 when in a steep dive, as the carburettor-fed Merlin could not respond to the negative 'g' condition as well as the fuel-injection DB601 engine of the Bf 109. The Bf 109 had an initial acceleration away from the Spitfire, as the negative 'g' condition caused the fuel in the float chamber of the Merlin's SU carburettor to be temporarily flung to the top of the chamber, preventing fuel from being metered to the choke and so causing the engine to lose power. Once the float chamber was correctly oriented with no negative 'g', the fuel flooding the top of the chamber then returned to its normal position and caused a rich-mixture 'cut'.

At RAE Farnborough a lady scientist named Miss B. Shilling came up with a simple device, called by all and sundry the 'Shilling orifice' which, although it did not cure the problem, eased it until other, newer, carburettors and fuel injection were employed. The device was basically a small metal diaphragm with a central calibrated hole that was inserted in the feed line to the carburettor. Thus when negative 'g' restricted the amount of fuel supplied from the carburettor, the 'Shilling orifice' allowed just enough fuel to be supplied to an acceptable level.

The Supermarine Spitfire was to have the honour of shooting down the first enemy aircraft on British soil during the Second World War, when on 16 October 1939 Spitfires of 602 and 603 Squadrons engaged He 111 bombers over the Firth of Forth, and a He 111 fell to the guns of 602 Squadron. It was also the first time that the Spitfire had fired its guns in anger, but it wouldn't be the last: it was just the start, for at the beginning of the Battle of Britain there were nineteen squadrons of Spitfires in Fighter Command.

Having previously mentioned the North American P-51 Mustang, it may now be worth briefly considering the controversy that has occurred post-war as to which is the better aircraft, the Spitfire or the P-51. First of all it must be appreciated that five years lay between the two designs, and in those five years great improvements were made both in the knowledge of aerodynamics and in production techniques; indeed, if one is to compare an aircraft with the Spitfire then the best candidate would be the Messerschmitt Bf 109. Returning to the Mustang and Spitfire, although great claims were made for the efficiency of the Mustang's laminar-flow aerofoil section, research by RAE Farnborough determined that these claims were debatable: laminar flow is dependent upon a clean aerofoil, which in practice is never possible.

The P-51, and only in its Merlin-powered versions, was without any doubt the finest long-range and all-round fighter of its period. The Spitfire was an interceptor as demanded by the RAF for the defence of the British Isles before 1939, and in that role was supreme. From there the two differ, both in build quality and production. The Mustang, with its lack of curved (in planform) mainplanes and tail unit, was without doubt the better production aircraft. Furthermore, being produced with flush-butted skin panels held by flush riveting it was also aerodynamically the better aircraft. However, the Merlin-powered Mustang did not see the light of day as a production aircraft until late 1942 – a little too late to have fought in the Battle of Britain.

2

Further Spitfire Development

Over its operational career the Spitfire was built or modified into a number of roles, as a low-level fighter, high-altitude fighter, strike fighter and photo-reconnaissance aircraft. At the same time, Rolls-Royce proved themselves to be the ace of developers, raising the Merlin's power and making it suitable for all these tasks. The first high-altitude development of the Spitfire was the Mark VI, as described earlier. This was followed by the Mark VII, the prototype of which was AB450 (a modified Mark V), which had a strengthened fuselage and was powered by a Merlin 60. Only seventy-five Merlin 60 engines were produced, the mark being a bomber engine intended for installation in the Wellington VI; only a few were installed experimentally in Spitfires to prove the concept that led to the Marks VII and VIII. The standard Mark VII in service was powered by a Merlin 61 or 64, and the HF VII by a Merlin 71.

Around 1941–2 the Spitfire's armament was a source of test and discussion as various protagonists tried to influence the authorities to favour various weapons; even Sholto Douglas, the head of Fighter Command, entered the contest, suggesting a Spitfire armed with twelve 0.303in machine guns! This idea was already dated as the Hurricane IIB had this armament, and enemy aircraft had been armoured against 0.303in bullets. Therefore, thoughts on Spitfire re-armament centred around the improved Browning 0.5in machine gun and the 20mm cannon, as well as the established mix-match of four 0.303in and two 20mm cannon.

The Merlin 60 and 70

The Merlin 60 series, encompassing the Marks 61 to 68, were all two-speed, two-stage supercharged engines. This series originated when the Air Ministry asked Rolls-Royce to develop an engine capable of powering a high-altitude version of the Vickers-Armstrongs Wellington bomber. At Rolls-

Royce, calculations determined that with a two-speed, two-stage supercharger and intercooler the power of a Merlin at 30,000ft (9,000m) could be doubled. This was achieved on test by matching the supercharger from a Rolls-Royce Vulture engine to feed a Merlin supercharger, following which detail design work started in March 1940. The new engine, designated the Merlin 60, was then developed into the Merlin 61 for fighter aircraft. This was hurried into production in March 1942 to power the Spitfire IXs that were urgently needed to combat the Focke-Wulf Fw 190 fighter, which was proving too capable an opponent for the Spitfire V.

The Mark 60 series of Merlins introduced the two-piece cylinder block/head onto British production lines. They had supercharger impellor diameters of 11.5in and 10.1in and spawned a variety of different supercharger gear ratios and reduction gear ratios over the different marks. Some models used the RAE/SU injection system and others the Bendix-Stromberg injection carburettor. The different models were as follows:

- Mark 61. Reduction gear ratio 0.42:1. SU float or RAE/SU anti-G carburation. Coffman starter crankcase to accommodate cabin blower. Supercharger gear ratios 6.39:1 and 8.03:1. Maximum combat power rating 1,565bhp at 3,000rpm and +15psi boost at 11,250ft (3,430m) in MS gear.
- Mark 62. Reduction gear ratio 0.42:1. SU float or RAE/SU anti-G carburation. Supercharger gear ratios 5.52:1 and 8.41:1. Maximum combat power rating 1,280bhp at 2,850rpm and +9psi boost at 9,000ft (2,700m) in MS gear.
- Marks 63 and 64. Reduction gear ratio 0.477:1. Carburation by RAE/SU. Supercharger gear ratios 6.39:1 and 8.03:1.
- Mark 66. Reduction gear ratio 0.477:1. Carburation by Bendix. Supercharger gear ratios 5.79:1 and 7.06:1

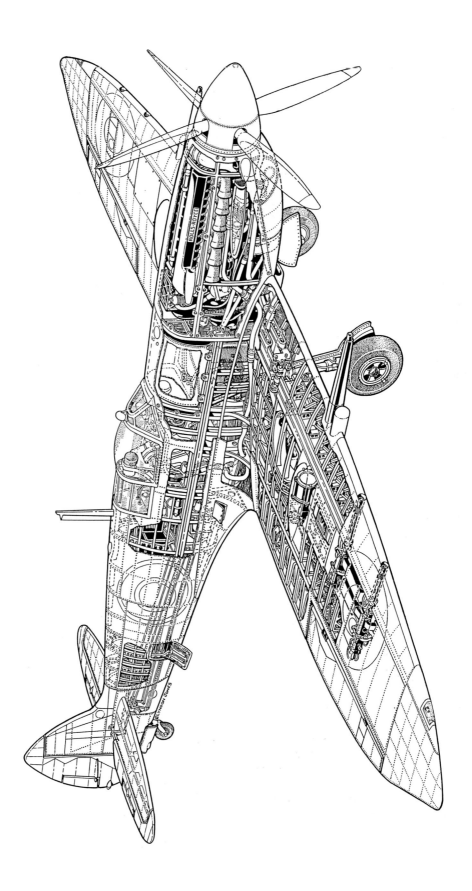

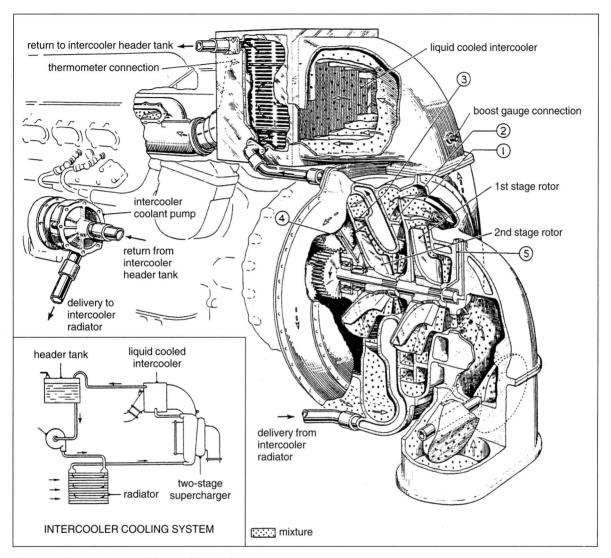

The two-speed, two-stage supercharger and intercooler.

The Mark 70 series closely follow the Mark 60, but the Marks 72 and 73 had their intercooler header tanks integral with the intercooler. The Marks 70–77 had supercharger gear ratios 6.39:1 and 8.03:1. The Mark 77 (like the Mark 64) had a cabin supercharger drive.

Following consultations between Rolls-Royce and the Ministry, it was decided to up-rate the Mark 61 by increasing combat boost from +12psi to +15psi. This was followed by a change in the supercharger gear ratios to provide an increase in performance at low and medium altitudes – the areas in which the Fw 190 excelled. With these changes the engine was redesignated the Mark 66, the high-altitude engines (Marks 61 and 63) being retained in production for the photographic-reconnaissance variants and Mark VII high-altitude fighters.

The development of the two-speed, two-stage Merlin brought the need for an intercooler (in US terminology an 'aftercooler') in the supercharger system, to lower the temperature of the compressed air-fuel mixture, both to prevent premature

Specification – Rolls-Royce Merlin 66

Bore and stroke	5.4 × 6.0in (137 × 152mm)
Cubic capacity	1,649cu in (27.02ltr)
Compression ratio	6.0:1
Reduction gear ratio	0.477:1
Supercharger gear ratios	MS 5.79:1
	FS 7.06:1
Nett dry weight	1,645lb (746kg)
Propeller	Rotol four-blade R12/4FS/4
Fuel octane rating	100/130
Carburation	Bendix-Stromberg
Spark plug	Lodge RS 5/5
Take-off rating	1,315bhp at 3,000rpm with +12psi boost
Combat rating	MS 1,705bhp at 3,000rpm with +18psi boost at 5,750ft (1,750m)
	FS 1,580bhp at 3,000rpm with +18psi boost at 16,000ft (4,900m)

detonation and to raise the volumetric efficiency. An intercooler matrix of high enough efficiency was not then available in the UK, which problem was passed to RAE Farnborough. The scientists there produced a satisfactory design combining both strength and high efficiency, and this was passed to Rolls-Royce to convert into production form.

A further problem associated with the two-speed two-stage Merlin occurred in flight. This was the 'leading-up' of the spark plugs if low charge temperatures were encountered under low-cruise conditions at height: this caused the lead inhibitor to separate in the induction and deposit on the sparking plug ends. This problem led to the fitting of charge-temperature gauges in the cockpit to ensure the pilot maintained the charge temperature above a certain point.

During the panic caused by the Fw 190's superiority to the Spitfire V, Rolls-Royce Hucknall and Supermarine converted a number of Spitfire Vs into Mark IXs by re-engineering them with Merlin 61 engines.

A converted Mark V aircraft was tested at both A&AEE and AFDU (Air Fighting Development Unit) and received favourable comment, and the first unit with the Mark IX was 64 Squadron, which became operational with the type in July 1942. The Mark IX was viewed by the Ministry as a stopgap fighter until delivery of the Mark VIII, which was to have a stronger airframe. However, the Mark IX stayed in production until the end of the war, whilst the Mark VIIIs mainly saw service overseas.

Re-engined Airframes

The Spitfire Mark IX was produced in both LF and HF versions, as well as a special HF powered by a Merlin 70 (supercharger gear ratios MS 6.39:1 and FS 8.03:1).

The Fw 190 had progressed from a difficult time with its engine installation to become a feared opponent in its Fw 190-A5 form onwards. At an all-up take-off weight of 8,474lb (3,843kg) its maximum speed at 18,000ft (5,500m) was 408mph (656km/h), with a rate of climb from 1,000m to 5,000m (3,300ft to 16,400ft) of 830m/min (2,715ft/min). This compares with the production Spitfire Mark IX's performance of 409mph at 28,000ft (658km/h at 8,500m), with an average rate of climb to that height of 2,654ft/min (809m/min). The Fw 190's original inadequate performance at altitude was a point of concern to the Technisches Amt (the German equivalent of the RAE), which led to the introduction of the MW-50 and GM1 nitrous-oxide boost systems. As the Spitfire IX was able to compete against the Fw 190 at high altitude it was decided to restrict the Mark V to lower-level operations.

Even so, the Spitfire V was no match for the Fw 190, and two modifications were introduced to help it remain competitive: the wingtips were clipped to improve manoeuvrability at low-level, and the supercharger impellor of the Merlin 45 was cropped. These modifications originated in the Middle East where the Spitfire V's performance over the desert was inferior to that of the Bf 109F and -G, and the Fw 190. Rolls-Royce sent R.W. Harker out to discuss possible improvements with Air Vice Marshal Dawson, OC Maintenance at HQ Middle East Command. Harker was asked how to raise the boost to 18psi at 3,000rpm at 10,000ft (3,000m). He cabled Rolls-Royce for advice and was told that ⅜in should be cropped off the supercharger impellor diameter. Dawson immediately ordered three

A&AEE test data of an early Spitfire IX/Merlin 1

Engine	reduction gear ratio 0.42:1
Supercharger	two-speed two-stage
Gear ratios	MS 6.39:1
	FS 8.03:1
Impellor diameter	MS 11.5in (292mm)
	FS 10.1in (257mm)
Nett dry weight	1,640lb (744kg)
Take-off power at sea level	1,280bhp at 3,000rpm, +12psi boost
Combat power	MS 1,565bhp at 3,000rpm, +15psi boost at 11,250ft (3,430m)
	FS 1,390bhp at 3,000rpm, +15psi boost at 23,500ft (7,200m)
Aircraft wingspan	36ft 11in (11.25m)
Wing area	242sq ft (22.48sq m)
Length	30ft (9.14m)
All-up weight at take-off	7,400lb (3,356kg)
Wing loading	30.6lb/sq ft (149.38kg/sq m)
Max speed at 12,000ft (3,700m)	363mph (584km/h)
Time to 12,000ft	3.5min
Max speed at 28,000ft (8,500m)	409mph (658km/h)
Time to 28,000ft	10.38min
Max speed at 32,000ft (9,800m)	395mph (636km/h)
Time to 32,000ft	13.25min

Spitfire IX and XVI marks and engines

F.IX	Merlin 61, 63 or 63A engine
LF.IX and IXE	Merlin 66 engine
HF.IX and IXE	Merlin 70 engine
LF.XVI	Packard Merlin 266 engine

Merlins modified, and at the same time the Spitfire's wings were 'clipped' by removing their detachable wing tips. Also, a locally designed air filter was substituted for the rather large standard filter. Tests revealed a 22mph (35km/h) increase in speed and an improved rate of roll.

Authorization was then given for aircraft to be modified locally without referral to the A&AEE and AFDU – which somewhat upset those establishments. However, after the modifications were tested in the UK and proven correct, a large number of Spitfire V airframes and engines were converted. The engine was then designated the Mark 45M and the aircraft became the Spitfire Vc. In this guise it was in general used for low- to medium-altitude fighting and escort duties. As most of the airframes converted were 'tired' and reputed to have already flown 500–1,000 hours, it was claimed that the 'c' stood for 'clipped, cropped and clapped'.

A further modification took place in the Middle East where Junkers Ju 86P high-altitude reconnaissance aircraft were over-flying the Nile Delta and the Spitfire V was unable to reach their altitude. As

OPPOSITE PAGE: *Spitfire MkIX MJ730 flown by Wg Cdr Forbes-Wilson.* P.W. PORTER

Specification – Spitfire Marks IX and XVI

Wingspan	standard 36ft 10in (11.23m)
	clipped 32ft 7in (9.93m)
Wing area	(standard) 242sq ft (22.48sq m)
Aerofoil section	NACA 2200 series
Mean chord	6ft 6.8in (2m)
Incidence	2 degrees at root
Dihedral	6 degrees
Length	early aircraft 31ft (9.45m)
	later aircraft 31ft 4¼in (9.56m)
Tailplane width	10ft 6in (3.2m)
Tailplane area (later aircraft)	33.84sq ft (3.14sq m)
Elevator area (later aircraft)	13.74sq ft (1.28sq m)
Fin area	4.5sq ft (0.42sq m)
Rudder area (later aircraft)	10 sq ft (0.93sq m)
Undercarriage track	5ft 8½in (1.79m)
Oleo struts	Vickers oleo-pneumatic
Fuel capacity	maximum internal 85gal (387ltr)
	drop tanks 30/45/50/90/170gal (137/205/228/410/774ltr)
Oil tank capacity	
standard	7.5gal 934ltr)
long-range	14.4gal (65.5ltr)
coolant system	14.5gal (66ltr)
hydraulic system	1.06gal (4.8ltr)
Cut-out pressure	1,150lb/sq in (80kg/sq cm)
Pneumatic pressure	300lb/sq in (21kg/sq cm)
Electrical system	12V two-wire
Engine	*Mark IX* Merlin 66
	Mark XVI Merlin 266
Propeller	type Rotol: four-blade
	type/pitch range: constant-speed, 35 degrees
	diameter: 10ft 9in (3.28m)

Flt Lt Beauchamp, an ex-Rolls-Royce engineer on the staff of Air Commodore Smylie (the RAF's senior engineer officer in the Middle East), had some specially tapered SU carburettor needles in his possession, an engineering solution was embarked on. The cylinder blocks were machined to raise the compression ratio, the pistons were scalloped to give valve clearance, and the special needles were fitted in the carburettors. Two Spitfires were modified, one having radio and no armament and the second with armament but no radio. When the next Ju 86P appeared and proceeded on its normal photographic sortie the two Spitfires were vectored onto it, and shot it down.

The requirement for a four-cannon wing had originally been catered for by the 'Universal' wing on the Spitfire Vc, although most home-based squadrons with these aircraft used two 20mm cannon and four Browning 0.303in machine guns, as it had been found impossible to heat the outer cannon bay satisfactorily. To introduce a four-cannon aircraft powered by the two-speed, two-stage Merlin 61 engine, Supermarine designed the Spitfire VIII. This was an LF version of the Mark V using the stronger 'B' airframe and powered by the Merlin 66. It was fitted with the 'Universal' wing that could accommodate four 20mm Hispano-Suiza cannon or the normal two 20mm cannon and four 0.303in Browning machine guns. It was fully tropicalized and had extra fuel in the wing roots to raise the capacity to 124gal (27.3ltr). It also had a retractable tailwheel and, originally, extended wing tips. Its all-up weight was 7,000lb (3,200kg). The modifications introduced on this airframe delayed its entry into service, and so the Mark IX joined the operational squadrons first. The Mark VIII was mainly used on overseas service, but without the extended wing tips. By the end of 1943 the main Spitfire orders were for the Marks VIII and IX.

The Spitfire Mark IX was the main production version to combat the German fighters, and with the capture of a complete and serviceable Fw 190A-3, the AFDU carried out a fighter affiliation exercise between a Spitfire IX and the Fw 190 to determine

43

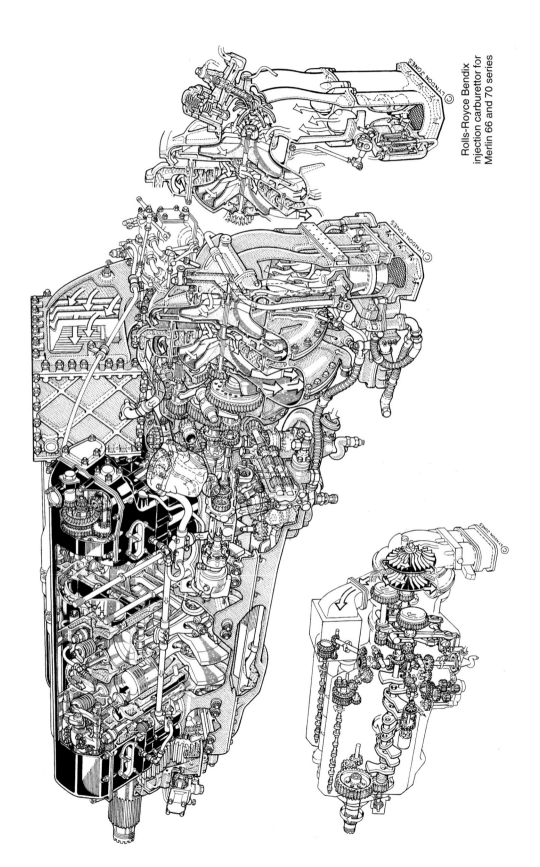

Rolls-Royce Bendix
injection carburettor for
Merlin 66 and 70 series

© LYNDON JONES

Merlin 61, 66 and 70.

44

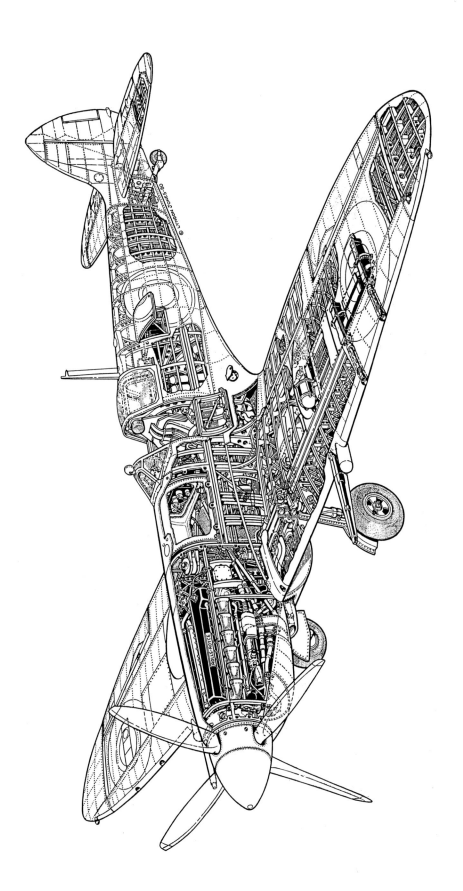

Spitfire IX.

Spitfire VIII A58-758, owned by Colin Paye in Australia. P.W. PORTER

Spitfire LF.IX.

each type's superior points. The following were highlighted:

- The Spitfire IX was superior to the Fw 190 at heights from 8,000–15,000ft (2,400–4,600m) and above 22,000ft (6,700m).
- The Fw 190 was superior to Spitfire IX at heights between 18,000–22,000ft (5,500–6,700m) and below 3,000ft (900m).
- The Spitfire IX was slightly faster in climb overall up to 23,000ft (7,000m).
- The Fw 190 was faster in the dive, and more manoeuvrable except in turning.
- The Spitfire IX out-turned the Fw 190 without any difficulty.

The Spitfire Mark XVI was a Mark IX fitted with a Packard Merlin 266. Some had the four-cannon armament, but most had the 'E' wing of two 20mm cannon and two 0.5in Browning machine guns. The Merlin 66 and 266, with the introduction of 100/150 grade fuel allowed boost to be increased to +25psi. This raised the low-level power to 2,000bhp in MS gear, and was originally classed as a 'Special Operations Only' measure to increase the low-level

'dash' speed of aircraft powered by Merlin 66s, 266s and Packard Merlin V-1670-7s, to allow them to overhaul the German V-1 flying bomb.

In regard to aircraft handling in general and engine control on take-off and approach, Flt Lt J.C.M. Wood (who flew Spitfire F.IXs and F.XVIs with 43 and 93 Squadrons) comments:

Once familiarized with this mark of Spitfire and its very few quirks, such as its trimming and engine handling demands, it was a very pleasant aircraft to fly with few, if any, real vices. Aerobatics were a delight and tight manoeuvres, either at high speed or hauling around in a tight turn at the stall judder, with its pronounced warning, did not pose any real problems to the initiated. Recovery from most 'unintentional manoeuvres' such as stalling/flicking out of a tight manoeuvre, and spins were straightforward. To the initiated, handling the IX/XVI was, up to a point, carefree. However, two phases of flying, the take-off and landing approach, could be troublesome and warrant comment. The apparently relatively low maximum take-off boost of +9psi produced from the propeller considerable torque, gyroscopic forces, etc., consequently full right-trim and rudder was necessary

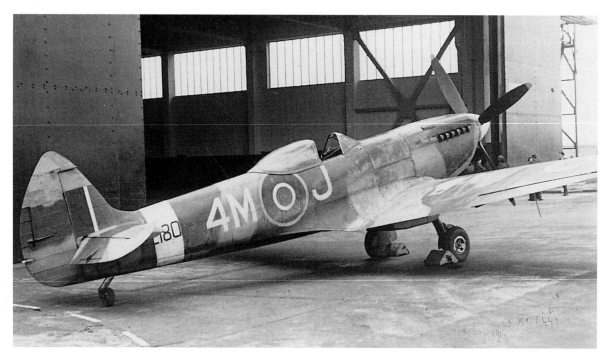

Spitfire XVI TE180 of 695 Squadron at Horsham St Faith in 1948. P.W. PORTER

Spitfire XVI TE392, minus cannon, in use post-war. R. DEACON

and opening the throttle had to be unhurried, smoothly controlled and in accord with the rudder control available at the aircraft's current speed. To exceed +9psi boost much before lift-off and reaching sufficient control speed risked running out of rudder control with a dire swing following. At all times it was essential that power applied was in accord with airspeed to provide control. Another aspect even more critical, being in the approach phase when initiating an overshoot, when care had to be taken not to apply excess power for the relatively slow approach speed, otherwise and most probably a torque stall would result, this being an uncontrollable roll and yaw – into the ground!

Further to this, the *Pilot's Notes* for the Spitfire IX and XVI states:

At training and normal loads +7 to +9psi boost is sufficient for take-off. After take-off, however, boost should be increased (where applicable) to +12psi to minimize the possibility of lead fouling the spark plugs.

The Different Spitfire Models

At this stage it might be worth listing the basic wing and airframe designations and propeller types of the different Spitfires, so as to make clear the different marks and their basic differences:

Wing Designation

'A' – the original wing, this had eight 0.303in machine guns.
'B' – two 20mm cannon and four 0.303in machine guns.
'C' – termed the 'Universal wing', this could accommodate either four 20mm cannon or two 20mm cannon and four 0.303in machine guns.
'E' – two 20mm cannon and two 0.5in machine guns.

Airframe Designation

'A' – the original airframe, accommodating the Merlin II, III and XII engines. It formed the basis of Marks Ia, Ib, IIa, IIb, PR.IV, Va, Vb, VI, PR.VII and XIII.

49

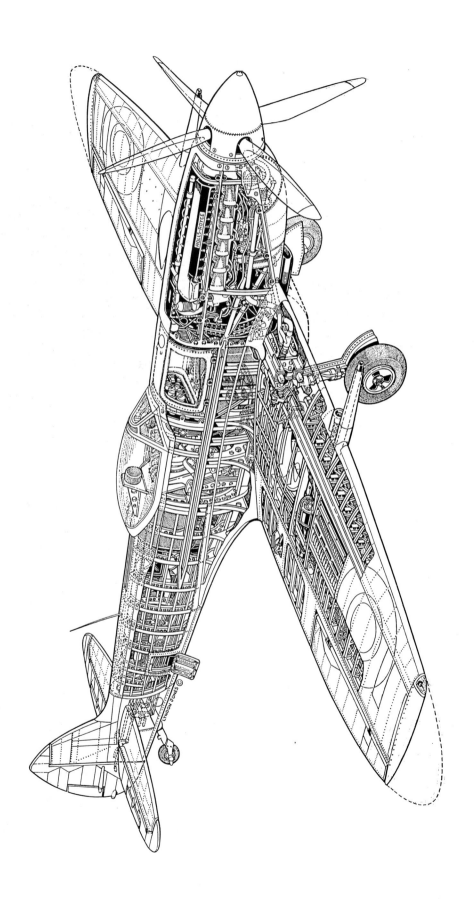

Spitfire XVI.

Spitfire VII X4786. Note the washed-out camouflage and roundel. MAP

'B' – designed for the Mark III, this was the basis of Marks Ic, Vc, PR.XI and XII.
'C' – Marks VII, VIII and XI.
'D' – Marks 21, 22 and 24.

Propeller

The standard types of propeller varied over the different marks of Spitfire and occasionally, due to local shortages overseas, this varied again; but the following is the standard type against aircraft mark number.

Mark I – two-blade, fixed-pitch wooden, or two-position de Havilland three-blade or de Havilland three-blade constant-speed.
Mark II/III – three-blade Jablo material Rotol constant-speed.
PR.IV/VII – three-blade de Havilland constant-speed.
Mark V – three-blade Rotol constant-speed, or de Havilland bracket type, or hydromatic.
Mark VI – four-blade Jablo material Rotol constant-speed.
Mark VII/VIII/IX – four-blade Rotol hydulignum constant-speed.

PR.X/XI – four-blade Rotol hydulignum constant-speed.
Mark XII – four-blade Jablo material Rotol constant-speed.
PR.XIII – three-blade de Havilland constant-speed.
Mark XIV – five-blade Rotol constant-speed.
Mark XVI – four-blade Rotol constant-speed.
Mark XVIII – five-blade Rotol constant-speed.
PR.XIX – five-blade Rotol constant-speed.
Marks 21/22/24 – five-blade Rotol constant-speed.

Photographic Reconnaissance Spitfires

These came into being during 1939–40, after a buccaneering entrepreneur-type character named Sydney Cotton, in conjunction with F. Winterbotham of the Secret Intelligence Service (SIS, or MI6), had shown the need, pre-war, for clandestine, high-speed, high-altitude photo-reconnaissance (PR) using a Lockheed 12 which Cotton himself flew, as owner/pilot. He then had to, with the enthusiastic involvement of a Fg Off M. Longbottom, convince the Air Ministry of the need for a high-speed photo-reconnaissance aircraft to replace the Bristol-Blenheims then being used for

Spitfire FR.XVII TP265 in what appears to be desert camouflage. MAP

this task, which were suffering losses. The proposal put forward for the conversion of Spitfires to the photo-reconnaissance role, when they were in short supply, must have initially seemed heresy to the Air Council. The proposal was, however, accepted, and the Spitfire PR aircraft became another tool in RAF Air Intelligence.

The first Spitfires converted were Mark Is and were produced in versions designated A, B, C, D, E and G, all unarmed and painted a duck-egg green all over. Their airframes were cleaned up, with all joints filled in and rubbed down, painted and polished. These early marks were fitted with extra fuel tanks to increase range, and were used by the first PR unit (PRU) deep into enemy airspace to provide photographs for Allied intelligence. The PRU was based at Hendon, but operated from major airfields in France prior to the 1940 Armistice, and from British airfields including Alconbury, Newmarket and Wyton. The PRU later formed the basis for other photoreconnaissance units, as the war progressed.

Some of the later marks of PR airframes were produced as such, whilst others were converted from fighter types. All had two main tanks in the fuselage forward of the pilot, whilst some had mainplane leading-edge fuel tanks, and others an additional fuel tank behind the pilot. The main fuel tanks were pressurized by exhaust air from the vacuum pump, with an aneroid valve preventing pressurizing until 20,000ft (6,000m) was reached.

The fuselage airframe construction followed standard Spitfire practice of stressed skin over four main longerons, frames and intercostals. The mainplanes were standard with stressed-skin, a single main spar and a light auxiliary rear spar. Some airframes had non-retracting tailwheels up to the Mark XI, when later versions of this mark were fitted with a retracting type. Individual characteristics of the marks were:

PR.IV – two leading-edge tanks, each of 66gal (300ltr) plus normal two main fuel tanks. 18gal (82ltr) oil tank. TR1133 or TR1143 radio. Cameras in fuselage. Merlin 45 or 46. Three-blade propeller.

PR.VII – rear fuselage 29gal (132ltr) fuel tank plus normal two main fuel tanks. 5.8 gal (26.4ltr) oil tank. Armament carried. No radio. Cameras in fuselage. Merlin 45 or 46. Three-blade propeller.

PR.XI – two leading-edge fuel tanks, each of 66gal (300ltr) plus normal two main fuel tanks. 14.4gal (65.5ltr) oil tank. Merlin 61, 63, 63A or 70. Four-blade propeller.

PR.XIII – similar to PR.VII, but provision for 30gal (137ltr) drop tank to replace rear fuselage fuel tank. Merlin 32. Three-blade propeller.

The two-speed, two-stage superchargers of the Merlin engines of the photo-reconnaissance Spitfires were as standard and automatically changed from MS to FS gear at a pre-determined altitude. These varied with the engine type, and these heights could also be varied by the fitting of a different type of altitude switch. The intercooler system was connected to the supercharger system so that the MS gear was engaged

A Spitfire PR.IC of the PRU detached to RAF Alconbury in 1940.

A Spitfire PR.IC of the PRU detached to RAF Wyton in 1940.

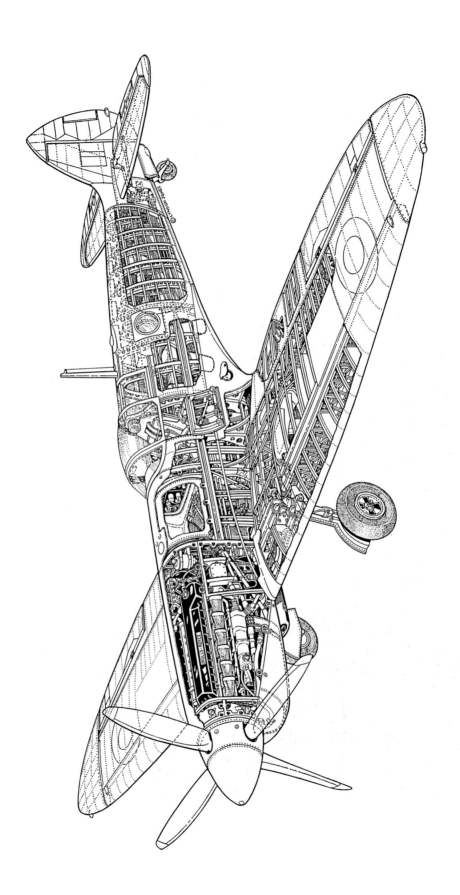

Spitfire PR.XI.

Spitfire PR.XIX.

Merlin 61–70 supercharger change heights

Engine	Change up to FS	Change down to MS
Merlin 61	15,250ft (4,650m)	13,750ft (4,200m)
Merlin 63, 63A	21,000ft (6,400m)	19,500ft (5,950m)
Merlin 70	19,500ft (5,950m)	18,000ft (5,500m)

General dimensions of PR.IV, VII, XI and XIII

Wingspan	36ft 10in (11.23m)
Wing area including ailerons	242sq ft (22.48sq m)
Incidence	2 degrees
Dihedral	6 degrees
Mean chord	7ft 1in (2.16m)
Aileron total area	18.9sq ft (1.76sq m)
Flap total area	15.5sq ft (1.44sq m)
Tailplane span	10.5ft (3.2m)
Area including elevators	31.46sq ft (2.92sq m)
Tailplane incidence	0
Elevator total area	13.26sq ft (1.23sq m)
Fin area	4.61sq ft (0.43sq m)
Rudder area	8.23sq ft (0.76sq m)
Undercarriage track	5ft 8.5in (1.74m)
Height, top of fin, tail raised	10ft 11in (3.33m)

Specification – Merlin 70 (Spitfire PR.XI)

Reduction gear ratio	0.42:1
Supercharger gear ratio	MS 6.39:1
	FS 8.03:1
Supercharger impellor diameter	MS 12in
	FS 10.1in
Nett dry weight	1,645lb (746kg)
Take-off power at sea level	1,250bhp at 3,000rpm, +12psi boost
Combat rating	MS 1,655bhp at 3,000rpm, +18psi boost at 10,000ft (3,000m)
	FS 1,475bhp at 3,000rpm, +18psi boost at 22,250ft (6,780m)
Maximum climb power	2,850rpm, +12psi boost
Maximum cruise power	2,650rpm, +7psi boost

automatically when the charge temperature became excessive, but could be re-set by a push-button on the instrument panel. The standard heights for the altitude switches were as set out in the table (*top*).

Between these various marks of PR Spitfire, certain dimensions varied slightly, but the main dimensions applicable to all four marks were as in the table (*above left*).

As improvements were incorporated in later marks of Spitfire, new versions were developed for the PR role. The first PR version powered by the Merlin 61 was the Mark XI; this had the extra 66.5gal (302ltr) of fuel in the wing leading edge, an enlarged oil tank under the nose, a rounded windscreen and a retractable tailwheel. This model was followed, later on in 1944, by the Mark X, which was essentially similar to the Mark XI but with a pressurized cabin and a Lobelle sliding hood.

Increased Airframe Strength

As the Spitfire was developed through various marks and as speed increased over the years, the greater power and higher speeds caused increased structural loads, and inadequate wing torsional stiffness caused twisting that seriously reduced aileron effectiveness. This problem was solved by progressive alterations to the design – such as the local application of thicker sections of the mainplane spars – and the use of higher-strength materials. The mainplane spar booms consisted of a series of duralumin tubes telescoped into each other and stopped off at intervals, which lent themselves to being modified in length and to changes of material; this occurred throughout the development life of the Spitfire.

The next development was the Mark XVIII, for which Supermarine used extruded sections of DTD364 machined on the taper. The stressed-skin construction permitted the strengthening of the skin by increasing the gauge where necessary. On the re-design of the mainplane for the Spitfire 21, an increase in strength of 47 per cent was obtained by ensuring rigid load-carrying joints at all points of access to the torsion box and also by increasing the gauge of the wing plating.

The Griffon-powered Mark XVIII was produced in both standard-wingspan and clipped-wing versions. It had reduced-span, metal-covered ailerons, increased-area fin and rudder, and elevators with extended horns. Flt Lt A.W. Paterson, who flew around 600 hours on the type over a period of two and a half years with 60 Squadron in the Far East, recalls:

> To look at it was certainly more beautiful than earlier marks, with its longer, tapered nose, teardrop canopy, larger and more shapely fin and rudder.
>
> Starting the engine was quick and easy with the Coffman cartridge starter system – if all went well. If one had given more strokes of the priming pump than the temperature required (usually 80–90°F ambient in Malaya) impressive sheets of flame poured from the stub exhausts. Setting too much throttle before starting could result in the tail lifting as the prop revved fast when the engine fired, with the possibility of the five-bladed propeller touching the ground. So I got into the habit of holding the stick right back with the left leg, pressing the starter and booster coil buttons, which were on the right, with the left fingers, and keeping the right hand free to push the priming pump handle only as the engine fired, perhaps having given it a touch beforehand.
>
> On take-off there was no need to use anything like full throttle, +7psi boost being ample; but even so the propeller generated enormous torque (and gyroscopic effect) with consequent yawing tendency, and it was necessary to set full left rudder to keep the aircraft straight (one tyre still wore out sooner than the other).

> Handling in the air was generally very pleasant and easy, though not, I believe, as good as the XVI. Except in some situations the aircraft was very docile, e.g. it could only be persuaded to spin with reluctance. There was usually plenty of stall warning from a quite marked rudder judder. The difficulties were the marked tendency to yaw if large throttle movements were made, and also the constant changes in rudder required with changes in airspeed. One could get a nasty yaw – if one was not ready to catch it – when the auxiliary rear fuel tank behind the seat emptied. It had no gauge, so the drill was to fly on it until the engine cut, then turn off the rear fuel cock and then turn on the main, whereupon the engine cut in again – usually! (The rear fuel tank was only filled when necessary for a longer than usual flight, since it made the aircraft a bit unstable in pitch.)
>
> Again, constant attention to trim was necessary in an attacking dive, whether for gunnery or, most of all, in dive bombing. Which we usually tried to do in a 60-degree dive, starting from 7–8,000ft. Otherwise the large speed change resulted in a skidding effect which pointed the gunsight away from where the aircraft was going.

Flt Lt John Wood comments on diving speeds:

> I corresponded with Jeffrey Quill about this and was given some very interesting facts that included the following. From the Spitfire Mark I onwards every production Spitfire was dived to the design maximum speed (V_D) of 470mph IAS. From the Mark 21 onwards this was increased to 525mph IAS. The Spitfire was regularly dived in excess of this by the test pilots. Quill also stated the Spitfire was superior to the Bf 109 in diving speed, but the Bf 109 had an opening advantage to the Merlin Spitfire in its initial dive acceleration, but that its controls were terribly heavy above 400mph.

It must however be stated that in the early days not all pilots were wildly enthusiastic about the Spitfire. For instance, during the Battle of Britain there were some pilots who preferred the Hurricane, as it was a better gun platform. Group Captain Wray DFC, who was a widely experienced pilot from Blenheims to Tempests, summarizing his own experiences to the author, said that although he liked the Spitfire, he considered the Mustang to be 'the finest all-round fighter aircraft of World War Two'.

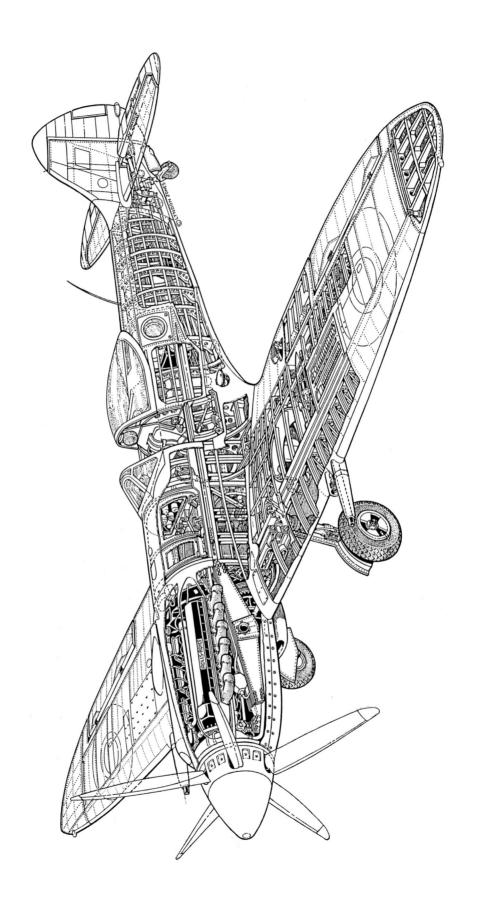

Spitfire FR.XVIII.

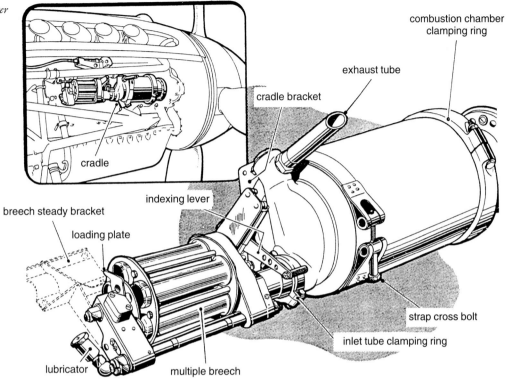

The Coffman starter and breech on the Griffon engine.

combustion chamber clamping ring

exhaust tube

cradle bracket

cradle

indexing lever

breech steady bracket

loading plate

strap cross bolt

inlet tube clamping ring

lubricator

multiple breech

Early Griffon Engine Development

The Griffon engine originally started life as a de-rated version of the Rolls-Royce 'R' engine, with the prototype tested on the bench in 1933. It was then put on hold until January 1939, when the company was considering an engine to replace the Merlin, that would be a direct fit into the same aircraft installation. It had already been realized that the Griffon would be the ideal engine, but with Merlin-size cylinders. The exigencies of the period gave insufficient time to carry out this re-design, but as the Griffon's length was excessive for installation in the Spitfire, detail planning was carried out to make a partial re-design so that it could be a direct replacement for the Merlin. The camshaft drive, magneto drives and magnetos were moved to the front of the engine, in the same lateral plane as the reduction gear.

The first wartime Griffons were running on the test beds in November 1939, but the crankshafts fractured in two during the tests. A relative newcomer to the design office wrote to Hives and pointed out that the Griffon's crankshaft rotated in the opposite direction to the Merlin's, but had the same spiral. Hives had a new, re-designed crankshaft manufactured that was based on the different spiral; this was tested and installed, and the problem solved – a self-inflicted injury!

Two early problems encountered when testing the Griffon involved the supercharger. One concerned the step-up gear, whose second part did not give a balanced drive. The second concerned the supercharger drive itself, which centred on Fairchild hydraulic clutches. It was found that these, after around ten hours on test, became packed with sludge due to the oil being centrifuged during the revolving of the clutch housing. As at that time it was not possible to include a centrifuge in the design, a completely new clutch was designed to replace the Fairchild clutch. This was a housing that revolved at up to 12,000rpm and contained one set of swing-type clutchweights, which engaged each of two clutches by means of a twin hydraulic ram. This ram was within a large-diameter shaft, but was held stationary against a cover containing the two-way operating valve.

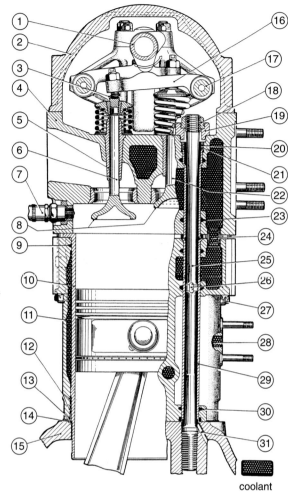

coolant

The Griffon cylinder block.

1. camshaft
2. rocker cover
3. hardened tip
4. cylinder head
5. valve guide
6. inlet valve
7. sparking plug
8. corrosion resistant faces
9. rubber ring
10. wide-flange liner
11. cylinder skirt
12. coolant glands
13. sealing collar
14. rubber ring
15. crankcase
16. valve rocker
17. rocker spindle
18. cylinder block holding-down nut
19. clamp
20. circlip
21. stud tube retaining nut
22. exhaust valve
23. rubber ring
24. coolant transfer ferrule
25. cylinder block securing stud
26. flats for oil drain
27. nut securing skirt to head
28. coolant inlet
29. stud tube (oil drain)
30. rubber ring
31. oil drain to crankcase

Specification – Rolls-Royce Griffon II

Bore	6.0in (152mm)
Stroke	6.6in (168mm)
Capacity	36.7ltr
Fuel grade	100/130
Compression ratio	6.0:1
Reduction gear ratio	0.451:1
Take-off rating at sea level	1,620bhp at 2,750rpm
Maximum power rating	MS 1,730bhp at 2,750rpm at 750ft (230m)
	FS 1,490bhp at 2,750rpm at 14,000ft (4,300m)

The first part of the supercharger drive was originally carried at the front of the engine, with a gear mounted on the front end of the crankshaft and driving a pinion via a long shaft. This was not liked for manufacturing reasons, and so on later versions of the Griffon this step-up gear train was moved to the rear of the engine.

Griffon-Powered Airframe Development

Supermarine's design team had been investigating the possible installation of a Griffon engine into the Spitfire airframe from early 1939, and had raised their Specification 466 covering this. During October 1939 this was submitted to the Air Ministry as the Type 337 for a Griffon-powered Spitfire. Following this, on 9 November, N.E. Rowe of DTD minuted the Director of Requirements (DOR) with the details of the Supermarine scheme. Nothing further appears to have surfaced until around March/April 1941 when the Air Staff consulted and compiled a specification for a Griffon-powered Spitfire, and on 23 May 1941 Specification F.4/41 was issued for the Spitfire IV. Some of the requirements were:

- maximum speed not to be less than 410mph (660km/h) at 22,000ft (6,700m);
- take-off over a 50ft (15m) barrier not to be more than 500yd (460m); and
- landing run over a 50ft barrier to be about 700yd (640m).

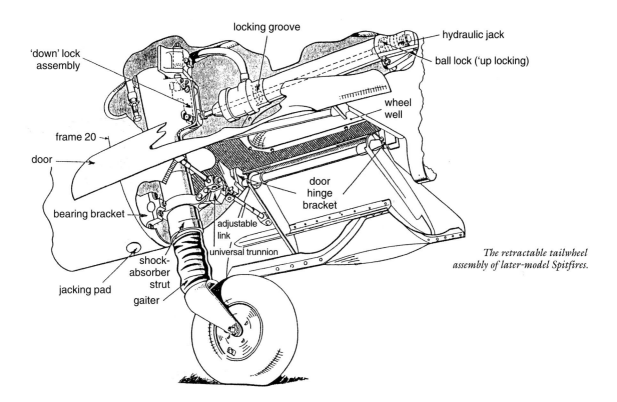

The retractable tailwheel assembly of later-model Spitfires.

Modifications to the existing 'B' airframe were:

- the engine mounting would need to be changed and the cowlings re-designed;
- the fuel and cooling systems would need some alteration; and
- minor strengthening of the wing spar would be needed.

Two Mark III airframes, DP845 and DP851, were set aside for conversion. In late 1941 a Griffon RG2SM engine was delivered to Supermarine and installed in DP845. It was found during the engine installation that several parts of the engine protruded through the original cowling line: Rolls-Royce had to re-design the cowlings to bring these protrusions within the lines of the aircraft. With the increased engine power came the inevitable need for strengthened longerons to take the heavier engine, and increased cooling capability. With the introduction of the two-stage supercharger came twin radiators, one combining glycol and oil-cooler matrixes, and the other glycol and intercooler matrixes.

The original concept of the Spitfire IV powered by a single-stage Griffon began to grow, as things developed, into a more extensively re-designed aircraft powered by the two-speed, two-stage Griffon. This was probably hastened by the appearance of the Fw 190 on the Channel Front, which had originally been mis-identified as a modified Curtiss 75 Mohawk. It was soon realized that the Fw 190 was a more potent enemy fighter with excellent lateral manoeuvrability and good low- and medium-altitude performance, though in its early stages inhibited by an overheating and unreliable BMW 801 engine.

The two airframes were converted to Griffon power with the wingspan at 36ft 10in (11.23m) and aircraft overall length of 31ft 10in (9.7m), with an enlarged rudder area. DP845 first flew on 27 November 1941 powered by a (single-stage) Griffon II. DP851 was developed further than DP845 and so made its maiden flight later, on 8 August 1942. It was then further developed towards the Spitfire 21 concept, of which more later. DP845 was designated a Mark IV, but was later re-designated a Mark XII as the Mark IV designation was allocated to the PR range.

Pilot's Notes for the standard Spitfire XII gave the approximate stalling speeds with 'engine off' at normal AUW of 7,400lb (3,360kg) as follows:

- undercarriage and flaps 'down' 74mph (120km/h) ias;
- undercarriage and flaps 'up' 82mph (132km/h) ias.

With the installation of the Griffon engine in the Spitfire, Supermarine took the opportunity to improve the forward vision by lowering the nose-line, and also to incorporate some speed-enhancing features, for instance:

- retractable tailwheel saved 5mph (8km/h);
- clipped wing tips saved 1mph (1.6km/h);
- new rear-view hood saved 1mph (1.6km/h);
- propeller root fairings saved 4mph (6km/h);
- plain ailerons saved 6mph (10km/h); and
- multi-ejector exhaust saved 4mph (6km/h).

In flight the Spitfire XII handled somewhat similarly to the Mark V, but longitudinally it was more stable as its CG was further forward. Rudder control was heavier and aileron forces greater. In production form the Mark XII's rudder control was improved and the need for constant trimming was corrected. It was an excellent aircraft in its role as a low-level fighter as it was fast low down and very manoeuvrable, being capable of 372mph (600km/h) at 5,000ft (1,500m).

The Mark 21 was the next step in Spitfire development, and was a large stride forward, the concept growing from the Mark IV prototype, DP851. Supermarine's designation for the Spitfire Mark 21 was Type 356 and the design time involved in developing it would be 168,050 hours, the next highest time after the Spitfire prototype. As well as the design being influenced by armament trends, Joe Smith and his team wanted to improve the lateral manoeuvrability of the Spitfire. To achieve the latter, the torsional stiffness of the wings needed to be improved to reduce or prevent aileron reversal. A taller and wider undercarriage was required to allow the fitting of an 11ft-diameter (3.35m) propeller to absorb the thrust from the Griffon 61 or 65 engine. A taller undercarriage meant that to retract it into the same space in the mainplane a means had to be found to have both a normal-length undercarriage leg and a long oleo extension!

A&AEE test data for Spitfire XII DP845

Wingspan	36ft 10in (11.23m)
Length	30ft 10in (9.7m)
All-up weight at take-off	7,415lb (3,363kg)
Wing loading at AUW	30.6lb/sq ft (149.4kg/sq m)
Engine	Griffon IIB
Supercharger	single-stage, two-speed
Propeller	four-blade, 20ft 5in (6.22m) diameter
Maximum speed (TAS)	
at sea level	346mph (557km/h)
at 4,000ft (1,200m)	364mph (586km/h)
at 10,000ft (3,000m)	370.5mph (596km/h)
at 12,000ft (3,700m)	370mph (595km/h)
at 24,000ft (7,300m)	394mph (634km/h)
Climb	6.7min to 20,000ft (6,000m)
	rate of climb 2,230ft/min (680m/min)
	12.95min to 30,000ft (9,100m)
	rate of climb 1,110ft/minute (340m/min)
Ceiling	38,200ft (11,600m)
Stalling speed (engine off)	65mph (105km/h) ias with all 'down' (engine off)
	75mph (121km/h) ias with all retracted

This was achieved by a linkage that reduced the oleo extension length as the undercarriage retracted. The DP851 prototype was, however, only a half-way house on the way to what Supermarine was after, so a major re-design took place to increase wing stiffness, increase the fuel load and raise the aileron reversal speed.

When fitted with a single-stage Griffon engine, the airframe was designated the Mark 20; when fitted with a two-stage Griffon it would be designated Mark 21. However, with the two-stage Griffon not entering production until August/September 1943

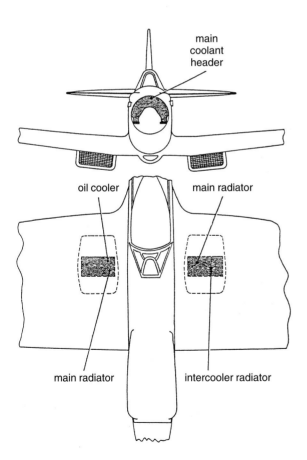

PROPELLER

MARK	TYPE	BLADE	DIAMETER	
			FOOT	M
IX AND XVI	ROTOL	4	10'9"	(3.28)
SPITFIRE 21	ROTOL	5	11'	(3.35)
22 AND 24	ROTOL	2X5	11'	(3.35)

equire-
ed.
or sec-
gan in
rted to
-speed
essen-
te the
trials
d the
imum
00m)
/min
at the
Mark
or an
h an
ed to

oil cooler   main radiator

main coolant header

main radiator   intercooler radiator

Radiator and oil cooler disposition on Spitfire Marks 22–24.

Mark VIIIG JF319 was developed by Supermarine to a standard for submitting for test at A&AEE Boscombe Down. This aircraft was fitted with Griffon RG5SM serial number 1282, with +18psi boost. This drove a Rotol 10ft 5in-diameter (3.17m) propeller through a 0.5:1 reduction gear. The aircraft's all-up weight was 8,400lb (3,800kg). The performance of this aircraft was:

maximum speed	MS gear 389mph (626km/h) at 16,000ft (4,900m) FS gear 447mph (719km/h) at 25,000ft (7,600m)
climb to 20,000ft (6,000m)	just over 5 minutes
climb to 40,000ft (12,000m)	15 minutes

The Type 366 was the Griffon-powered Spitfire XII, and was the first Griffon-engined production mark to go into service. However, it was the Type 379 Spitfire XIV which would be the first Griffon-powered Spitfire to go into large-scale production. The Mark XIV featuring the two-stage, two-speed Griffon 65 engine. The longer and more powerful engine meant lengthening the nose, with the top cowling incorporating blisters to accommodate the cylinder heads; the oil tank was also re-positioned, from under the crankcase to a position in front of the main fuel tank and behind the fireproof bulkhead.

Handling of the Griffon-Spitfires with their longer noses and heavier engines required even more careful throttle and brake handling when taxiing, and it was essential that the stick was held fully back. On take-off it was an entirely different beast to the less powerful Merlin-Spitfire: full-left rudder trim and full-left rudder was essential on the initial take-off run. Lift-off took place at around 80–90kt (150–165km/h) without any difficulty, providing the propeller was kept up off the runway! A climb performance comparison of typical Mark XIV and Mark XXI aircraft at A&AEE gave the results shown in the table (*see* p. 64).

Whilst no other enemy aircraft, except the Japanese A6M 'Zero', could out-turn the Spitfire, both the 'Zero' and the Fw 190 had a higher rate of roll, with the latter having exceptionally well-harmonized controls.

Spitfire JP321 was experimentally fitted with a Rotol six-blade contra-rotating propeller. (Some

Climb performance comparison of Spitfire XIV and XXI

	Mk XIV	Mk XXI
Time		
to 12,000ft (3,700m)	2min 51sec	2min 54sec
to 30,000ft (9,100m)	8min 21sec	8min 51sec
Rate of climb		
at 12,000ft	3,600ft/min (1,100m/min)	3,570ft/min (1,100m/min)
at 30,000ft	2,390ft/min (730m/min)	2,030ft/min (620m/min)
Maximum speed		
at 12,000ft	388mph (624km/h)	411mph (661km/h)
at 30,000ft	443mph (713km/h)	436mph (702km/h)

early Spitfires had been fitted with contra-rotating propellers in which the translational bearing failed, causing the rear propeller to go out of control.) With the enlarged tail surfaces and other modifications, and powered by a Griffon 65 driving a five-blade Rotol propeller, the type was designated the Spitfire XIV, and the Air Staff authorized it to replace the outstanding Mark VIII orders. The first production Mark XIV was RBl40.

Flt Lt J.C.M. Wood commenting on the later Spitfires:

I flew both the Merlin- and Griffon-engined [XIV/XIX] marks. Handling of both types in the air was, in general, most pleasant and tractable with possibly the Merlin-powered Mark IX/XVI having the edge in this respect. The comments in the earlier section dealing

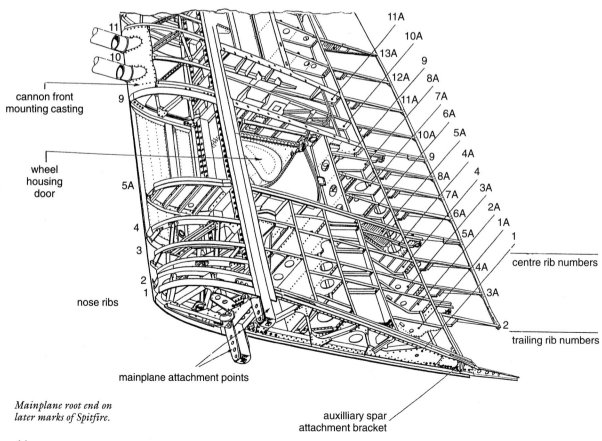

Mainplane root end on later marks of Spitfire.

64

with the handling and general flying of the Merlin-powered IX/XVI also apply to the Griffon Spitfires, but these later Spitfires, being heavier with greater power, demanded a little more in the handling and used up, not surprisingly, a little more sky in some manoeuvres, but were generally similar in their turning ability and roll rates.

The Marks XVI/XIX, being later and more powerful were faster, had a higher rate of climb, a better zoom climb, and had a higher acceleration in the dive. As regards maximum diving speeds, the Griffon series had the slightly higher limiting TAS/Mach number of the two in the dive, and both types could boast as being the only operational fighters, in operational trim, to have official diving speed limitations equating to a Mach limitation of 0.85 at the higher levels.

Regarding the more critical phases of operation of take-off and approach. The Griffon's seemingly relatively low maximum take-off boost of +7psi nevertheless produced, from the large five-bladed propeller, enormous torque, gyroscopic, asymmetric blade and helical slipstream effects which demanded full-left rudder trim and full-left rudder. Another critical stage of flight was on the approach when overshooting, for it was essential not to increase power in excess of the rudder control available at the relatively low approach speed. But if excessive power was used a torque stall resulted, causing the aircraft to roll and yaw to starboard uncontrollably and dive fatally.

Regarding cruise setting. With both the Merlin and Griffon Spitfires the technique was to set the maximum obtainable boost in MS, not exceeding maximum continuous weak mixture boost, then reduce the rpm to obtain the required speed. With increase of altitude the required speed in MS would not be attainable as boost fell, even with full throttle and maximum cruise rpm, so a change to FS gear had to be made to restore boost and lower rpm.

The prototype Mark 21 was PP39 and its performance was the fastest yet, but its handling was not satisfactory.

With the Spitfire 21 came a new wing that was 47 per cent stiffer, carried more fuel and had a heavier armament. The airframe had a theoretical aileron reversal speed of 825mph (1,327km/h), as opposed to the earlier types' 580mph (933km/h). On take-off the Griffon's powerful torque required a great deal of rudder to control it, and the starboard wing

was liable to dip until airspeed increased. It climbed to 40,000ft (12,200m) in just over ten minutes. The lightness of the controls at high speeds was greatly improved; however, in slow rolls the ailerons were ineffective, and rolls and aileron turns at 500mph (800km/h) ias or above had to be made with care.

A development of the Mark 21 was the Mark 22, which had a completely new and larger tail unit that increased the aircraft length by 3in to 31ft 11in (9.73m). This tail unit brought a vast improvement in handling compared with the Mark 21, which had been criticized by A&AEE pilots as being 'unstable in the yawing plane'. From the Mark 22 was developed the Mark 24, with a cut-down rear fuselage and an all-vision cockpit canopy. It was considered to be the ultimate Spitfire in a combination of manoeuvrability, handling, speed, climb and ceiling. Late production Mark 24 aircraft were fitted with the short-barrelled Hispano-Suiza Mark V 20mm cannon.

The initial introduction of the Rolls-Royce Griffon had been as a single-stage, two-speed version for Fleet Air Arm aircraft, but for the installation of

Specification – Spitfire 21

Wingspan	36ft 11in (11.25m)
Wing area	243.6sq ft (22.63sq m)
Wing loading	38lb/sq ft (186kg/m)
Aspect ratio	5.68
Undercarriage track	6ft 4¼in (1.94m)
Engine type	Griffon 61
Fuel rating	115/145
Take-off rating	1,900bhp at 2,750rpm +18psi at sea level
Military rating	MS 2,035bhp at 2,750rpm at 7,000ft (2,100m)
	FS 1,820bhp at 2,750rpm at 21,000ft (6,400m)
Propeller	Rotol five-blade, 11ft (3.35m) diameter
Total fuel capacity	120gal (545ltr)
Armament	four 20mm cannon
Operational all-up-weight	9,124–9,305lb (4,138–4,220kg)

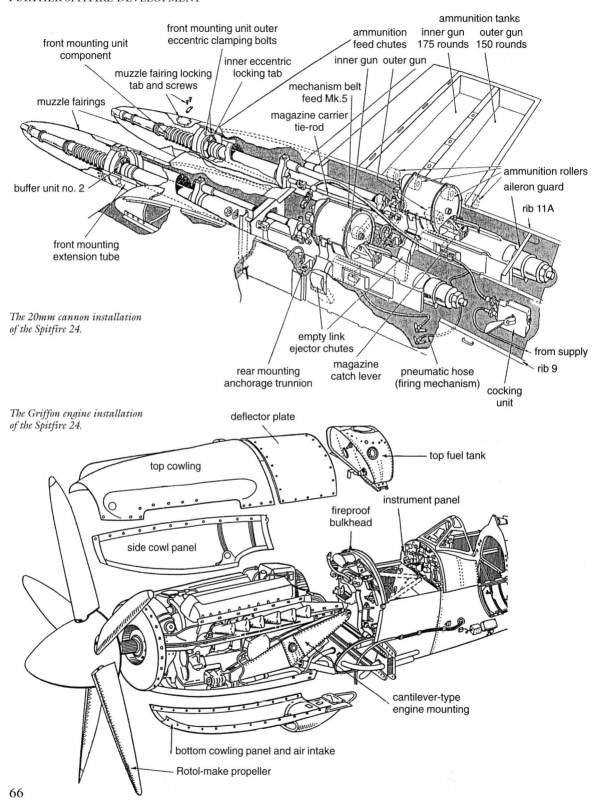

front mounting unit
component

front mounting unit outer
eccentric clamping bolts

muzzle fairing locking
tab and screws

inner eccentric
locking tab

ammunition
feed chutes

ammunition tanks
inner gun   outer gun
175 rounds   150 rounds

inner gun outer gun

muzzle fairings

mechanism belt
feed Mk.5

magazine carrier
tie-rod

buffer unit no. 2

ammunition rollers
aileron guard

rib 11A

front mounting
extension tube

*The 20mm cannon installation
of the Spitfire 24.*

empty link
ejector chutes

rear mounting
anchorage trunnion

magazine
catch lever

pneumatic hose
(firing mechanism)

from supply

rib 9

cocking
unit

*The Griffon engine installation
of the Spitfire 24.*

deflector plate

top fuel tank

top cowling

instrument panel

fireproof
bulkhead

side cowl panel

cantilever-type
engine mounting

bottom cowling panel and air intake

Rotol-make propeller

66

Manufacturer's data for Spitfires 22 and 24

Wingspan	36ft 11in (11.25m)
Wing area	243.6sq ft (22.63sq m)
Wing loading	40.5lb/sq ft (198kg/sq m)
Aerofoil section	NACA 2200 series
Aspect ratio	5.68
Incidence	+2 degrees at root
Dihedral	6 degrees
Standard mean chord	7ft 2.3in (2.19m)
Aircraft length (horizontal)	32ft 11in (10/03m)
Tailplane span	12ft 10in (3.91m)
Area with elevators	42.56sq ft (3.95sq m)
Fin area	9.95sq ft (0.924sq m)
Rudder area	10.55sq ft (0.98sq m)
Undercarriage track	6ft 8in (2.03m)
Powerplant	Griffon 61 or 64
Power loading	4.17lb/bhp (1.89kg/bhp)
Propeller type	Rotol R14/5F5/2 five-blade, 11ft (3.35m) diameter
Tare weight	7,160lb (3,250kg)
All-up weight	9,900lb (4,500kg)
Maximum fuel capacity	*Mark 22* 210gal (955ltr)
	Mark 24 276gal (1,255ltr)
Maximum speed	MS gear 412mph (663km/h) at 5,000ft (1,500m)
	FS gear 450mph (724km/h) at 19,600ft (6,000m)
Rate of climb	MS gear 4,900ft/min (1,500m/min)
	FS gear 4,100ft/min (1,250m/min)
Service ceiling	43,000ft (13,100m)

Specification – Griffon 61

Bore	6.0in (152mm)
Stroke	6.6in (168mm)
Capacity	36.7ltr
Supercharger	two-speed two-stage centrifugal
Supercharger gear ratios	MS 5.84:1
	FS 7.58:1
Weight/power	0.93lb/bhp (0.42kg/bhp)
Piston speed	3,025ft/min (922m/min)
BMEP	288lb/sq in (20kg/sq cm)
SFC	0.50lb/bhp/hr (0.23kg/bhp/hr)
Fuel grade	100/130 rating
Carburation	Bendix-Stromberg 9T/40/1
Maximum fuel demand	179gal/hr (814ltr/hr) at +18psi boost
Take-off rating	1,900bhp at 2,750rpm with +18psi boost at sea level
Military rating	MS 2,035bhp at 2,750rpm with +18psi boost at 7,000ft (2,100m)
	FS 1,820bhp at 2,750rpm with +18psi boost at 21,000ft (6,400m)
Military rating	MS 2,375bhp at 2,750rpm with +25psi boost at 1,250ft* (380m)
	FS 2,145bhp at 2,750rpm with +25psi boost at 16,000ft* (4,900m)
Maximum climb	MS 1,490bhp at 2,600rpm with +9psi boost at 13,500ft (4,100m)
	FS 1,365bhp at 2,600rpm with +9psi boost at 26,500ft (8,100m)

*higher power rating using 115/145 grade fuel +25 psi boost

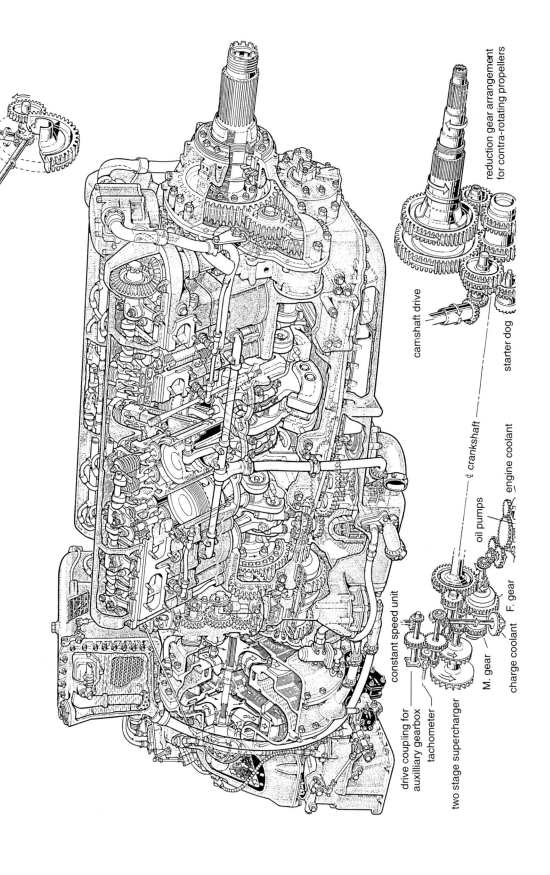

Griffon Marks 61–65.

magneto drive

camshaft drive

reduction gear arrangement
for contra-rotating propellers

camshaft drive

starter dog

¢ crankshaft

engine coolant

oil pumps

M. gear   F. gear

charge coolant

constant speed unit

drive coupling for
auxilliary gearbox

tachometer

two stage supercharger

the Griffon in the Spitfire the Air Ministry required a two-stage, two-speed version, and so the Mark 61 was introduced. The 60 series engines had interconnected throttle and propeller controls, and an automatic gear change.

Progressive Improvement

From an aerodynamic and flying aspect the Spitfire must be considered a classic. However, Mitchell designed it as a flying machine, and it was left to Joe Smith and his team to make it into a production fighter design, and from the manufacturing and maintenance points of view the Spitfire was far from a 100 per cent success. The elliptical wings created problems for production, and the wing design and engine installation made maintenance far from easy in comparison with, say, the Hurricane. The Browning 0.303in machine guns and the 20mm cannon, with their ammunition boxes and trays, were a problem for the armourers: the various pieces of armament had been squeezed in almost as an afterthought. The narrow track of the undercarriage reduced the aircraft's stability on the ground, and this resulted in many collapsed undercarriages.

An important point needs to be made about the Spitfire's diving performance, as quite often the terms 'maximum diving speed' and 'initial acceleration in a dive' are confused. The initial dive acceleration of the Bf 109 series was faster than the Merlin Spitfire's, but the Griffon Spitfire was certainly superior in this respect. As regards diving speeds – that is, the sustained diving speed – both the Merlin and Griffon Spitfires were supreme in this respect above about 20,000ft (6,000m), and in a prolonged dive the Spitfire could overhaul both the Bf 109 or Fw 190.

In case the reader should get the impression from the various modifications made to the Spitfire during its life, that Supermarine was always trying to catch up with the opposition, it should be pointed out that in war both sides are trying to better their opponents. So it was in the Second World War: first Britain held the lead in fighter superiority and then Germany, but at no time was there a period when Supermarine were unable to field a new Spitfire to take on and beat the opposition. At Rolls-Royce the design and development team were always able to stretch the Merlin and Griffon to give power to the Spitfire and other aircraft.

The Spitfire's construction did not change a great deal over the various marks, the main changes being in the wings. These were of NACA 2200 series with a thickness/chord ratio of 8 per cent at the mean chord and 6 per cent at the tip. The original mainplanes were of single main-spar construction with an auxiliary spar at the rear, the single main spar forming a 'D'-shaped torsion-box structure with the thick-skinned leading edge. The main spar itself was a built-up series of square tubular duralumin booms telescoped into each other and stopped-off at intervals outwards as the main-spar thickness thinned towards the tip, the two booms being joined by a single web. The mainplanes were improved in various ways over the years, to accept different armament and equipment for various roles, and were stiffened to reduce the flexing. With the re-design of the Mark XVIII onwards a change was made to the spar construction, in that Supermarine used extruded-section DTD 364 machined on the taper. The stressed skin permitted the increasing of the gauge where extra strength was required.

The Mark XVIII was basically a Mark XIV with strengthened wings and undercarriage, and a revised fuel system. Stronger longerons were fitted in the fuselage to allow it to accept heavier loads (mainly the engine); but these were still alterations to the basic airframe and shape, not wholesale re-design. Two versions were produced, the F.XVIII and the FR.XVIII, the latter not having clipped wings. A further photo-reconnaissance version was also produced, this being a Mark XIV fitted with modified Mark Vc mainplanes, and with a universal camera installation.

The Griffon installation in these later series was noteworthy for its large semi-cantilever engine-mounting beam that replaced the original tubular cradle type. The longeron material was changed from duralumin to steel, and alterations were made to the size and shape of fin and rudder to cater for the increased weight, engine power and forward area.

Service Use

The Spitfire first entered service with 19 Squadron at Duxford on 4 August 1938 with more following at intervals to replace the squadron's Gloster Gauntlets. Arrangements were made at Duxford to carry out intensive flying on K9789 so as to help eliminate teething problems. At the outbreak of war on 3 September 1939 there were nine Spitfire squadrons on the RAF's inventory. Many of the Spitfires employed in 1939 were, like the Hurricanes, still fitted with two-blade fixed-pitch propellers and with very little armour protection, so that during early 1940 there was a wholesale flap on to rectify this situation.

During the Battle of France the Spitfire fighter units were not stationed in France, although the PRU aircraft were. With many of the airfields used by the RAF's Advanced Air Striking Force and Air Component being nothing more than rough stubble strips, it was obvious that the more robust Hurricane, with its wide-track undercarriage, was better suited to operations in the field.

When the Battle of Britain began there were nineteen operational Spitfire squadrons on Fighter Command's order of battle, with others on the point of conversion. The operational units were: 54, 64, 65, 74, 92, 234, 609 and 610 Squadrons in 11 Group; 19, 66, 222, 266 and 611 Squadrons in 12 Group; and 41, 72, 152, 602, 603 and 616 Squadrons in 13 Group. The Spitfires, with their speed and manoeuvrability, were more able to cope with the Bf 109s, although it must be remembered that due to the tactics employed by Fighter Command (Hurricanes concentrating primarily on enemy bombers), more enemy aircraft were shot down by the Hurricanes during the battle.

Following the Battle of Britain Air Vice Marshal Trafford Leigh-Mallory and Air Chief Marshal Sholto Douglas took over command of 11 Group and Fighter Command, respectively, and in 1941 they started offensive operations with Bomber Command called 'Circuses' over the Low Countries and France. Contrary to Douglas's reports, these were not only a waste of time, as the small bomb loads (approximately 1,000lb (450kg per aircraft) dropped by the Blenheim bombers caused little damage, but the Luftwaffe in the main refused to accept combat unless conditions were favourable to them. A typical 'Circus' was six to twelve Blenheims escorted by around twelve to fifteen fighter squadrons. Luftwaffe pilots mostly kept out of range, and then went in and picked off stragglers, with the result that RAF losses – including Spitfires – were well in excess of the Luftwaffe's fighter losses. As the Bf 109's armament included cannon, they could attack a target successfully out of range of the British 0.303in machine guns, so contradicting Bader's theories.

The Spitfire was basically a home-defence interceptor, not a long-range escort fighter, but during its service various long-range fuel tanks were developed and fitted. The introduction of the Bf 109F and -G, as well as the Fw 190, meant problems for both both Supermarine and Rolls-Royce, for with the B109F

came heavier armament, a higher ceiling and a higher top speed than the then-current Spitfire, and more so in the Western Desert. As was to be expected, both British companies replied with new or modified machinery that swung the air war back in the RAF's favour – and so air superiority swung backwards and forwards between the Luftwaffe and the RAF.

There was very little difference in the air in the performance between the Spitfire II and V, but the difference in handling between the two marks was remarkable, the metal-covered ailerons of the Mark V almost doubling the rate of roll at high speed and reducing the stick pressure, so improving lateral manoeuvrability and easing the pilot's workload.

By early 1942 it was obvious that the 'Circus' operations were accomplishing very little to deplete the Luftwaffe over France, and Fighter Command were suffering losses similar to those the Luftwaffe had suffered over Britain during the Battle of Britain, without causing similar significant bomb damage. In a seven-week period 174 Spitfires were lost against claims of 137 German aircraft shot down, and we now know that these claims were inflated. During 1941 524 Spitfires were lost against 103 enemy fighters, hardly the success that Leigh-Mallory and Douglas claimed.

Due to these operations a requirement was raised for Spitfires to operate in the air-sea-rescue (ASR) role, so a number of Mark IIs were modified with a small rack for smoke bombs under the port wing, with two flare chutes aft of the cockpit that housed a small dinghy and a food container. These aircraft were designated Mark IIc and were operated by Fighter Command's 275, 276, 277, 281 and 282 Squadrons. They also quite often flew escort to ASR Walruses going over to make a pick-up of a downed pilot in the Channel.

The Spitfire's role as close-escort to the Blenheim bombers over Europe 1941–2 inhibited its offensive capability, which could have been exploited on fighter sweeps and intruder patrols, as had originally been envisaged by Leigh-Mallory's predecessor, Keith Park.

The Spitfire was operated overseas in the various theatres right through to 1945, and beyond. In the Middle East and Far East the huge air filter that was needed degraded its performance, and its undercarriage was again to prove the limiting factor as regards airstrips. However, in the Far East the Spitfire at last brought a more competitive edge to the battle against the Japanese Mitsubishi A6M 'Zero'

Spitfire experimental N33, powered by the Merlin XX; it did not go into production. MAP

Spitfire F.Mk IX of No.331 Squadron Norwegian Air Force. BJORN OLSEN

fighter, especially with the introduction of the Spitfire VIII; and its 20mm armament proved most effective in ground-attack against Japanese armoured vehicles, defence posts and railway engines. Brian Buckley, a Spitfire pilot with 67 Squadron in the Far East:

> When the squadron was equipped with Spitfires [from Hurricanes] in February 1944 the situation changed markedly, the Spitfire being much more manoeuvrable and with a better ceiling.

By the end of the war the Spitfire 21 was a most effective, heavily armed fighter, but would serve with only four squadrons, as construction contracts were cancelled. The same thing happened to the Marks 22 and 24, although one RAF unit, 80 Squadron, continued operating the Mark 24 from Hong Kong until 1952.

Post-war it was considered that there was need for a two-seat, high-speed, single-engined fighter trainer for export, so a number of Spitfires were converted into two-seat trainers with the rear seat having a raised position and hood. Four 0.303in machine guns were fitted for gunnery training, with a camera gun also installed. The first conversion was originally a Mark VIII, which on conversion was designated Type 502 and registered N.32; a number were purchased by the Irish Air Corps.

Some Spitfire Vs were used for experimental purposes. For instance: AB457 had liquid-oxygen injection to the engine; BR114 was used for high-altitude tests; and BR372 was modified to have wing dive brakes. A turn-up for the Spitfire story was, however EN830: this had been captured by the Germans and modified by them with a Daimler-Benz DB605A engine for flight tests to check the cooling system.

Conclusions

The Spitfire as a point-defence fighter or interceptor was excellent, as an escort fighter it was limited by its small fuel load, even with drop tanks. Its

Spitfire trainer prototype N32. MAP

armament and engine power was steadily improved without too much degrading of aircraft handling, although some pilots felt that the later Griffon-powered Spitfires were 'not really Spitfires'. It was, however, like the Bf 109, operated throughout the Second World War in its fighter role, and with a gradual improvement in its maximum speed and armament.

Ease of maintenance did not improve, as performance and handling were the determining factors. It was only really during the war years that consideration was given in aircraft design to ease of maintenance in the field, so that this feature only became a requirement in aircraft that were designed during the latter stages of the war and after. (The exceptions to these were some of the larger fighter aircraft, like the USA's Republic P-47 Thunderbolt, where some consideration had been given in the design to ease the groundcrew's workload.

The Spitfire's wing– although a construction and maintenance problem – had a lower thickness/chord ratio than the wings of other Allied fighters of the period, and so its profile drag at high Mach numbers was less, with shock waves forming at a higher critical Mach number.

The best 'operational' conversion of the Spitfire was in modifying the Mark IX into a tanker, an unofficial adaptation after D-Day for the carriage of

Manufacturer's data for the Spitfire Trainer

Wingspan	36ft 10in (11.23m)
Wing area	242sq ft (22.48sq m)
Overall length	31ft 4½in (9.56m)
All-up weight at take-off	7,400lb (3,360kg)
Wing loading	30.6lb/sq ft (149.5kg/sq m)
Power loading	4.23lb/bhp (1.92kg/bhp)
Maximum speed	MS gear 362mph (583km/h) at 9,000ft (2,700m)
	FS gear 393mph (632km/h) at 20,000ft (6,000m)
Rate of climb	MS gear 4,570ft/minute at 7,000ft (2,100m)
	FS gear 3,890ft/minute at 18,000ft (5,500m)
Service ceiling	40,000ft (12,000m)

Strong's Triple-X beer kegs on the wing bomb racks for the RAF troops in Normandy – approval of the modification being given at ground level by the airmen concerned!

3

The Seafire

With the disastrous finish of the 1940 Norwegian campaign and the demonstration by 46 and 263 RAF Squadrons' pilots that they could land their unhooked Hurricanes on the deck of HMS *Courageous*, the Admiralty decided that they needed Hurricanes to replace the Fleet Air Arm's existing, uncompetitive, fighters. This was followed in late 1941 by a request from the Admiralty for Spitfires, modified to operate from aircraft carriers.

Work was started that December, with 250 Spitfires being transferred from the RAF to the FAA. Then, just before Christmas, Spitfire Vb BL676, having been fitted with an arrester hook and slinging points, started deck-landing trials on HMS *Illustrious*. It was obvious to any aircraft engineer that the Spitfire airframe was not suitable for the rough and tumble of carrier landings, and its narrow track undercarriage spelt trickery and doom for anything other than a good landing. However, such logic did not come into the equation: there was a war on and the Fleet Air Arm needed a viable, fast fighter. BL676's trials on *Illustrious* were deemed to have passed off satisfactory, and so orders were placed for two variants. The first was the Seafire Ib based on the Spitfire Vb with 'B'-type wings, the second the Seafire IIc based on the Spitfire Vc with 'C' wings. The name Sea Spitfire had originally been used, but the carrier's crew soon reduced this to Seafire, and this was later officially recognized.

Great care was taken to ensure that the Seafire's weight was not much greater than the equivalent Spitfire, due to the extra equipment and strengthening points required for the crane slinging points (for lifting the aircraft on board ship) and arrester hook. It was accepted that the drag from these would reduce the maximum level speed slightly. To get the Seafire models operational quickly, neither the Seafire Ib nor the IIc were fitted with folding wings. The contract work for conversion was carried out by AST Ltd of Hamble and Cunliffe-Owen of Eastleigh. The Seafire Ib was a fairly direct adaptation of the existing Spitfire

Vb, an 'A'-frame arrester hook being secured to the bottom longerons at fuselage frame 15 with local strengthening added. Naval radio equipment and IFF was also added – but no semaphore flags! The simplicity of the conversion was such that the weight increase was only 5 per cent and the drag from the external fitting only reduced the maximum speed by around 5–6mph (8–10km/h). The Admiralty had originally wanted the four-cannon armament for the Seafire, but the extra weight was too great, as with the standard armament the take-off run had proven too long for carrier operation.

The IIc was the first major Seafire model, and these were built on the production line as Seafires. On this model, catapult points were installed as well as the arrester hook. An external fish-plate was fitted in the fuselage aft of the pilot's bulkhead to strengthen this area, as this was where the arrester hook stresses were felt.

Further carrier trials were carried out aboard HMS *Victorious* during March–April 1942 while sailing off the Orkneys. These were carried out by experienced pilots, who sorted out a number of problems regarding carrier landings, not least of all being the view ahead on the approach. With the Seafire in the 'three-point landing' position approaching the aircraft carrier, the view forward was obscured by the long nose. From these trials the curved final approach pattern was adopted, which allowed the pilot to keep the carrier and 'batman' in view until rolling out level before touchdown.

Though the Merlin 46 was used on both Seafire marks there was a difference in maximum speed, the Mark IIc's being about 15mph (24km/h) slower than the Mark Ib, due partly to the Mark IIc's all-up weight being about 6 per cent greater than the Mark Ib's, and partly to the extra drag of the added modifications. A number of IIc aircraft were converted to L.IIc by the installation of the Merlin 32 and a strengthened undercarriage. The Seafire Ib aircraft were first embarked in HMS *Furious* in

October 1942, as this carrier had a larger-than-normal aircraft lift and so could accommodate the non-folding wings.

In Service

The Seafire was at the time one of the fastest carrier aircraft, but it was far from being ideal for that role. Its disadvantages were due to its land-based ancestry, for instance its lack of robustness and load-carrying capability, and its narrow-track undercarriage. The Spitfire had been designed for interception duties operating from equipped airfields, whereas the Seafire's base was a short deck that failed to stay still in the vertical plane; and the Seafire's construction and design inhibited the carriage of large quantities of fuel or bombs.

Far more Seafires were damaged or lost in service due to their weaknesses than to enemy action. Its main weakness, which it shared with the Spitfire, was without any doubt its narrow-track undercarriage, which sheared off at the pivot points on heavy landings. A wrinkling in the fuselage skin was a sign of service and too much stress at that point: if the distortion was minor and beyond local repair, the Seafire was despatched to a repair yard. If at sea, then any major buckling in the fuselage resulted in the aircraft being jettisoned over the side.

During repair work on damaged propellers of RAF Spitfires, tests were carried out to determine how much of a damaged propeller blade could be cropped and the aircraft still able to fly. This resulted in a maximum crop being laid down, with all blades being equally cropped on the damaged propeller. This repair would apply particularly to the Fleet Air Arm's Seafires, where deck 'pecking' was a frequent cause of unserviceability.

As most naval fighter interception in and around European waters took place below 10,000ft (3,000m), enemy torpedo bombers slipping in at a lower level still, it was decided that the benefit of the Seafire powered by a Merlin 46 having its maximum speed at 20,000ft (6,000m) was not required. A

Specification – Supermarine Seafire Ib

Engine	Merlin 45 (usually a Merlin 46, but the data here was from a Seafire tested by A&AEE that happened to have a Merlin 45 fitted)
Take-off rating	1,145bhp at 3,000rpm with +12psi boost
Combat rating	1,415bhp at 3,000rpm at 11,000ft (3,400m)
Wingspan	
normal	36ft 10in (11.23m)
clipped	32ft 7in (9.93m)
Wing area	
normal	242sq ft (22.48sq m)
clipped	234sq ft (21.74sq m)
Length	30ft 2½in (9.2m)
Armament	two 20mm cannon and four 0.303in Browning machine guns
Weight	empty 5,910lb (2,680kg)
	loaded 6,718lb (3,047kg)
Maximum speed	295mph (475km/h) at sea level
	355mph (571km/h) at 13,000ft (4,000m)
	341mph (549km/h) at 19,000ft (5,800m)
Rate of climb at sea level	2,700ft/min (820m/min)
Time to 20,000ft (6,000m)	8min

A Seafire on final approach to HMS Formidable, *almost hanging on its propeller!*

A Seafire from HMS Battler *caught its hook on the barrier whilst landing on HMS* Attacker *in 1943, and crashed into parked aircraft. Note its engine in the foreground!* P.W. PORTER

decision was then made to re-engine all Merlin 46-engined Seafires with the Merlin 32. This was confirmed by the installation of a Mark 32 engine in the much-modified ex-Spitfire L1004. The satisfactory service trial of L1004 was followed by the conversion of Seafire IIcs to L.IIc standard. The Merlin 32 had a cropped supercharger impellor and at 3,000rpm with

Specification – Seafire L.IIc

Empty weight	6,106lb (2,769kg)
Loaded weight, normal	7,006lb (3,177kg)
Engine type	Merlin 32
Take-off rating at sea level	3,000rpm with 18psi boost
Combat rating	1,640bhp at 3,000rpm at 1,750ft (530m)
Maximum speed	316mph (508km/h) at sea level
	335mph (539km/h) at 6,000ft (1,800m)
	328mph (528km/h) at 19,000ft (5,800m)
Rate of climb at sea level	3,300ft/min (1,000m)
Time to 5,000ft (1,500m)	1.7min
Radius of action	140 miles (225km)

+18 psi boost at 3,000ft (900m) it churned out 1,640bhp. With this power in hand, the three-blade propeller was replaced with a four-blade one.

As three of the Royal Navy's major armoured aircraft carriers (HMS *Illustrious*, *Formidable* and *Victorious*) had small lifts they could not accommodate the early fixed-wing Seafires in their hangars, which meant that the aircraft had to be arranged on-deck on outriggers exposed to the elements – whose salty contents were far from kind to aeronautical objects and materials.

From the conception of the Seafire, Supermarine had been quite aware of the need for wing folding, and had retained the first production Seafire IIc for the necessary development work. To keep the weight penalty down it was decided to go for manually operated wing folding rather than power operation, though the weight penalty was still 125lb (57kg) per aircraft. A certain amount of wing 'stiffness' was lost, but the torsional rigidity was maintained at 90 per cent of the IIc's wing design factor.

Folding wings on the Seafire were first introduced on the F.III, which was powered with the Merlin 55 driving a four-blade propeller. The prototype conversion was MA970, which started its trials in the middle of November 1942. On this model, production of which commenced in March 1943, there was a gain of 20mph (32km/h) over the Mark IIc at all heights and an initial rate of climb of 4,600ft/min (1,400m/min). Its folding wings were jointed in two places in each wing, the major joint being inboard of the inboard cannon mounting and the second at the wing-to-wing-tip joint. In the interests of simplicity and weight-saving Supermarine and the Fleet Air Arm decided on manual unfolding and locking of the wings. The Seafire L.III was powered by a Merlin 55M, which had a low-altitude supercharger with a cropped (9.5in/240mm) impellor, and the normal exhaust was replaced by the ejector type. This gave performance as detailed in the table (*bottom*).

Specification – Merlin 55 (Seafire III)

Reduction gear ratio	0.477:1
Supercharger gear ratio	9.089:l
Supercharger rotor diameter	10.25in (260mm)
Nett dry weight	1,400lb (635kg)
Cylinder block	two-piece
Take-off rating	1,185bhp at 3,000rpm, +12 psi boost
Combat power rating	1,470bhp at 3,000rpm at 9,250ft (2,820m)
Maximum climb power	2,850rpm, +9 psi boost
Maximum cruise power	2,650rpm, +7 psi boost

A Seafire taking off from HMS Formidable, *just over the forward lift.*

Specification – Supermarine Seafire III

Engine	Merlin 55 or 55M
Take-off rating	1,185bhp at 3,000rpm with +12psi boost
Combat rating	*Mk 55* 1,470bhp at 3,000rpm at 9,250ft (2,800m)
	Mk 55M 1,585bhp at 3,000rpm at 2,750ft (840m)
Fuel capacity, internal	85gal (386ltr)
Overload	90gal (410ltr) drop tank
Weight, empty	6,204lb (2,814kg)
Loaded	7,104lb (3,222kg)
Overload (with 90gal drop tank)	7,950lb (3,605kg)
Maximum speed	348mph (560km/h) at 6,000ft (1,800m)
Maximum initial climb	4,160ft/min (1,270m)
Time to 5,000ft (1,500m)	1.9min
Time to 20,000ft (6,100m)	8min
Maximum tactical altitude	24,000ft (7,300m)
Service ceiling	31,000ft (9,450m)
Maximum range with 90gal drop tank	513 miles (825km)

In the light of the experience of the Norwegian campaign, the Air Ministry asked Supermarine to develop Spitfire floatplanes with a view to operating from fjords, lakes, and so on. As far as is known there were five aircraft converted:

Mk I R6722 reconstructed as a floatplane in 1940;
Mk VB W3760 (Merlin 45 engine) reconstructed as a floatplane in 1943;
Mk V EP751 reconstructed as a floatplane in 1943;
Mk V EP754 reconstructed as a floatplane in 1943;
Mk IXB MJ892 reconstructed as a floatplane in 1943.

These were special conversions of the Spitfire with twin floats and ventral fins to increase the vertical stabilizer area but, as far as is known, none went operational.

Sometimes Seafires, due to tactical considerations, had to be operated from escort carriers, which were smaller and slower than the fleet carriers from which the type usually flew: this made damage and loss to Seafires almost inevitable. At Salerno in Italy, where Seafires flew from escort carriers to provide close support for the Allied invasion forces, the wind was light and the rate of attrition was consequently high. There were some fifty deck crashes, for with only a 15kt (28km/h) wind over the deck the Seafire L.IIc's maximum vertical touchdown velocity of 7ft/sec (2.1m/sec) and 3.5-degree descent path made a crash-landing almost a certainty. This resulted in the availability of the Seafires on the second day of the landings being down to 38 per cent, no fewer than forty-two having been written off during the day.

The clean, beautiful lines of the Seafire did mean that there was no built-in drag, and without air brakes or spoilers there was no controllable drag available to the Seafire pilot to allow him to make small corrections on his approach speed. To aggravate the situation the finely balanced controls and an aft CG made the pilot's control of his approach difficult. The result of this was what one pilot called 'controlled crashes' when referring to landing a Seafire on an aircraft carrier.

The Seafire's narrow-track undercarriage and lack of robustness compared with US carrier aircraft was unfavourable – but once in the air a Seafire was a Spitfire as regards handling. While the Seafire had a high rate of turn and excelled in the rolling plane, as well as being able to reverse its turn quickly, it was not comparable to Japan's A6M 'Zero' in this regard. The 'Zero' has excellent manoeuvrability, especially when flying at around 180mph (290km/h), so Allied fighter pilots were warned against dogfighting with it. The

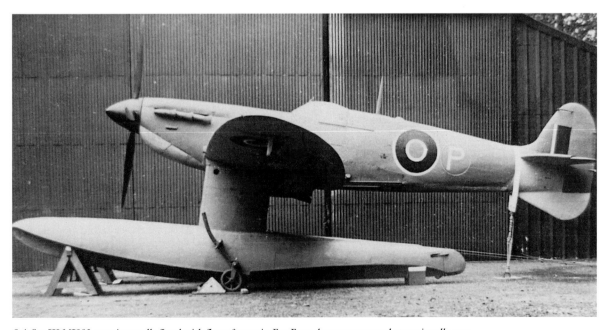

Spitfire IX MJ892 experimentally fitted with floats for use in Far East; these were not used operationally. MAP

Seafire Mark 47 VP428 at the 1948 SBAC Show at Radlett. P.W. PORTER

Seafire could, however, out-climb the 'Zero', so that diving and zoom climbing became part of a Seafire pilot's repertoire in combating the 'Zero'.

Griffon-Powered Seafire

The first prototype Seafire with a Griffon engine was NS487, and this was the origin of the Type 377 Seafire XV, which was built to specification N.4/43. This mark was something of a hotchpotch in its conception, having the L.III airframe allied to the wing-root fuel tanks of the Spitfire IX, the retractable tail-wheel and enlarged vertical surfaces of the Spitfire VIII. It was powered by the Griffon VI, which had a combat rating of 1,815bhp at 4,500ft (1,400m) and 1,730bhp at 13,000ft (4,000m) with +15psi boost. These modifications, along with the fact that the Griffon's was left-hand rotation, as opposed to the Merlin's right-hand rotation, caused the aircraft to track to starboard – that is, towards the carrier 'island' area! – requiring full rudder trim and rudder application on take-off.

The Seafire XV was quite an improvement over the previous marks. Various modifications were tried out to improve its deck-landing characteristics, with both Lt Cdr E. Brown and Lt Cdr Jeffrey Quill (seconded to the Fleet Air Arm) having made recommendations that could be carried out to update and improve the Seafire and its operation. These included a strengthened undercarriage, long-stroke oleos with less rebound, large-area flaps, and improved hook-damping.

On trials, the large-area flaps proved ineffective but the long-stroke oleos were a vast improvement. The adoption of metal-covered ailerons made a control improvement, but it was pointed out that the manufacturing quality needed to be improved. Another improvement came with the major modification, carried out by Westland, of cutting the aft fuselage down to the level of the longerons and fitting a 'teardrop' pilot's cockpit canopy (coupe hood). Another introduction was the sting-type hook with large chord rudder, which was initially trialled on NS490 by Lt Shea-Simonds and Lt Cdr Quill.

The first production Seafire XVs were accepted for service with a strengthened 'A'-type arrester hook on the first few hundred aircraft, whilst the second prototype (NS490) fitted with the sting-type hook went for trials at RAE Farnborough. A new type of throttle box was also fitted that allowed coarser throttle movement, with the gate set at +10psi and combat as +15psi boost. Unfortunately the Griffon 6's MS supercharger clutch had a nasty habit of slipping at high revs and boost settings, which made taking-off from a carrier decidedly dicey. Therefore the Seafire XVs were barred from carrier operation until early 1947, when a modified clutch had been fitted. Once modified, the Griffon 6 proved a reliable engine and was retained for powering the Type 384 Seafire XVII.

A number of the improvements, including the teardrop canopy, were incorporated on the last of the Seafire XVs, which almost brought them up to Mark XVII standard. The Seafire XVII was a direct descendant of the Mark XV, the prototype being a rebuild of Mark XV NS493. This aircraft incorporated a 24V electrical system to replace the previous 12V, provision for wing-mounted rocket projectiles or bombs, a JATO rocket installation for assisted take-off, and a curved windscreen covering the bullet-proof glass.

The fuselage decking aft of the production Seafire XVII's cockpit was cut down and a frameless coupe hood was fitted. A new, strengthened undercarriage and attachments were also fitted, in which the oleos had a longer stroke and were much stronger: this offered not only greater propeller-to-deck clearance, but also a lower rebound ratio, so absorbing the 'bounce' so common with the previous marks of Seafire. A number were also later modified with two F24 cameras, one vertical and one oblique, for photo-reconnaissance duties.

Final Developments

With the re-engineered Spitfire 21 entering service, the Admiralty naturally gave consideration to the possibility of converting the Mark 21 for naval use, as this mark employed a contra-rotating propeller that cancelled out propeller torque. The Mark 21's features were considered against Specification N.5/43 by the Admiralty, but their expectations had been heightened by the Fleet Air Arm's experience of US naval aircraft and it did not fulfil their requirements. Next came the prototype Seafire 45 (TM379) against Specification N.7/44. This was an adaptation of the Spitfire 21 mated to new wings and powered by a two-stage Griffon. On this mark the aileron control was less effective, the forward view had deteriorated and the stalling characteristics had worsened; it was considered a development aircraft, as the aim was for a production Mark 46 (Type 388) that would incorporate a number of new features. This again was a development aircraft, and was in fact again TM379, with the minimum of navalization.

The Mark 46 was really the second stage in the evolution of the FR.47, as the difference between this and previous Seafires mainly concerned the propeller

and the tail-unit assembly. Two Seafire 45s, LA442 and LA444, started trials, powered by a Griffon 85 engine driving a six-bladed contra-rotating propeller. Service trials found the handling transformed with no swing on take-off, loops without rudder correction, and reduced flexing of the wings. 'Wet points' were provided on the mainplanes for the carriage of drop tanks, which now raised the fuel capacity to 228gal (1,036ltr). As an interim development aircraft, only twenty-four of this mark were built and none went into squadron service.

Specification – Supermarine Seafire F.XVII

Wingspan	36ft 10in (11.23m)
Wing area	242sq ft (22.48sq m)
Overall length	32ft 3in (9.83m)
Engine type	Griffon 6
Take-off power	1,735bhp at 2,750rpm with +9 psi boost
Combat power rating	MS 1,815bhp at 2,750rpm with +15psi boost at 4,500ft (1,400m)
	FS 1,730bhp at 2,750rpm at 13,000ft (4,000m)
Fuel capacity, normal	100gal (455ltr)
Drop tank	50gal (230ltr)
Empty weight	7,015lb (3,181kg)
Loaded weight, normal	8,010lb (3,633kg)
Overload (with drop tank)	8,781lb (3,982kg)
Maximum speed	358mph (576km/h) at sea level
	372mph (599km/h) at 9,500ft (2,300m)
	383mph (616km/h) at 23,000ft (7,000m)
Climb time to	
10,000ft (3,000m)	2.5min
20,000ft (6,000m)	6min
Operational ceiling	31,000ft (9,450m)
Radius of action	220 miles (354km)

By the date this mark had emerged the war was over and there was little urgency to introduce the Mark 47 as a production aircraft. Apart from the first fourteen production aircraft, the Mark 47 had hydraulically folding wings, a Griffon 88 engine, large-area flaps and tall tail vertical surfaces. It was fitted with the six-blade contra-rotating propeller that entirely cured the swing and wing stalling on take-off. The heavier Griffon also cancelled out the tail heaviness and the need for weights. The sting-type arrester hook replaced the previous 'A'-frame, and hanging lower it made the hooking-on more positive.

The Mark 47 was the ultimate development of the Seafire, yet its construction differed little from that created by Mitchell and the classic Spitfire shape remained, except for the massive Spiteful tail (*see* Chapter 4). It was considered by its pilots to be a much better aircraft to deck-land than its predecessors, with better stability once on the deck. It was, however, found to have a rather sensitive rudder, the cockpit still had no heating and so was cold at high altitude, and the lateral vision was reduced. Set against that, its control response and manoeuvrability was excellent, with a 360-degree turn at 10,000ft (3,000m) being completed in 26sec, with a rate of climb superior to other piston-engined carrier aircraft.

Conclusions

The Seafire, like the Spitfire, was not an easy aircraft from the maintenance point of view, and aboard a carrier major maintenance was even worse than ashore. As all major components carried aboard a carrier were 'bare', changing a component such as a wing meant transferring all the equipment and wiring from the damaged component to the new one – and this in the restricted space of a carrier hangar and with the vessel itself rolling and tossing.

The Spitfire was basically a short-range, land-based interceptor fighter, so as the basis for a naval aircraft design it was unsatisfactory. The Seafire's offensive capability, apart from its guns, was restricted by its limited ability to carry external stores, and it was not a good weapons platform due to the structural flexing of its airframe. Its short endurance became a worry in the back of a pilot's mind when looking for his mobile base in bad weather, or waiting his turn to land on.

One of a number of outstanding naval aviators who flew the Seafire, in a number of marks and combat engagements, was Lt Cdr Peter Lamb. He survived seven Seafire 'prangs' and went on post-1945 to fly Sea Hawks as CO of 810 Squadron FAA, and then as chief test pilot with Saunders-Roe test flew the SR.53, mentioned in Chapter 7.

In comparison with other naval fighters, the Seafire's low- to medium-altitude performance was classed as 'respectable'. Its acceleration and rate of climb were phenomenal: it could reach a given altitude faster than any other Allied carrier aircraft, which was a great tactical advantage as an interceptor. It was however, handsomely surpassed in diving by the heavier, radial-engined US fighters, who also had the range and endurance that the Seafire/Spitfire series lacked. As an all-round carrier fighter the Seafire was not in the same league as the American Bearcat, Hellcat and Corsair, but it met the Royal Navy's need when there was nothing else available.

Specification – Supermarine Seafire 47

Wingspan	36ft 11in (11.25m)
Wing area	243.6sq ft (22.63sq m)
Length	34ft 4in (10.47m)
Wing loading, normal	41.9lb/sq ft (204.59kg/sq m)
Powerplant	Griffon
Power loading	4.29lb/bhp (1.95kg/bhp)
Fuel capacity, internal	153gal (696ltr)
Maximum speed	353mph (568km/h) at sea level
	452mph (727km/h) at 20,500ft (6,250m)
Maximum initial climb	4,790ft/min (1,460m/min)
Time to 20,000ft	4.9min
Service ceiling	43,100ft (13,000m)
Maximum range	1,475 miles (2,373km)
Empty weight (equipped)	8,680lb (3,937kg)
Normal all-up weight	10,300lb (4,671kg)
Maximum combat take-off weight	12,530lb (5,682kg)
Take-off distance in 30mph (50km/h) wind	378ft (115m)

4

Transition Period

Spitfire XI minus propeller and reduction gear at RAE Farnborough after a test dive to Mach 0.92.

At first glance there appears little connection between the Spitfire and Supermarine's Swift jet fighter of the 1950s, except for the manufacturer's name, yet there does run a fine thread through the designs between the two, even though the compactness of the Spitfire is in direct contrast to the large, rotund shape of the Swift. This thread will become obvious as the text runs through the end of the Spitfire's career and the transition period.

As they completed work on the Griffon-powered Spitfire marks, Joe Smith and his team were also gradually pressing on with various aerodynamic improvements, trying to improve the Spitfire and to develop it along other parameters. Some of their research paralleled other research at various government establishments during the early years of the War. This had already foreseen that increasing speeds with the types of aerofoil then in use would result in increasing drag, and this would eventually limit maximum speeds. Further to this, as speeds increased the 'compressibility' of the air would create shock waves across the mainplane and tail surfaces, which would change the control surface characteristics. It was

found that at Mach 0.85 the greater part of the drag increase was caused by direct shock-wave losses.

In the USA NACA had produced a series of aerofoil profiles, all with the intention of reducing drag by maintaining low drag (or 'laminar flow') as far across the aerofoil chord as possible. On the NACA laminar-flow aerofoil series the greatest thickness of the aerofoil was located much further back along the chord than previously. Britain's first introduction to the laminar-flow aerofoil was with the P-51 Mustang, an outstanding aircraft that brought with it high speed, long range and manoeuvrability. However, since the War it has been determined that extensive laminar flow was not in fact developed on the Mustang's aerofoil, but the cooling drag was much lower than normal due to the large, ducted radiator. This used a large-area matrix with a slow-speed airflow through it, and was based on experiments carried out at RAE Farnborough by F. Meredith's section.

RAE Farnborough was one of the establishments involved in high-speed research and its problems. This started in 1939, with studies of compressibility

SIB P-51H LAST PRODUCTION of P-51

Comparison – Spitfire 24 and Mustang P-51D

	Spitfire 24	*Mustang P-51D*
Wingspan	36ft 11in (11.25m)	37ft ¼in (11.28m)
Wing area	243.6sq ft (22.63sq m)	233.19sq ft (21.66sq m)
Aerofoil section	NACA 2200 Srs	NAA-NACA
Standard mean chord	7ft 2.3in (2.19m)	6ft 10.17in (2.09m)
Incidence	2 degrees	–1 degree
Dihedral	6 degrees	5 degrees
Tailplane		
Span	12ft 10in (3.91m)	13ft 2.33in (4.02m)
Area	42.56sq ft (3.95sq m)	41.03sq ft (3.81sq m)
Incidence	1 degree	2 degree
Dihedral	nil	nil
Elevator area	17.39sq ft (1.62sq m)	13.05sq ft (1.21sq m)
Fin & rudder area	20.50sq ft (1.9sq m)	20.02sq ft (1.86sq m)
Rudder area	10.55sq ft (0.98sq m)	10.41sq ft (0.97sq m)
Aircraft overall length	32ft 11in (10.03m)	32ft 3¼in (9.84m)
Engine	Griffon 61/64	Packard-Merlin V1650-7
Take-off power	1,520bhp	1,490bhp
Wing loading	40.5lb/sq ft (198kg/sq m)	40lb/sq ft (195kg/sq m)
Power loading	4.17lb/bhp (1.89kg/bhp)	6.9–7.5lb/bhp (3.13–3.4kg/bhp)
Undercarriage track	6ft 8in (2.03m)	11ft 10in (3.61m)
Fuel capacity	186gal (846ltr)	184gal (836ltr)
Armament	four 20mm cannon	six 0.5in machine guns
Maximum speed at 20,000ft	449mph (722km/h)	437mph (703km/h)
Rate of climb at sea level	4,900ft/min (1,500m/min)	3,475ft/min (1,060m/min)
Service ceiling	43,000ft (13,000m)	41,900ft (12,800m)
Range	580 miles (930km)	950 miles (1,530km)
Tare weight	6,923lb (3,140kg)	7,125lb (3,230kg)
Normal loaded weight	9,182lb (4,164kg)	11,100lb (5,034kg)

effects on aircraft performance made by collecting and collating data from high-speed fighters in dives during tests in both the USA and UK. This was extended in 1941–2 to include investigation into Spitfire airframe distortion under severe aerodynamic loads. Following this, further research into high-speed aerodynamics commenced from 1942 onwards, both in the RAE Farnborough high-speed tunnel and with the Aerodynamics Flight. A number of reports were issued including Report and Memorandum 2222 (R&M 2222) which compared wind-tunnel test results and flight-test results into compressibility effects in flight. The R&M 2222 report acknowledged the contributions of numerous scientists, and of Sqn Ldrs A.F. Martindale, B.H. Maloney and J.R. Tobin of the Aerodynamic Flight, who had put their lives on the line in diving various aircraft beyond their design speeds.

These RAE investigations into high-speed flight increased in 1943 as aircraft with higher-powered engines and fairly high wing loadings became available. The tests involved aircraft such as the Spitfire, Mustang and Thunderbolt, and the effect that different parts of the airframe had on drag; but were mainly concerned with the compressibility of air, the Spitfire and low-drag aerofoils. These early researches into high-speed flight allowed for few errors and computing the Mach number still presented some difficulty, so it is to RAE Farnborough's credit that their instrument engineers developed what became the first Machmeter.

High-Speed Trials

High-speed flight trials with Spitfires began in 1943 at RAE Farnborough and continued through 1944, with similar tests conducted on other aircraft. The aircraft were of course completely instrumented to the science of the day. The Spitfire type used for the tests were basically of two marks, the PR.XI and the F.21. The PR.XI had a better surface finish than the Mark 21, and for the diving tests its all-up-weight (AUW) was approximately 6,500lb (3,000kg). The Spitfire F.21 resembled the PR.XI fairly closely, but the wing area was about 2 per cent greater, its radiator was larger and the fuselage at the front was larger to accommodate the Griffon engine. For the trials the F.21's AUW was 9,100lb (4,100kg) with a wing loading of 36lb/sq ft (176kg/sq m). As the underwing pressure head on the Spitfire could give inaccurate readings in the test conditions, due to position and compressibility errors, it was replaced by a new pressure head in the leading edge of the wing, which would give smaller errors.

The flight trials report gave details of the preparation of the aircraft and the sequence of the tests, as well as the briefing of the pilots. The maximum angle of dive was usually 45 degrees, with a few as steep as 60 degrees. The dive was maintained until the maximum Mach number was achieved; this was then held for a few seconds before a gentle pull-out was started. A series of tests carried out by Sqn Ldr J. Tobin to compare the high Mach-number characteristics of

a number of aircraft showed that the Spitfire achieved an indicated Mach number 0.92 (corrected to just under 0.9), as against Mach 0.8 for the Mustang Mark I. It was later found out that, of all the aircraft tested, the Spitfire was the only one that was drag-limited, several of the American aircraft being limited by high-frequency vibration of the ailerons and aileron system, usually referred to as aileron 'buzz'.

These flight trials at high Mach-number dives were carried out under strict RAE instructions, as it was known that compressibility brought with it a number of complications in handling the aircraft. The aircraft was accelerated to maximum level speed, then trimmed and the stick eased forward to achieve the dive angle. Once the dive was steady and the Mach number had increased there was a loss of lift and so the nose went down: the pilot then had to pull on the stick to hold the aircraft at the correct dive angle. Normally the elevator trim tab would then be used to offset the load, but the RAE instruction was not to use the trim tab, so as to prevent possible structural failure. This was because, as altitude was lost and the atmospheric temperature increased, the Mach number would decrease and lift would return, this could be quick enough in conjunction with the elevator 'up' trim to result in a fast pull-out and structural failure. Thus a high Mach-number dive would start with the stick forward to initiate the dive, then as Mach 0.73 was reached it would be necessary to pull on the stick to maintain the dive angle – when it was estimated that the pilot would be applying a pull equivalent to 60lb (27kg) – and with the Mach number decreasing as height was lost the pilot would first ease the load on the stick, then revert to pulling back to ease out of the dive.

On 27 April 1944 during a compressibility research dive on Spitfire EN409, Sqn Ldr Martindale went into the record books by achieving a speed of over 600mph (965km/h). He eased the aircraft into a dive at an angle of 45 degrees at 40,500ft (12,350m) and planned to pull-out at 27,000ft (8,200m). Martindale's report states:

I glanced at the altimeter again and saw it drop from 28,000 to 27,000 and knew I was past the high speed. I began to think of easing out of the dive when there was a fearful explosion and the aircraft became enveloped in white smoke. I incorrectly assumed that a structural failure had occurred, as I knew this to be a danger. The aircraft shook from end to end. I knew I could not bail out at such speed so I sat still. The aircraft was doing nothing startling. The screen and hood were now quite black and I could see nothing. Automatically I eased the stick back. After a time I discovered by looking backwards through a chink in the oil film that I was climbing. The airspeed was obviously falling as the noises were dying down. I realized instantly that I could now bail out and opened the hood. It had not jammed.

I then realized that the aircraft was under partial control at least and so switched off the camera which had been winking away all the time. I began to think I might get the aircraft down and so save the film and all the special apparatus. I still did not know what had happened as I could not see through the windscreen.

I pointed the aircraft towards base and called up on the radio. It was working. I tried to look around the screen but my goggles were whipped away. After a time the screen cleared a little. The engine clearly was not going and I could see no propeller. Bits of engine were sticking out and the engine seemed to have shifted sideways. I reported this to base.

Arriving over Odiham at 10,000ft, Martindale steered the aircraft to arrive over Farnborough at 6,000ft. Following instructions from RAE Farnborough Flying Control a 'wheels-down' landing was made there. The gliding back to base had been accomplished without too much difficulty according to Sqn Ldr Martindale – a testimony to his skill in handling the aircraft in a damaged state. (Prior to his RAF service Martindale was a Rolls-Royce test pilot, and would later return to this work.)

Sqn Ldr Martindale's report concluded (after landing) with the following:

I looked at the aircraft and saw that the propeller and reduction gear had gone. A rod was through the side. A main engine bearer had buckled. The leading edge of the wing root was dented and the tailplane looked as though it had had a severe strain.

The Spitfire had reached a speed of 600mph (965km/h), and from the data obtained RAE established that at approximately Mach 0.825 there was a large increase in drag and that the aircraft had reached a true Mach 0.92, at which point the pilot was applying a pull of 80lb on the stick. The recording indicated failure of the reduction gear due to overspeeding of the propeller, caused by loss of engine oil to the constant speed unit during the final part of the dive.

Shortly after this incident the same pilot was repeating the same experiment, but with another Spitfire. This time the engine supercharger burst and the aircraft caught fire. As Farnborough airfield was covered with 10/10th cloud a forced landing had to be quickly made, so Martindale elected to carry out a wheels-up landing at Worplesdon near Guildford. Hitting overhead power cables just before touchdown, the aircraft crashed and caught fire. Even though he suffered an injured back, Martindale removed the recording camera from the aircraft before retreating to a safe distance. For his test-flying Martindale was awarded an Air Force Cross just after the first incident.

Whilst the Spitfire Mk XI had reached Mach 0.92, the P-47 Thunderbolt was at the other end of the scale and suffered 'frozen controls' at a much lower

T/C ratios and Mach limits of six test aircraft

aircraft	aerofoil section	thickness/chord ratio		Mach limit
		(root)	(tip)	
Mustang I	low-drag	0.15	0.11	0.79
Mustang III	low-drag	0.15	0.11	0.82
Spitfire IX	NACA 22XX	0.13	0.07	0.85
Spitfire XI	NACA 22XX	0.13	0.07	0.92
Spitfire XXI	NACA 22XX	0.13	0.07	0.88
Meteor F.1	ECXX /064040	0.12	1.10	0.8

Mach number. R&M No. 2222 listed the details and results of the tests (*see* table p.84).

These flight trials at high Mach numbers, carried out with extreme danger to RAE test pilots, were a further step in the region of transonic flight and contributed enormously to the knowledge of flight handling and the effects of compressibility. This contributed to the design of the Spiteful, which would eventually be involved in the trials, but would make a larger contribution to the Attacker and Swift. RAE Farnborough's contribution to the knowledge of aircraft handling, both normal and at high Mach numbers, is very rarely acknowledged in print – maybe a hangover from the days when it was the Royal Aircraft Factory and C.G. Grey's criticisms in *The Aeroplane* magazine damned it! Nevertheless, most manufacturers have benefited from its contributions to aviation knowledge.

Amongst a number of improvements to the Spitfire, one that was made to the Mark 21 would be incorporated in the Spiteful and Attacker. This was a system of levers to compress the oleos as the undercarriage retracted, so as to accommodate the lengthened leg in the same space in the wing.

During the first half of the Second World War all improvements in aircraft speed were achieved by improvements in engine power, not aerodynamically. At Supermarine, as at other British aircraft manufacturers, only small aerodynamic changes were made, and these were usually related to the aircraft's role. However, Supermarine's design staff had reached the conclusion that, with the steady growth of both the Merlin and Griffon engines, the Spitfire's wing would soon reach the limit of its aerodynamic potential. They were also aware that, though previously they had been able to ignore the effect of the compressibility of the air, as flight speeds were now exceeding Mach 0.6–0.7, the changes in air density that occurred around the aircraft or wing were becoming important and compressibility could no longer be ignored. Another point was that in the area around an aircraft or wing the local air velocity could be equal to the local velocity of sound, and at high Mach numbers a local supersonic flow could be formed, with a shock wave formed at the downstream boundary of the area.

The RAE would again come to Supermarine's aid, as did the National Physics Laboratory (NPL), when a low-drag wing was considered for the Spitfire. Low-drag wing sections, termed laminar flow (*see* p.81), had been one of a number of developments at the NACA of the USA. This would result in a whole series of wind-tunnel tests at the RAE and NPL, covering aerofoil sections, radiator ducts, wing incidence and Mach-number effects.

Spiteful/Seafang Development

At Supermarine two lines of research were embarked on. One was a collaboration between S.R. Hughes of Supermarine and Dr S. Goldstein of the NPL, and would result in the Type 371 aerofoil, a completely new laminar-flow (low-drag) wing. The other led to the Type 372 aerofoil, a modification to the existing Spitfire wing in which the leading edge was lifted. This latter modification was carried out on Spitfire Mk VIII JG204; however, flight trials were disappointing and so further development along these lines was discontinued. The laminar-flow wing, in comparison with other wings of the period, was a thin wing with its maximum thickness further back, so it had to be both stronger and heavier. This type of wing demanded not only greater accuracy in manufacture and surface finish, but it had the penalty of reduced space for fuel, guns, ammunition and undercarriage stowage. In the case of the Spiteful, the wing loading increased to 43lb/sq ft (210kg/sq m).

The Type 371 aerofoil was designed specifically for the Spitfire and was designed to maintain laminar flow as far back as possible across the chord, the aerofoil having maximum thickness at approximately 42 per cent chord. The problem with a laminar-flow aerofoil is that the smallest alteration to the surface affects the airflow, so that it is not only necessary to have well-fitting skin joints, but also to eliminate things like scratches on the skin – even dead flies on the leading edge! In service of course these things occur, so the practical benefits of laminar flow are never up to the theoretical level expected, but were definitely improved when machined wing panels became the norm.

In issuing Specification F.1/43 for a fighter aircraft the Air Ministry created for Supermarine the requirements for their successor to the Spitfire, which would become the Spiteful. In 1943 jet propulsion was largely unproven, so even though the jet's future looked promising (especially under the pressure of war), it was essential that the Air Ministry had newer piston-engined aircraft developed until jet-propelled aircraft became not only viable, but reliable as well. So the Spiteful must be seen in this context, as well as being the continuation of the design line.

Spiteful RB518. MAP

When NN667 was presented to the A&AEE for trials, the unit's report was far from flattering. Generally, the airframe was considered below average for finish, with too much time required for routine operations such as refuelling and re-arming due to inaccessibility. Also criticized were the following:

- the fuselage skin was butt-jointed, which would make it difficult to obtain a superfine paint finish, and the joint filling was tending to dry and fall out;
- the cannon's truncated cone fairings' attachments and the wing access panels were badly located and secured;
- the trailing edges of the rudder and elevators were poor, with cracks already appearing;
- the aileron controls had to be disconnected when re-arming; and
- the pilot's view of the instruments was very good, but the cockpit had too many dirt traps and projections.

The suggested modifications and improvements ran to a whole foolscap page, and in the case of the trailing edges of the rudder and elevator and the construction of the wing tips, the report also went on to say:

... some of the defects due to poor workmanship, and perhaps design, could be avoided if light alloy castings were substituted for the present abrupt bends.

The criticism of the fuselage skinning was overcome on later aircraft by overlapping the sheet skin and blending, with chamfering of the top sheet at the fin–fuselage joint; this improved both the finish and the jointing.

After NN664 had completed its first flight on 8 January 1945, the Ministry placed an order with Supermarine for 150 production Spitefuls to Specification 1/43/PI/SU. By this date it would appear that the RAF's only interest was possibly in the Spiteful's low-drag wing and handling characteristics. The evaluation of the aircraft and its handling problems, and the imminent end of the war, no doubt contributed to its demise: on 5 May 1945 the Ministry cancelled the order. Three Spitefuls were retained by Supermarine and three others were used by service establishments; the remainder went into store at No. 6 Maintenance Unit at Brize Norton.

Two versions of the Spiteful had been proposed originally: the F.XIV powered by a Griffon 69 driving a Rotol five-blade propeller; and the F.XV powered by a Griffon 89 or 90 driving two three-blade, co-axial, contra-rotating propellers. The final version was the

F.XVI, of which only one (RB518) was built. During 1946 this was powered by a Griffon 101, a three-speed, two-stage supercharged engine driving a five-bladed propeller. During its various trials at Supermarine it was fitted with a number of different types of propeller. One of these was a five-blade propeller with blades of NACA aerofoil section: with this fitted, RB518 achieved a speed of 487mph (784km/h) at 33,600ft (10,250m). Next installed was a Griffon 121 engine driving a contra-rotating propeller with blades of Clark Y aerofoil section, with this 470mph (756km/h) was achieved at 30,600ft (9,300m). However, before a full evaluation could be carried out RB518 suffered a forced landing (its seventh!). This time the engine failed and the pilot put it down on Chilbolton airfield; the undercarriage was forced through the mainplanes, causing severe damage. The aircraft was considered beyond economic repair and this was put beyond any doubt when the salvage crane lifting the aircraft dropped it and caused further damage.

Engine Development

The two-stage, two-speed Griffon series that started with the Mark 61 was nearing the end of a line of classic aero-engines. The supercharger layout was basically two superchargers in tandem with an intercooler system independent of the main coolant system, the supercharger changeover selection being controlled by atmospheric capsule.

Because of the cylinder sizes of the Griffon (6.0 × 6.6in as against the Merlin's 5.4 × 6.0in) it was not possible to run at the same high boost pressures as the Merlin on 100/130 grade fuel, because detonation would occur. When higher boost pressures were employed on the Griffon, 115/145 grade fuel was required: thus fuel technology contributed to raising the power on this range of engines.

The final development of the Griffon engine range was the 100–130 series, of which only a few examples were built. This series employed a two-stage, three-speed supercharger and used 115/145 grade fuel.

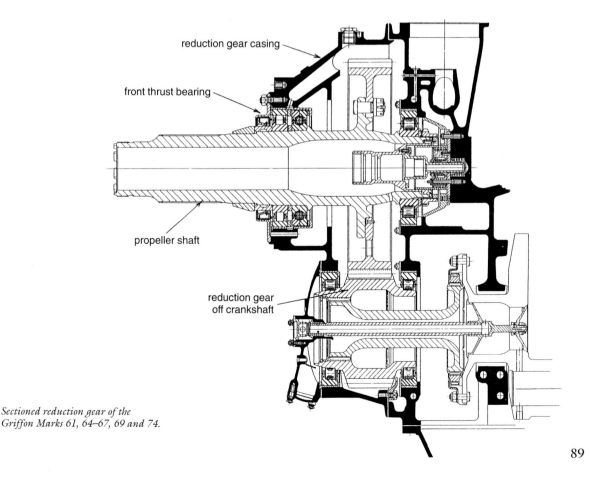

reduction gear casing

front thrust bearing

propeller shaft

reduction gear off crankshaft

Sectioned reduction gear of the Griffon Marks 61, 64–67, 69 and 74.

The Mark 121 drove a six-blade, co-axial, contra-rotating propeller. The Mark 101 had the same type supercharger as the Mk 121 but had a reduction gear of 0.451:1 and a single propeller shaft. The Mark 105 was similar to the Mark 101 but had a reduction gear ratio of 0.51:1 and a contra-rotating propeller similar to the Mark 121's.

Specification – Griffon Mk 69

Cubic capacity	2,239cu in (36.7ltr)
Overall length	81in (206cm)
Overall width	29½in (75cm)
Nett dry weight	2,090lb (948kg)
Reduction gear ratio	0.451:1
Propeller shaft	No.5 SBAC
Supercharger gear ratio	MS 5.84:1
	FS 7.58:1
Supercharger impellor diameter	
	MS 13.4in (34cm)
	FS 11.3in (29cm)
Carburation	Bendix-Stromberg 9T/40/1
Maximum BMEP	286lb/sq in (20kg/sq cm)
Mean piston speed	3,025ft/min (922m/min)
Power/weight ratio	0.941lb/bhp (0.427kg/bhp)
Fuel grade	115/145
Take-off power SL	1,540bhp at 2,750rpm with +12psi boost
Military rating	MS 2,375bhp at 2,750rpm with +25psi boost at 1,250ft (380m)
	FS 2,145bhp at 2,750rpm with +25psi boost at 16,000ft (5,000m)
Maximum climb	MS 1,490bhp at 2,600rpm with +9psi boost at 13,500ft (4,100m)
	FS 1,365bhp at 2,600rpm +9psi boost at 26,500ft (8,100m)

Seafang Development

Supermarine had on 7 October 1943 raised their Specification 474 covering the Type 382. This was a development of the Seafire XV incorporating the laminar-flow wing and powered by a Griffon 61 engine. The documents covering this development were passed to the Ministry of Aircraft Production (MAP), but no interest appears to have been shown until 1945, when the Air Ministry raised Specification N.5/45 for a single-seat fighter for the Fleet Air Arm. This was followed on 21 April 1945 by a contract to Supermarine for two prototypes of the Seafang, as the navalized version of the Spiteful was to be known. This was followed on 7 May 1945 with a production order for 150 Seafangs – rather strangely, this was two days after the cancellation of the Spitefuls!

The first production Seafang, VG471, followed the fifth Spiteful off the production line and was allocated to RAE Farnborough for trials as the F.31. This airframe had 3 degrees more dihedral than the early Spitefuls, and the mainplane had a more rounded leading edge. The result was a sharp wing drop to 80 degrees and a 'clean' stall at 109mph (175km/h). On 15 January VG471 was despatched to RAE Farnborough, where arrester proofing trials began in February. These were terminated when the rudder skin wrinkled during off-centre arrests at 2.7g retardation. Although repairs were carried out, further damage occurred during more trials, so the aircraft was returned to Supermarine's High Post works for modifications.

Test pilots found the Seafang directionally unstable on the ground, but this difficulty was eased because the aircraft had excellent brakes and a tail-wheel lock. It was also found advisable to keep the tail down on the take-off run, as in the horizontal position the aircraft only had 10in (25cm) propeller clearance. Whilst the flight controls were considered light and effective in the normal speed range, the aircraft had the vicious stall mentioned previously with the Spiteful, which could, under combat conditions, prove highly undesirable.

The final arresting proofing trials were completed on 30 April 1946 with dummy deck landing trials carried out by Lt Cdr Mike Lithgow at RNAS Ford. The Admiralty's requirement for a deck-landing assessment of the aircraft was cleared by 1 May 1946, when during the trial the Seafang demonstrated a satisfactory approach speed of 95kt (176km/h). On the basis of this deck-landing assessment the Admiralty

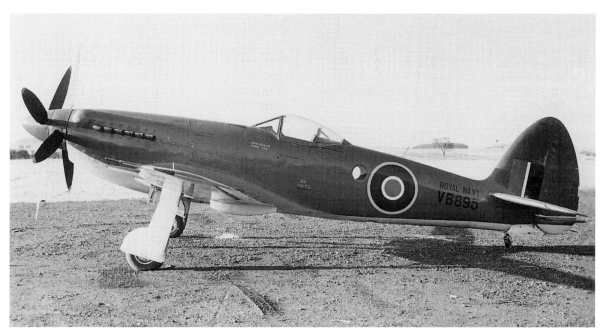

Seafang Mark 32 VB895. MAP

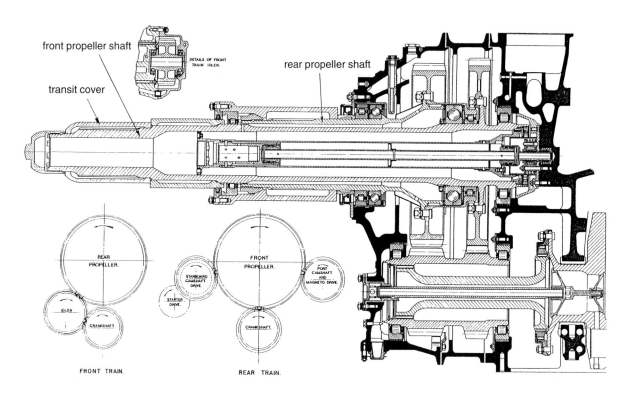

Sectioned reduction gear of the Griffon with contra-rotating propellers.

Data of Rolls-Royce Griffon Mk 121

Compression ratio	6.0:1
Reduction gear ratio	0.4423:1
Nett weight dry	2,100lb (950kg)
Weight/bhp	0.86lb/bhp (0.39kg/bhp)
Fuel grade	115/145
Specific fuel consumption	0.46lb/bhp/hr (0.21kg/bhp/hr)
Piston speed	3,025ft/min (922m/min)
Maximum BMEP	314lb/sq in (22kg/sq cm)
Supercharger gear ratios	
low	5.720:1
medium	6.735:1
high	7.703:1
Take-off power	1,900bhp at 2,750rpm with +24psi boost
Military rating	
low	2,440bhp at 2,750rpm at 6,000ft (1,800m)
medium	2,300bhp at 2,750rpm at 15,750ft (4,800m)
high	2,085bhp at 2,750rpm at 23,000ft (7,000m)
Maximum cruise	
low	1,300bhp at 2,400rpm at 16,250ft (4,950m)
medium	1,250bhp at 2,400rpm at 24,000ft (7,300m)
high	1,165bhp at 2,400rpm at 31,750ft (9,700m)

Manufacturer's data on Seafang

Wingspan	35ft (10.67m)
Wing area	210sq ft (19.5sq m)
Wing loading	48.8lb/sq ft (238kg/sq m)
Width, wings folded	27ft (8.23m)
Length	34ft 1in (10.39m)
Tare weight	8,000lb (3,600kg)
Normal weight	10,450lb (4,750kg)
All-up-weight with 180 IG drop tank	11,900lb (5,400kg)
Power plant	Rolls-Royce Griffon
Power loading	4.40lb/bhp (2kg/bhp)
Maximum speed	MS gear 428mph (689km/h) at 5,500ft (1,700m)
	FS gear 475mph (764km/h) at 21,000ft (6,400m)
Rate of climb	MS gear 4,630ft/min (1,410m/min) at 2,000ft (600m)
	FS gear 3,970ft/min (1,210m/min) at 17,200ft (5,250m)
Service ceiling	42,000ft (13,000m)
Take-off in 30mph (50km/h) wind	457ft (139m)

decided that the Seafang left a lot to be desired compared with the Seafire 47.

With this failure to impress the cancellation of the Seafang programme was almost a foregone conclusion. Apart from the lack of interest by the Ministry, the fact was that jet fighter aircraft were now viable and reliable. Along with this was the policy of the post-war Labour Government of 1945, which would be a reduction of spending on the armed forces.

During March 1946 Lt Cdr Eric Brown flew Seafang F.31 VG474, which was being used to develop controls for the Attacker (*see* Chapter 5). It had been fitted with power-operated ailerons with 30 per cent feedback of feel and Brown considered that this modification was superb in improving the aileron control. On 1 July 1948 Brown flew the same aircraft again, this time fitted with Attacker-type ailerons, in which spring tabs replaced the balance tabs. In Brown's opinion this change made the ailerons as near to perfect as possible in lateral control over the speed range up to the limiting dive speed.

The failure of the Spiteful and Seafang to reach full production status, followed by the cancellation of the

Comparison – Spiteful and Seafang

	Spiteful F.XV	*Seafang*
Wingspan	35ft (10.67m)	35ft (10.67m)
Wing area	210sq ft (19.5sq m)	210sq ft (19.5sq m)
Length	32ft 11in	(10.03m) 34ft 1in (10.39m)
Tailplane span	12ft 10in (3.91m)	12ft 10in (3.91m)
Weights		
Empty	7,350lb (3,330kg)	8,000lb (3,600kg)
Normal loaded	9,950lb (4,500kg)	10,450lb (4,750kg)
Max. loaded	11,400lb (5,200kg)	11,900lb (5,400kg)
Wing loading	47.4lb/sq ft (231kg/sq m)	49.8lb/sq ft (243kg/sq m)
Power loading	4.19lb/bhp (1.9kg/bhp)	4.4lb/bhp (2kg/sq m)
Maximum speed		
at sea level	409mph (658km/h)	397mph (639km/h)
at altitude	483mph (777km/h) at 26,000ft (8,000m)	475mph (764km/h) at 21,000ft (6,400m)

two types, gave the critics cause to comment that without Mitchell's genius Supermarine was without creative ability. This is by no means fair to Joseph Smith and his team, for they had developed the Spitfire far beyond the original concept and role, and they were no doubt hamstrung by cutbacks at the war's end. Unfortunately for the Supermarine team, their first design after the death of Mitchell came at the cross-roads betwixt piston-engine and pure-jet propulsion. That this was mixed with an unproven aerofoil section turned out to be disastrous, yet it added to their knowledge about transonic flight. It must be said, in hindsight, that with the Me 262, Meteor and Vampire jets already in service, it should have been obvious to aircraft designers that the day of the piston-engined fighter was over.

At Supermarine Joe Smith and his team had a number of projects on their drawing boards, some based on the Spiteful, some more advanced, but none became production hardware. Ever mindful of what Rolls-Royce produced in engine and engine power, Smith, with the unveiling of the Eagle 24-cylinder engine, projected the Type 391. This was a low-wing monoplane on Spiteful lines, powered by the Eagle and with wing-root air intakes and radiators – but it remained on the drawing board.

Spitefuls and Seafangs in Use on Trials

VB895 (Used for development of Attacker)
14/10/46 High Post on tests with power-folding of wings and long-stroke undercarriage;
28/4/47 RAE Farnborough on arrester trials;
16/5/47 Chilbolton on deck-landing trials;
20/5/47 STU Ford on deck-landing trials;
11/5/48 extensively damaged by explosion in port wing during trials at A&AEE, wing damage assessed as Category E;
19/5/48 Chilbolton for repair;
10/8/48 A&AEE on gun-clearance trials.

VG474
25/5/46 A&AEE on take-off trials and deck-landing assessment;
20/10/46 on test for external fitments.

VG475
15/8/46 drag and boundary layer investigation at High Post;
20/10/48 struck off charge as spares for other Seafangs.

5

The Attacker

Development

With the cessation of hostilities in Europe in May 1945 the Allies had access to a wealth of research data from various German research establishments. Contrary to popular belief, not all of it was practical, and not all of the Allies' own research was out of date. However, one area of German research that raised a huge amount of interest concerned flight at high Mach numbers, and the necessity of swept-back aerofoils to delay the onset of compressibility. This seemed to have initiated a certain amount of panic in the corridors of power and, with the economic axe now being wielded, created an excuse to cancel a number of projects that did not have sweepback. The first to go was the Miles M.52 supersonic aircraft, the reason given being that it was not fair to ask test pilots to risk their lives – they were not even asked!

The post-war Labour Government was as complacent about defence as the pre-war Labour Party; yet strangely enough, maybe for prestige reasons, it was at the same time prepared to finance the development and production of an atom bomb – without a modern long-range bomber to carry it! In concentrating on the atom bomb the government neglected the immediate defence of the United Kingdom, whose skies were protected in the post-war years by an assortment of outdated Vampires and Meteors. Thus, with the disagreement in 1948 between the USSR and the Western Allies, followed by the Berlin blockade and then the Berlin Airlift, it was realized too late that the RAF needed modern fighters.

Brian Buss was an aeronautical design draughtsman with Tiltman Langley Laboratories and was involved with the design/development of the Supermarine 510–535 series and Swift designs:

> The Germans were far ahead of the Allies in the last war, as far as aeronautical design was concerned, particularly where they found the layout of wings using sweepback, or sweepforward, could off-set to

some degree the problems of transonic flight. The result of this research work was already in the hands of the USA and Russia, as soon as the war was over in May 1945, if not before. At this date a Labour Government was swept into power in the UK with grandiose social programmes with little thought for financing manned research into high-speed flight, and Mosquito-launched models off Lands End had to suffice with dire results. Consequently the UK was left far behind, for by October 1947 the prototype US F-86 swept-wing Sabre took to the air, while the Attacker F.1 with Spiteful-type straight wings and Nene engine had only flown just three months before. This was around the same time as the MiG-15 first took to the air. The UK lost probably three years in the advances made in this area of technology, during which the war clouds were once again gathering around the world.

During this early post-war period, with a lack of government research finance, most British aircraft manufacturers had little knowledge of the difficulties that would be encountered in breaking into the transonic and supersonic regions of flight. As regards heavy bomber design, Geoffrey Lee of Handley Page had, with a number of other aviation colleagues, been to Germany and viewed the German research data and research. He would return to the UK and propose to the Air Ministry a tailless swept-wing bomber project, that would eventually result in the issue of a specification that produced the Victor and Vulcan bombers. However, British fighter aircraft designers appeared not to appreciate the rapid changes that took place with the airflow pattern around the aerofoil as Mach 1.0 was approached, and the consequent effect this had on the handling, control and stability characteristics of aircraft.

It also appears from specifications issued at the time that the Air Staff of the period were not exactly bursting with enthusiasm, as well as finding it difficult to formulate their requirements, though the latter may have been due to the financial pressures applied by their political masters. Into this political atmosphere and financial restraint was launched the Jet-Spiteful, later to be renamed the Attacker, which first flew in 1946.

The issue of Specification E.10/44 for an experimental fighter gave Supermarine the incentive to move from the failed Spiteful/Seafang aircraft to gaining a foothold in the emerging jet-fighter arena. It also gave Supermarine the opportunity to build a flying test bed on which to gain experience. Following the DTD inspection of a partly completed mock-up, a draft requirements list was issued to Supermarine. Then, in early 1945, a complementary specification, E.1/45, was issued for a navalized version of the E.10/44. Against these two specifications Supermarine were given contracts to produce three prototypes, the second and third to be navalized but without folding wings.

Gloster, Hawker and Supermarine all showed interest in the specifications, though it was for an experimental aircraft in the fighter role, not for a production fighter. Gloster had produced their GA.2 jet fighter prototype to a previous specification, which had then been re-numbered E.1/44. The GA.2 was a single turbojet-powered monoplane with taper on both the leading and trailing edges of the mainplane. The airframe was of robust construction with a tricycle undercarriage. However, the Royal Air Force showed no interest in this aircraft or the Attacker.

The Supermarine Project Team's response to the Air Staff specifications was their Type 392 against Supermarine Specification 477. This was basically a jet-powered offspring of the Spiteful, and was provisionally known as the 'Jet-Spiteful'. It used the Spiteful's Type 371 laminar-flow wing, with mechanically linked inner and outer trailing edge flaps matched to a new fuselage. It was proposed to MAP by Joe Smith that, to simplify and speed production, the fuselage should be of circular cross-section, as simple as possible and with a plenum chamber for the engine installed behind the pilot. The fuselage was of quite pleasing appearance throughout, and was modified at frame 8 to provide engine air intakes for the engine. The use of the Spiteful's 371 wing led to the use of a tailwheel-type undercarriage. Though the use of the Spiteful's mainplane and undercarriage would simplify and speed up production, it could also be a recipe for disaster, and was hardly in the modern trend. From this one can but wonder how much pressure was put on Joe Smith and his team to get a jet fighter quickly from the Supermarine section of a wide manufacturing empire.

A pre-production order for twenty-four Type 392 Jet-Spiteful aircraft was approved on 9 July 1945, these being six to E.10/44 as landplanes and eighteen to E.1/45 that would be suitable for the Royal Navy's Fleet Air Arm; this latter specification was developed into the Attacker. With the end of the Second World War and with the adverse reports

Attackers aboard HMS Eagle.

An Attacker overshooting HMS Eagle after a dummy landing pass, with everything down and dangling.

on the Spiteful's handling in regard to its wing stalling characteristics (*see* Chapter 4), the Admiralty requested that work on the naval order be cancelled. Work on the three prototypes was however allowed by the Ministry to proceed as a matter of expediency. The engine considered for the project was the Rolls-Royce RB41.

With the cancellation of the order a relatively simple, conventional and strong aircraft was delayed by four or five years before reinstatement and service entry, by which time it was obsolescent. If there had been no delay then the Attacker could have been giving jet-handling experience on carriers over that period. When the cancellation order arrived at Supermarine the first prototype, TS409, was nearing completion at Hurst Park. TS409 first flew on 27 July 1946 from Boscombe Down, piloted by Jeffrey Quill. The flight trials that followed showed that the jet-aircraft phenomenon known as 'snaking', a form of directional instability, was evident with TS409. The 'snaking' was reduced by 'beading' the rudder from its top to the bottom of the tab. TS409 made the Attacker's first appearance at the SBAC Show at Radlett in September 1946.

Aileron development for the E.10/44 had commenced on the Spiteful, but delays ensued as it was found that the slotted ailerons with geared balance tabs became too heavy as speeds increased over 400mph (640km/h). Further investigation of handling characteristics was therefore embarked on to improve controls for the E.10/44 (Attacker).

The Rolls-Royce RB41 Nene

During February 1944 Rolls-Royce began new gas turbine designs, the first being the RB40. The turbine end of this was a 2.6 scale-up of the B37 Derwent 1, intended to produce 5,200lb (2,400kg) thrust. Nine combustion chambers were fitted. The basic design features of the RB40 were outlined to N.E. Rowe of the MAP, but at a meeting attended by Joe Smith and other members of the Supermarine and Rolls-Royce teams, Smith made it clear that the RB40's 55in (140cm) diameter was too large for their submission to the E.10/44 specification. The result of this was a down-sizing of the engine by Rolls-Royce to give a diameter of 49.5in (126cm) to produce a thrust of 4,200lb (1,900kg). The engine was designated the RB41 Nene and was a simple low-pressure turbojet engine with a thermodynamic design that resembled the Derwent V's, although it had greater mass flow and thus more thrust.

The Ministry of Aircraft Production issued a specification early in 1944 for a jet engine having a minimum thrust of 4,000lb (1,800kg), a maximum overall diameter of 55in (140cm) and the weight

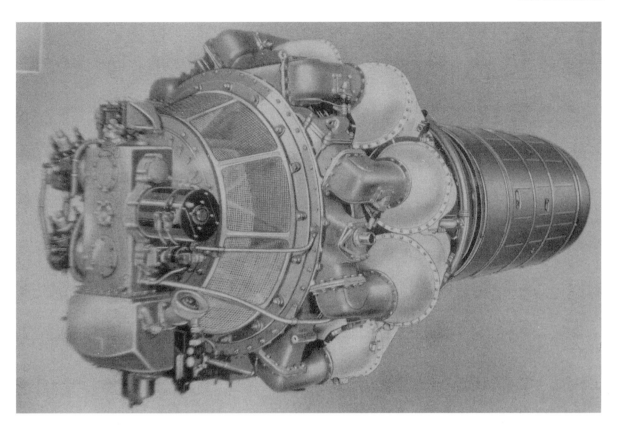

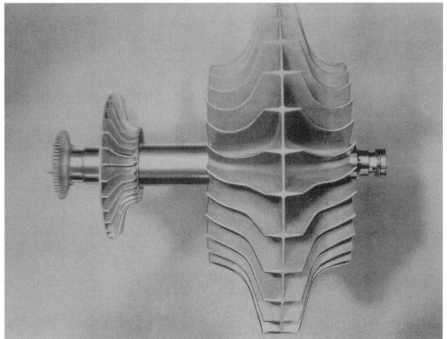

ABOVE: *The Rolls-Royce Nene gas-turbine engine.*

RIGHT: *The double-sided compressor assembly of the Nene engine.*

The turbine assembly and drive shaft of the Nene engine.

Specification – Rolls-Royce Nene Mark 1

Diameter	49.5in (125.73cm)
Length to end of turbine	63.9in (162.31cm)
Length including exhaust cone	96.8in (245.87cm)
Weight less jetpipe	1,550lb (700kg)
Compression ratio	4:1 static
Compressor diameter	25.8in (65.53cm)
Compressor peripheral velocity	1,530ft/sec (470m/sec)
Turbine rotor, mean blade tip speed	1,070ft/sec (330m/sec)
Turbine material	Jessop G.l8B steel
Turbine blade material	Nimonic 80 alloy
Fuel specific gravity (Avtur)	0.806
SFC, sea level static	4,000lb (1,800kg) thrust 1.055lb/lb/hr
	5,000lb (2,300kg) thrust 1.065lb/lb/hr
Air consumption, 5,000lb (2,300kg) thrust	89lb/sec
Acceleration 2,500–12,300rpm	4.5sec

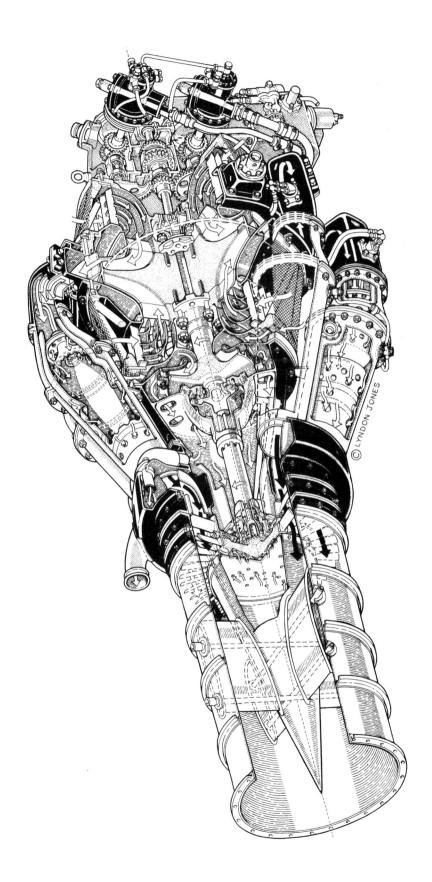

The Rolls-Royce Nene gas-turbine engine.

© LYNDON JONES

not to exceed 2,200lb (1,000kg). The Nene would fulfil those requirements.

The development of the RB41 Nene by Rolls-Royce introduced the 'big engine' (when compared to the Derwent), for it was 50 per cent bigger and delivered a nominal power (according to the Air Ministry specification) of 4,000lb thrust, or twice the thrust of the Derwent 1, which was just entering production. The design of the RB41 commenced at the beginning of May 1944 and the engine made its first test-bed run on 27 October that year.

The design had a double-sided, single-stage centrifugal compressor driven by a single-stage axial turbine. The compressor case had tangential outlets, and the right-angled outlet elbows had cascade vanes to smooth the airflow around the bends to the nine straight-through combustion chambers. Although the first Nene was run fitted with a Derwent wheelcase and a jury-rigged second fuel pump, a new wheelcase was designed to accommodate the two fuel pump drives. This had the oil pumps and filters buried in the sump, and made a neater front to the engine.

Problems appeared with the new RB41, one of these being ignition, which was by high-tension igniter plugs in the Nene's large combustion chambers. These gave trouble on starting, sometimes refusing to ignite. Later on, the torch igniter was designed and introduced, in which an ignited auxiliary fuel spray was directed into the combustion chamber to light-up the main fuel flow. This became a feature of most Rolls-Royce engines until the introduction of the high-energy surface discharge igniter. Another problem was resonance in the jet-pipe on starting. When this occurred, a resonance-organ effect could cause a back-pressure, which could sometimes prevent acceleration through the critical period.

The Nene from its original design thrust was soon up-rated to 4,500lb (2,000kg) thrust as the RN.1 and then to 5,000lb (2,300kg) on the production version, with a thrust of 5,500lb (2,500kg) being obtained on the test-beds. The 5,000lb thrust represented a compressor efficiency of 76 per cent, combustion system efficiency of 98 per cent and an expansion efficiency of 93 per cent. The Nene had an overall diameter of 49in (124cm) and a weight of 1,550lb (700kg), giving a thrust/weight ratio of 3.2:1 and thrust/frontal area of 375lb/sq ft (1,830kg/sq m). Thrust was ultimately raised to 5,400lb (2,450kg) on the Nene RN.6.

Specification – Rolls-Royce Nene Mark II

Diameter	49.5in (125.73cm)
Length to end of turbine	63.9in (162.31cm)
Length including exhaust cone	96.8in (245.87cm)
Frontal area	13sq ft (1.208sq m)
Weight complete	1,755lb (796kg)
Fuel specific gravity (Avtur)	0.806
Take-off power	5,000lb (2,300kg) ST/12,300rpm at sea level
Maximum power	2,120lb (960kg) ST/12,300rpm/30,000ft (9,000m)
Maximum climb power	4,500lb (2,000kg) ST/12,000rpm at sea level
Maximum climb power	1,960lb (890kg) ST/12,000rpm/30,000ft
Maximum cruise power	4,000lb (1,800kg) ST/11,600rpm at sea level
Maximum cruise power	1,790lb (810kg) ST/11,600rpm/30,000ft

At this time the Nene was the most powerful turbojet in the world, and was produced under licence by Hispano-Suiza in France and Pratt & Whitney in the USA. At a time when the USSR's own gas-turbine engine technology was basically nil and dependent on captured German jet engines, the first post-war Labour Government sold a number of Nene Mark 1s to the USSR: unlicensed production rapidly followed, under the designation VK-1, and so the USSR obtained from Britain the latest gas-turbine technology.

Attacker Testing and Production

Although development continued steadily the Admiralty showed little interest. The first E.1/45, Supermarine Type 398 TS413, made its first flight on 17 June 1947. This airframe was not provided with folding wings and differed from TS409 in a number of respects: the undercarriage oleo stroke had been increased from 9 to 11in (23 to 28cm);

lift spoilers and an arrester hook had been fitted; the fin size was reduced and the tailplane area increased; the flaps were modified and the ailerons altered to include balance tabs; and to improve engine performance the air intakes were modified.

After a series of Airfield Dummy Deck Landings (ADDLs), between 15–28 October 1947 the Attacker was aboard HMS *Illustrious* for deck handling and landing trials; these were carried out by Mike Lithgow for Supermarine, Lt Cdr E. Brown from the RAE and Lt S. Orr from A&AEE. For the deck-landings the lift spoilers in combination with the flaps were used to make powered approaches. No problems were encountered with the undercarriage, which completely scuppered the critics who had prophesied that the Attacker would be difficult to deck-land. As an added bonus to this, the undercarriage had shown no inclination to bounce and the test reports submitted on the aircraft were all favourable, with the main problem turning out to be the arrester hook on the V frame, which tended to shear and delayed testing until a suitable modification was made.

During March 1948 Mike Lithgow flying TS409 in full operational condition including armament, established a 100km (62-mile) closed-circuit record of 564.881mph (1008.89km/h). Starting and finishing from Chilbolton, Lithgow thus gave an indication of the type's performance. This was followed in April 1948 by Lithgow flying the prototype Attacker to Paris at the invitation of the French Air Force and Navy, during which flight he flew over the Arc de Triomphe at 600mph (965km/h) at fairly low level.

Meanwhile the decision had been taken to fit prototype TS409 with a DH Ghost engine. This, however, came to nought when, on 22 June 1948, TS413 crashed during naval arrester trials at A&AEE when being flown by Lt T. King-Joyce of the FAA. This resulted in TS409 being called in to be converted to the naval standard. The third prototype was TS416, which aircraft's production had been slowed down by orders of the Admiralty, whilst that august body made up its mind! It was not until September 1948 that an order was then placed for sixty Attackers with a need for quick production! TS416 was now to come into the picture as the Type 513, with its construction to include certain alterations for comparative trials, including the repositioning of the mainplane 13½in (34.3cm) further aft, a modified fuel system of

313gal (1,423ltr) instead of the previous 283gal (1,287ltr), a smaller fin, larger tailplane, and wider engine air intakes.

TS409, having been 'navalized', made its first flight in that condition on 5 March 1949, followed by twenty-two further flights for assessment of its flight handling. Following this, further flights were undertaken to give ADDL experience to FAA pilots, whilst at the same time carrying out an evaluation of the air-brake installation that had been added to decelerate the aircraft on the approach. This was followed by TS416 making its first flight on 24 January 1950; on 27 March it was at A&AEE on arrester-gear trials.

Between 8–16 February 1950 the two Attackers carried out thirty-three trial deck landings with four different pilots onto HMS *Illustrious* that proved the correctness of the air-brake installation. Following the deck-landing trials a number of modifications were introduced, including flat-sided elevators and lighter aileron controls.

One problem that was encountered on the original Attacker Mark 1 was that under certain sideslip conditions the rudder would 'lock over' and control would be lost, especially when the ventral fuel tank was installed. The dorsal fin fitted to the Mark 2 cured this, and was retrofitted on all previous aircraft.

On 23 May 1950 Les Colquhoun won the George Medal while flying WA409 in tests to assess the aircraft's behaviour and air-brake effectiveness at high Mach numbers. Two dives had been carried out successfully up to 400kt (740km/h), but when the airbrakes were deployed at 430kt (800km/h) on the third dive there was a vicious pitch-up followed by a sharp nose-down pitch. This had been accompanied by the departure of the starboard fold-up wing tip and the 'locking' of the ailerons. With application of full port rudder, Colquhoun could maintain a fairly straight and level flight. Then, with the undercarriage down and making a wide circuit on the rudder only, the approach to Chilbolton was made at 270kt (500km/h), reducing to 210kt (390km/h) as the flaps were lowered, with the touchdown at 200kt (370kt). The aircraft used most of the airfield and the port tyre burst during the last 100yd (90m), but the aircraft was saved and no further damage ensued.

By early 1950 the production Attacker line at South Marston was getting into its stride, with the first production example, WA469, making its first flight on 5 April 1950. The production Attackers

Operational limits of Nene Mark 3

	Maximum rpm	JPT limit	Time limit
Ground idling	2,500	550°C	unrestricted
Take-off	12,500	720°C	15 minutes
Operational necessity	12,500	720°C	15 minutes
Maximum intermediate	12,200	680°C	30 minutes
Maximum continuous	11,800	620°C	unlimited

Attacker R4000 of the Pakistan Air Force.

were fully navalized with folding wings and so on, and between 30 October and 24 November 1950 two of the early production Attackers carried out intensive deck-landing trials on HMS *Illustrious*. This was followed on 3 November 1952 with a production Attacker making its first flight in Canada on winterization trials.

The original production Attackers were powered with 5,100lb (2,300kg) ST Nene 3 engines, but with the introduction of the Attacker FB.2 came the Nene 102 (Nene 7). Attempts had been made during 1950 to sell the Attacker in the export market, with demonstration flights around the Mediterranean and Middle East countries being flown by Lithgow in TS409 accompanied by a Vickers Valetta, but to no avail. Then in August 1950 David Morgan flew TS409 on a visit to Pakistan, which resulted in an order for thirty-six un-navalized versions, designated Type 538.

Specification – Attacker F.1

Wingspan	36ft 11in (11.26m)
Wingspan, folded	28ft 11in (8.88m)
Wing area	226sq ft (21sq m)
Wing loading (normal loaded)	51lb/sq ft (249kg/sq m)
Aerofoil section	Supermarine 371/1 and /2
Standard mean chord	6.13ft (1.857m)
Dihedral	5 degrees
Incidence	2.5 degrees
Flap area	
Total	21.68sq ft (2.12sq m)
Inner	12.96sq ft (1.2sq m)
Outer	8.72sq ft (0.809sq m)
Aileron area (total)	17.23sq ft (1.6sq m)
Tailplane	
Span	16.9ft (5.151m)
Area	68.02sq ft (6.319sq m)
Dihedral	10 degrees
Incidence	2.25 degrees
Elevator area (total)	22.10sq ft (2.05sq m)
Fin and rudder area	33.02sq ft (3.067sq m)
Rudder area	6.72sq ft (0.624sq m)
Undercarriage track	14ft 6½in (4.282m)
Fuel capacity	
Main tank	82gal (372ltr)
Wing tanks	2 × 20½gal (93ltr)
Fuselage side tanks	2 × 73gal (332ltr)
Fuselage rear tanks	2 × 12gal (55ltr)
Total internal	293gal (1,332ltr)
Ventral tank	250gal (1,140ltr)
Total tankage	543gal (2,468ltr)
Hydraulic accumulator pressure	1,800psi
Pneumatic pressure	450psi
Brake pressure	150psi
Armament	four Hispano No. 3 Mark 5* 20mm cannon; 167 rounds per inboard gun, 145 rounds per outboard gun
Ejection seat	Martin-Baker Mark 2A

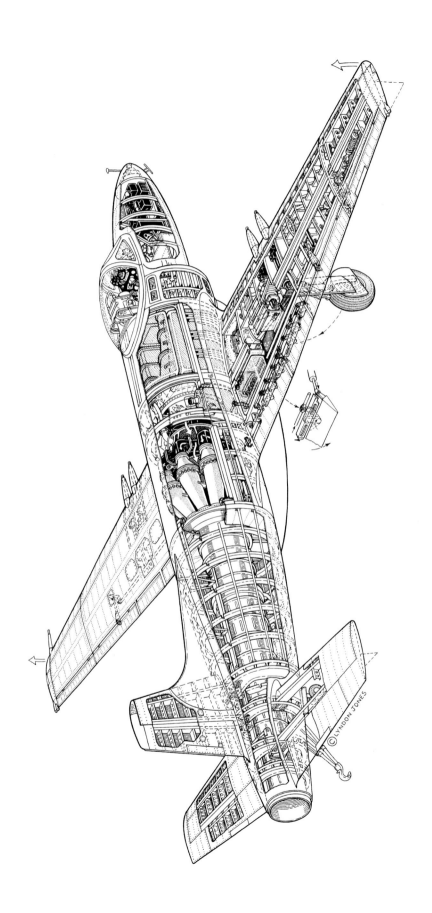

©LYNDON JONES

Attacker F.B.1.

The first Pakistani Attacker was handed over to their High Commissioner, His Excellency M.A. Ispahani, during a ceremony at South Marston on 6 March 1953. These Attackers had no provision for wing-folding, arrester gear or any naval equipment, but could carry a 90gal (410ltr) fuel tank on a pylon under each wing. The Type 538 was powered by a Nene 3 and had a stiffer, metal-framed pilot's canopy as standard.

The Rolls-Royce Nene was not only a superb engine but, being of the centrifugal type, was more robust than the axial-flow turbojets of the period in relation to ingestion of foreign objects, and the matching of the compressor to the turbine was that much easier. The first Attackers produced were the interceptor fighter version carrying the original armament of four 20mm cannon, but without provision for underwing weapon stores, although a 250gal (1,140ltr) belly drop tank was provided for. Apart from the naval requirement of folding wings, there was also provision for cata-pulting, slinging and two RATOG bottles each side of the fuselage.

In 1951 the Admiralty decided to introduce the Attacker as a fighter-bomber, to carry rocket pro-jectiles (RPs) or bombs under the wings. Fortu-nately Supermarine had foreseen this possibility and had built a load-carrying beam into the mainplane structure. The first Attacker FB.1 was WA529, which made its maiden flight on 7 January 1952. The first FB.2 was WK319, which made its maiden flight on 25 April 1952. Both versions had four 20mm Hispano-Suiza Mark 5* cannon with a Mark 3 belt-feed. Both the FB.1 and FB.2 had modifica-tions 124/125 allowing the carriage of eight RPs, modifications 126/127 for a pylon to carry a load not exceeding 1,000lb, while modification 147/155 introduced an additional RP station on each mainplane, so up to twelve projectiles could be car-ried. The FB.2 was manufactured with a dorsal fin (which was retrofitted to FB.1 aircraft), and also had the metal-framed cockpit canopy.

The first FAA unit to be equipped with the Attacker was 800 Squadron at Ford. For a trial peri-od this unit and 803 Squadron (formed 26 Novem-ber 1951) and 890 Squadron (formed 21 April 1951) were all equipped with only eight aircraft per unit. This inadequate complement was later altered when 890 Squadron aircraft and crews were absorbed by the other two units to make twelve-aircraft squadrons.

Construction

The main feature of the Attacker was its relatively straightforward design and construction. The fuse-lage was of circular section, with the exception of the nose forward of the air intakes, and all of stressed-skin construction. The wing front spar attachment points were mounted on frame 12 and the rear attachment points on frame 14, both these frames being of heavy, double-channel section con-struction. At the rear of the fuselage the fin-spar attachment points were at frames 23 and 25, the tailplane front spars were attached to frame 25 and rear spars to frame 27, and the tailwheel jack mounting point was also on frame 23.

The Nene engine was mounted in a pressure-sealed engine bay between frames 12 and 17, and was fed by a bifurcated air intake that incorporated boundary-layer bleeds at the 'D'-shaped air intakes (familiarly known as 'elephants ears'). The bound-ary-layer air-bleed system was incorporated in the air intakes against the fuselage sides: the boundary layer was passed through ducts to escape into the atmosphere via louvres in the intake surround behind, above and below the air intake. Fuel was carried in seven internal tanks, two in the wings and the remainder in the fuselage, the fuel being pumped to the engine by two Pulsometer booster pumps. Air for fuel transfer was fed from the engine compressor.

The mainplanes were also of stressed-skin con-struction with a heavy-gauge skin. The front spar was of built-up booms, flanged web plate, double-skin and skin attachment angles. On the naval ver-sions the outer portion of the mainplanes folded upwards to assist stowage aboard aircraft carriers. Inner and outer flaps were fitted with lift spoilers, between the flaps on the rear spar. Both ailerons were fitted with spring tabs, the starboard aileron also having a trim tab.

The tailplane was of quite conventional metal con-struction and stress-skin covered. It had 10 degrees' dihedral, with the elevators horn-balanced, each with a trim tab and the port elevator having a spring-tab as well. The rudder and elevator trailing edges coin-cided, with the rudder having an electrically oper-ated trim tab.

The flying controls were all conventional and man-ually operated. The rudder and aileron trim tabs were controlled electrically, and the elevator trim tab by mechanical linkage to the cockpit handwheel. The

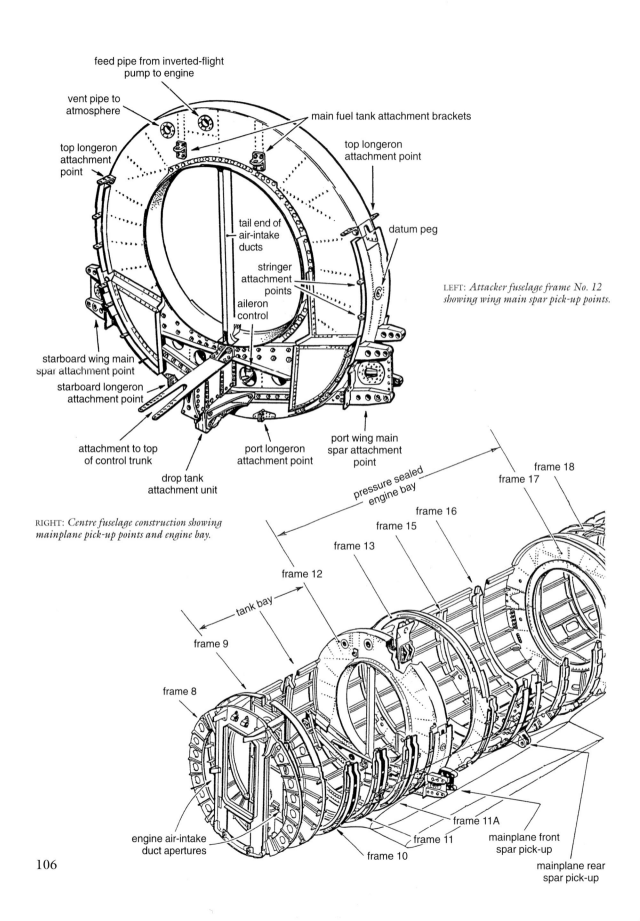

feed pipe from inverted-flight
pump to engine

vent pipe to
atmosphere

main fuel tank attachment brackets

top longeron
attachment
point

top longeron
attachment point

tail end of
air-intake
ducts

datum peg

stringer
attachment
points

aileron
control

LEFT: *Attacker fuselage frame No. 12
showing wing main spar pick-up points.*

starboard wing main
spar attachment point

starboard longeron
attachment point

attachment to top
of control trunk

port longeron
attachment point

port wing main
spar attachment
point

drop tank
attachment unit

RIGHT: *Centre fuselage construction showing
mainplane pick-up points and engine bay.*

pressure sealed
engine bay

frame 18
frame 17

frame 16

frame 15

frame 13

frame 12

tank bay

frame 9

frame 8

engine air-intake
duct apertures

frame 11A

frame 11

mainplane front
spar pick-up

frame 10

mainplane rear
spar pick-up

Attacker F.1 engine and airframe limitations

Engine limitations

Take-off	12,500rpm/max JPT 720°C; 15-minute limit
Combat	12,500rpm/max JPT 735°C; 10-minute limit
Intermediate	12,200rpm/max JPT 680°C; 30-minute limit
Maximum continuous	11,800rpm/max JPT 620°C; Unlimited
Ground idling	2,500rpm+/-100/max JPT 550°C
Oil pressure	20psi minimum in flight

Airframe limitations

Maximum speed	
with/without drop tanks	505kt (935km/h) or 0.78 Mach
air brakes in or out	505kt (935km/h) or 0.78 Mach
flaps fully down	190kt (350km/h)
undercarriage lowered	190kt (350km/h)
drop tank jettison	450kt (830km/h) maximum
canopy jettison	130kt (240kt) minimum
Weights	
tare	8,430lb (3,820kg)
basic	9,910lb (4,490kg)
maximum for take-off	14,600lb (6,600kg)
maximum overload take-off	17,350lb (7,870kg)
maximum for gentle manoeuvres only	14,600lb (6,600kg)
maximum permitted for all flying	13,300lb (6,000kg)
maximum for airfield landings	13,000lb (5,900kg)
maximum for arrested landings	11,300lb (5,100kg)
Maximum speed	512kt (950km/h) at sea level
Maximum rate of climb	6,350ft/min (1,935m/min) at sea level
Service ceiling	45,000ft (13,700m)

ailerons were operated by a combination of chain and rod, and the elevator and rudder by cable control. The trailing edge flaps were hydraulically operated, with the pilot's selector lever permitting any angle up to a maximum of 78 degrees down to be selected. The flaps could be used in combination with the lift spoilers as dive brakes, but in this configuration the flaps only went down to a maximum of 17 degrees, and it was impossible to raise the flaps without first retracting the spoilers. The spoilers were mounted on seven lever assemblies each side, four for each inboard spoiler and three for each outboard spoiler, the whole being actuated by a fuselage-mounted jack.

The hydraulic system was powered by an integral Type 116 engine-driven two-stage pump that supplied power to the main undercarriage and door jacks, the tailwheel jack and door, the brake flaps and lift

positions 3 to 16A rib attachments

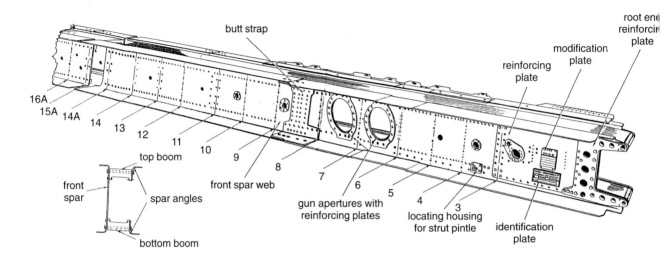

The root end Attacker main spar.

spoilers, the deck arrester hook and the mainplane folding. The deck arrester hook was of the 'A'-frame type and attached to the fuselage at frame 25.

Other features of the production aircraft included the Martin-Baker ejection seat (replacing the standard Supermarine seat) and provision for two RATOG bottles on each side of the fuselage. Two hooks were fitted for catapult launching, one in each wheel-well. Incorporated in the mainplane structure were strong-point beams, so that in the fighter-bomber role the incorporation of bomb-racks or rocket projectile beams posed no problem. In the case of the Type 538 Attacker for Pakistan, these beam-points were used for external fuel tank carriage for ferrying purposes.

The main undercarriage consisted of two Vickers oleo-pneumatic, long-stroke struts fitted with pre-retraction gear that, through a system of levers, compressed the oleo approximately 8in (20cm) as the undercarriage was raised. This was to meet Fleet Air Arm requirements of a greater touch-down rate of descent than that required by the RAF, the main oleo stroke being increased from 7in (18cm) to 10in (25cm). The tailwheel unit was based on the same oleo-pneumatic strut carrying twin tailwheels, with the tailwheel unit being held in the 'down' position by an internal lock in the tailwheel jack.

Attacker F.1 Flight Handling

(Taken from 'Pilot's Notes for the Attacker Mk F1')

(a) Take-off
No tendency to swing and rudder became effective at 50–60kt (IAS).

At typical service load tail was raised at 75–80kt and the aircraft flown off at 100–105kt. At maximum overload weight of 14,600lb the aircraft was flown off at 115–120kt.

Raise undercarriage, which should be locked 'up' before 190kt.

Maximum rate of climb, climb commenced using 12,500rpm, reducing to 12,200rpm after 15 minutes.

Recommended level speeds at typical service loads:

SL	310kt
10,000ft	285kt
20,000ft	260kt
30,000ft	240kt
40,000ft	215kt

When carrying a full ventral tank the speeds would be reduced by 20kt.

(b) Stalling

Warning of approach of stall was by slight airframe buffeting some 10kt above stall.

At typical service load undercarriage and flaps:

'up'	105kt
'down'	95kt

At full internal fuel and ammunition, empty drop tank undercarriage and flaps:

'up'	110kt
'down'	100kt

At all-up weight of 14,600lb undercarriage and flaps:

'up'	120kt
down	105kt

(c) Control Characteristics

Elevator, was heavy and effective at low speeds, lightened off at moderate speeds, became heavy again and less effective at high speed and high Mach nos. At high altitude and low IAS it was very light and effective for small movements, but heavy for relatively large movements in manoeuvring.

Ailerons, very light and effective gave a high rate of roll over most of speed range up to limiting Mach number, but became heavy as maximum speed was approached.

Rudder, was light and effective at low speeds but became heavy at high speeds, but did not affect manoeuvrability.

Air brakes, would open at any speed, introduced slight nose-down trim followed by marked nose-up trim. Operation of the spoilers when flaps not fully down would cause flaps to move in the direction of spoiler operation.

(d) Mach Number Characteristics

Up to Mach 0.74 there was no noticeable effect, but after this point a nose-down change of trim occurred and this increased progressively with increase in Mach no. At approximately 0.79 some buffeting was evident and increased up to 0.81, when the aircraft began slight pitching oscillations in a downward direction. In addition, on some aircraft, there was a strong tendency for a wing to drop. At these high Mach numbers the ailerons were heavy with reduced effectiveness. When flying at high Mach numbers with the engine throttled, some buffeting and vibration around the air intakes could be experienced, that could produce a fairly strong yawing action.

General

Two electrical LP fuel pumps were installed in the main fuel tank, one at the bottom for normal flight with one pump at the top for inverted flying.

The barometric pressure control (BPC) controlled the delivery pressure of the HP fuel pumps and so maintained the correct flow of fuel for given throttle settings under changing conditions. On Nene 102 engines, in addition to the BPC an acceleration control unit (ACU) was fitted to ensure satisfactory acceleration in the event of rapid throttle openings, thus reducing the possibility of surge and high JPTs.

The hydraulic pump operated the undercarriage, flaps, air brakes/lift spoilers, arrester hook and wing folding mechanism.

Service Use

On its entry into service the Attacker made Fleet Air Arm history by being the first jet fighter to become standard equipment in front-line naval squadrons, entering service with 800 Squadron at Ford on 22 August 1951. Sixty-one Attacker Is and eighty-four Mark 2s were built in batches WA469–WA498, WA505–WA534, WK319–WK342, WP275–WP304, WT851 and WZ273–WZ302. Pakistan's purchase of thirty-six were numbered R4000–R4035.

Attackers equipped 800, 803 and 890 Squadrons, and 736 Training Squadron, serving aboard Royal Navy aircraft carriers HMS *Albion*, HMS *Centaur* and HMS *Eagle*. Then, upon the entry into service of the Hawker Sea Hawk, the Attackers were transferred into RNVR Squadrons, 1831 RNVR Squadron being the first reserve unit to receive them. Due to the original cancellation of the aircraft the Attacker had a relatively short in-service life and became non-operational in 1957. Following disbandment of the RNVR Squadrons, the majority of the remaining aircraft were ferried to RNAS Abbotsinch, where they were scrapped. Only WA437 escaped the axe, and resides today at the Fleet Air Arm Museum at Yeovilton.

Attackers on Ministry Fleet

TS409

1.48 loaned to firm for demonstration to the Air Attachés of France and Holland;
16.4.48 demonstration flights in France from 18–20.4.48;

1.10.48 accepted ex-contract for flight tests with Nene engine and installation of Ghost;

18.10.48 converted to naval requirements;

3.4.49 A&AEE, handling trials with dive brakes;

16.9.49 force-landed at Greenham Common with fuel lock;

31.10.49 starboard undercarriage failed to lower, aircraft landed on grass with port undercarriage down. Failure due to jamming of wheel fairing in mainplane;

18.12.49 handling and jettisoning trials with drop tanks;

6.1.50 A&AEE, handling trials with 250lb Menthol drop tank;

27.1.50 loaned to company for demonstration to AVM Ivelaw-Chapman, C-in-C Indian Air Force;

8.2.50 damaged at sea on HMS *Illustrious*, tail oleo collapsed on landing;

6.3.50 to A&AEE;

20.4.50 spinning trials with drop tanks;

10.5.50 aircraft loaned for demonstration to AVM Atcherley C-in-C Pakistan Air Force;

25.8.50 demonstration in Karachi;

25.1.51 trial installation of flat-sided elevator and reduction of rudder travel, flight trials at A&AEE;

22.2.51 fitment of dorsal fin;

28.2.51 A&AEE, continuation of flight trials with improved controls;

3.8.51 undercarriage failed to lower, aircraft belly-landed on airfield;

1.10.51 RAE, crash barrier trials.

TS413

13.10.47 deceleration trials on HMS *Illustrious*;

22.6.48 naval arrester trials at A&AEE;

22.6.48 aircraft crashed category EE at Burford village;

18.10.48 converted to naval requirements;

20.5.49 struck off charge.

TS416

27.3.50 at A&AEE on arrester gear trials;

9.5.50 authority given for RATOG installation at Vickers;

21.8.51 at RAE on arrester gear trials.

WA469

30.11.50 at A&AEE for handling and gunnery trials;

9.5.50 aircraft damaged;

30.7.51 precautionary landing following engine failure;

10.3.52 at A&AEE on gun firing trials at high altitude and high Mach numbers.

WA470

22.11.50 intensive deck landing trials for A&AEE at STU Ford.

WA471

13.3.51 preparation for check RATOG and catapult trials at RAE;

19.9.51 at RAE on RATOG trials.

WA472

26.10.50 at STU Ford for intensive deck landing trials.

WA475

21.6.51 performance trials of Mark l0 arrester gear.

WA483

14.2.52 RAE barrier trials.

WA485

7.6.51 Vickers, clearance of pressure cabin and TIs;

5.2.52 aircraft crashed in marshy ground and completely submerged.

WA508

16.11.51 Vickers, trial installation of modification 35 (provision for alternative fuel) and modification 171 (introduction of Nene 7);

5.4.54 trial installation of gun safety solenoid.

WA529

12.10.51 Vickers, handling and installation clearance of bombs and rocket projectiles;

29.5.52 Vickers, preparation for intensive trials;

28.7.52 Winterization trials at CEPE Alberta, Canada;

26.6.54 RAE, proofing of strengthened arrester 'A'-frame and hook;

16.3.56 RAE Bedford, for arrester gear trials, side load check.

WK319

8.5.52 Vickers, trial installation of twelve-RP installation. Trials with bombs and RPs, RATOG and arresting at increased weight.

6

Types 510, 517 and 535

Even before the Attacker went into service, new experimental developments were in progress at Supermarine, as a result partly of research information and data, and partly a review of other aircraft manufacturers' products, within and outside the Vickers-Armstrongs' empire. From Germany had come the knowledge that with the Me 262 it had been necessary to use a nose-wheel undercarriage for a successful take-off, as had also been demonstrated by Glosters with their Pioneer, Meteor and GA.22, and by de Havilland with their Vampire series. Engine development had been inspiring, with thrusts increasing almost monthly, although problems were still being encountered and overcome. In particular, the surge lines and operating lines of axial-flow compressor units were often too close, and acceleration from idling was a problem.

In spite of the known research into swept-back aerofoils in Germany, as well as that at the RAE Farnborough and the National Physics Laboratory (NPL), there appeared to be a marked reluctance on the part of British companies manufacturing fighters to take advantage of such technology. Yet Handley Page's designer Geoffrey Lee, having personally viewed the German establishments and research, had already committed to paper a bomber design that incorporated sweepback and other innovations, which would eventually result in the Victor bomber.

By 1946 Britain's lead in jet-fighter design had already been challenged by developments in the USA and, despite the type's adoption into the Fleet Air Arm, the RAF had rejected the Attacker as a possible Meteor or Vampire replacement. As a result of this apparent lack of interest and new designs, various versions of the Meteor and Vampire continued in front-line service until well past obsolescence. Supermarine's design department were reviewing developments that were based on the Attacker layout and construction and, like Hawker Aviation, were interested in any new specification for a fighter aircraft for the RAF that might materialize.

However, it was not until 1946 that the Air Staff issued specification E.41/46 for a swept-wing development of the Attacker and E.38/46 for a similar development of the Hawker P.1040, but both specifications were only for experimental aircraft. Two prototypes of each aircraft were ordered, but whereas the Hawker P.1052 contender only had swept-back wings, the Supermarine prototypes had 40-degree sweepback on both wings and tailplane.

The Type 510

The two Supermarine prototypes were initially designated Type 510, and for some unknown reason followed Attacker practice in having a tail-wheel undercarriage, which was a throwback to the Spiteful and Attacker and failed to follow the tricycle undercarriage trend of the jet-powered aircraft of the period. The contract for the two prototypes was 6/Acft/1031 with the order placed on 12 March 1947. The two aircraft were built at Hurst Park and serial numbered VV106 and VV119.

The first aircraft completed was VV106, which was transported to Boscombe Down and made its maiden flight with Mike Lithgow at the controls on 29 December 1948. It was, incidentally, the first British jet-powered aircraft with swept-back wing and tail surfaces to fly. Unfortunately the test-flying was temporarily terminated on 16 March 1949 when a 'wheels-up' landing had to be carried out after an engine failure. This had started with severe engine vibration when power was reduced below 6,000rpm, and progressively got worse, accompanied by aircraft directional instability when taken down to 4,000rpm. However, the handling trials had already indicated that Supermarine had at last produced an aircraft capable of exceeding the Spitfire's Mach number limit of 0.92 – just! The Type 510 raised it to 0.93. There was, however, a limit to the aerofoil's maximum usable lift coefficient in the transonic range, although the low-drag wing, thanks to the sweepback, gave a considerable improvement in lift at high speed.

The trials also showed that the swept-back wing introduced longitudinal instability prior to the stall and this limited manoeuvrability at high altitude, as level-turn performance deteriorated due to insufficient engine power – such deficiencies obviously limiting the use of the aircraft. The Type 510 was otherwise fairly easy-handling and pleasant to fly. The records indicate that it was free from any tendency to 'snake', with the ailerons crisp and light, and giving a good rate of roll at low-to-medium altitude. This was in contrast to Hawker's P.1052, which suffered from a form of directional instability known as 'Dutch roll'.

By adapting the Attacker fuselage, complete with the per cent t/c ratio and a swept tailplane and fin, an experimental aircraft had been quickly produced by Supermarine. It therefore came as a surprise to Supermarine when, six months before VV106 flew and in spite of the P.1052's 'Dutch roll' problems, the Hawker follow-on design, the P.1067, was accepted straight off the drawing board with a contract following shortly afterwards, the production aircraft becoming the Hawker Hunter. This seems to bear out rumours at the time that, whereas Joe Smith considered the Types 535 and 541 (*see*

pp.114 and 116) to be experimental aircraft, the Air Ministry read things differently.

An RAE report on VV106 was critical of its poor finish and the unsealed gaps at the control surfaces, amongst other faults, although it was accepted that as the aircraft was a conversion of an Attacker, what was more important was that it enabled the flight characteristics of swept-back wings to be investigated. The aircraft was demonstrated at the 1949 SBAC Display Farnborough by Mike Lithgow, who stated that he had taken it up to Mach 0.9 without any trouble.

Following the SBAC Display VV106 was delivered to A&AEE Boscombe Down for handling trials. On 21 October 1949, following test pilots' complaints about its handling, Wg Cdr Wykeham-Barnes carried out a flight assessment of the aircraft. At two-thirds power the aircraft's flight characteristics were satisfactory, but lower power settings caused severe vibration with abrupt sideways nose movement of approximately 5 degrees. The aircraft was returned to the manufacturer for investigation and rectification, during which period Mike Lithgow was forced on 29 December to carry out a wheels-up landing following an engine failure.

With the repair completed testing recommenced on 10 May 1950, when the fault was traced to turbulence in the engine air intakes. The redesign involved changes to the boundary-layer bleed and

Supermarine Type 510 VV106 at RAE Farnborough in 1951. Note the pointed nose modification.

alterations to the front engine mounting. As the Admiralty was interested in a faster fighter than the Attacker, VV106 was programmed for carrier trials and suitably modified, which included the addition of an 'A' frame arrester hook. As such the Type 510 became the first fully swept jet fighter to land on an aircraft carrier, carrying out this operation onto HMS *Illustrious* on 8 December 1950 flown by Lt Elliott RN.

The trials were flown by Mike Lithgow and Lt Cdr D. Parker at an all-up weight at take-off of 12,700lb (5,760kg), and with the undercarriage oleos replaced with higher-rate ones of 16ft/sec (5m/sec). A series of take-offs were made using RATOG with four units grouped above and below the wing trailing edge, which resulted in an acceptable 500ft (150m) take-off run. The approach to the carrier was made at 124–134kt (230–248km/h) and the deck landings were considered acceptable with little oleo rebound action.

The last sortie was flown on 14 November by Lt Cdr Parker, but during a RATOG take-off, failure of a rocket caused VV106 to swing and its port wing struck a gun turret. Fortunately the pilot retained control and the aircraft was flown back to Boscombe Down.

Further development of the flight envelope continued with VV106. Tiltman Langley Laboratories, having relevant design capabilities, were contracted by Supermarine to help. Brian Buss was a design draughtsman with TLL and comments on VV106:

> It was limited by a change in lateral trim, when the stick had to be held hard over to counteract a low port wing. Also the sweepback introduced longitudinal instability before the high-speed stall and hence the aircraft could only be flown in level flight at high altitude, which did not augur well if it was to become a fighter aircraft.
>
> In order to maintain control at high Mach numbers it was suggested that a variable incidence (VI) tailplane be fitted that was adjustable in flight. This was considered to be an essential feature and it was decided to fit one on VV106. This was not immediately possible because in the post-war years, Supermarine had shed many of its design staff and all its personnel at that time were fully employed on other contracts. It was therefore urged by the Ministry to seek outside assistance and a contract was placed for this work with Tiltman Langley Laboratories on Redhill aerodrome.

The Type 517

Under Supermarine specification 515 dated 1 December 1948, a proposal was formulated around the Type 510, which basically stated that it should be capable of further development and of reaching speeds up to Mach 1.0. For this, and in order to maintain good and full control at such speeds, an adjustable tailplane was desirable, and to eliminate a possible cause of flutter the elevator spring tab was to be removed. VV106, having now returned to Supermarine, was stripped of naval equipment and spent some more time after repair at RAE on high-speed research. It was then returned to Supermarine for modification, which eventually resulted in the fitment to VV106 of another rear fuselage. In this major modification by Tiltman Langley Ltd the whole rear fuselage was hinged to move, and the variable-incidence tail proved an effective trimmer up to a limiting Mach number of 0.95. In this configuration the aircraft became the Type 517. When VV106 first appeared it had had a more sharp-pointed nose than the Attacker and square wing tips; it now had a shorter nose and an anti-spin parachute blister aft of the rudder. Brian Buss of Tiltman Langley:

> Rolls-Royce had designed a large ball-type jetpipe joint and TLL were required to design the rear fuselage around it with a fixed tailplane, all of which could move through +/−4 degrees. New short-chord nose balanced elevators and trim tabs were also designed and the variable incidence (VI) fuselage had to be operated by a Rotax actuator. The very cramped space around the tailpipe, and the need to ensure the elevator control runs remained unaffected by the rear fuselage movement, presented us with many headaches.
>
> It was found to be a powerful and effective method of trimming and speeds in excess of Mach 0.95 were achieved. However, the rate of actuation was found to be too fast, but the aircraft remained in experimental use until 1955.

Test-flying of VV106 as a Type 517 was carried out initially at RAE Farnborough, where the pilots' approval was given of the new configuration. Testing was briefly held up by a another successful 'wheels-up' landing on 14 December 1952 after an undercarriage extension failure. The aircraft was repaired and flying restarted on 2 September 1953 with Dave Morgan taking over the testing. The aircraft was eventually

Supermarine Type 535 VV119 at RAE Farnborough in 1951.

struck off charge and withdrawn from use on 14 January 1955, and allocated for use as an instructional airframe. Fortunately it was later saved to take its place at the RAF Museum Cosford.

The second Type 510 airframe, VV119, was similar to VV106, with a pointed nose and the rear fuselage built to accept reheat. It carried out its first flight from Boscombe Down, piloted by Mike Lithgow, on 27 March 1950. It was soon afterwards grounded for modification work and designated Type 528. For this, the length and diameter of the rear fuselage were increased to accommodate a larger jetpipe with reheat, with a special reduced-diameter tailcone at the exhaust exit. It had a lengthened nose with larger air intakes of a different, improved shape to VV106's, provision for wing armament, reduced-span ailerons and a reshaped wing trailing edge. The fuel system was also different and raised the fuel capacity to 400gal (1,820ltr).

The Type 535

VV119 was subsequently fitted with a nose-wheel undercarriage – a necessity with the use of reheat – although the tailwheel was retained to serve as a tail bumper. Now designated the Type 535, VV119

made its first flight in its new configuration on 23 August 1950 at Boscombe Down, and made its first public appearance at the 1950 SBAC Show. The early test-flights of the Type 535 showed that the change of rear fuselage had eliminated the elevator buffeting that had been experienced on the original configuration.

As a result of the tests further modification work was carried out, but the aircraft retained its type number. The longer nose caused some directional instability, to correct which a dorsal fin was added, as well as a new wing fitted with wing fences. Reheat was used for the first time on 1 September 1950.

At this point the Hawker Hunter prototype had still not flown, whilst at Supermarine the VV119 was ready for testing again. Brian Buss of TLL on the modified 535:

The Hunter would not take to the air for another year and, more seriously, war had broken out in Korea, so the pressure on Supermarine was intensified still further. The Type 535, as it was known, was far from a fighter in the true sense of the word. The lengthened nose replaced the original one and weights were added to the nose-wheel bay to balance the aircraft.

Particulars of the Types 510 and 535

	Type 510	Type 535
Wingspan	31ft 8½in (9.66m)	31ft 8½in (9.66m)
Wing area	273sq ft (25.36sq m)	295sq ft (27.41sq m)
Length	38ft 1in (11.61m)	42ft 11in (13.08m)
Maximum height	12ft 6in (3.81m)	12ft 6in (3.81m)
Maximum height, tail down	9ft 10in (3m)	9ft 10in (3m)
Internal fuel capacity		400gal (1,820ltr)
Drop tank fuel		250gal (1,140ltr)

Within another four months VV119 was modified yet again to become the Type 535, by the addition of a new wing and for a time wing fences, a dorsal fin fillet and reheat. It was the only Nene-powered aircraft so fitted. But once again no variable incidence tail. All these modifications, incorporated in double-quick time, illustrate the almost panic measures then being taken to make up for those lost years after the war. It was as if, were sufficient measures taken fast enough, then perhaps the Swift might be turned into an acceptable fighter. But this was certainly not the way to go about it, especially as the problems of transonic flight had not yet been overcome in the UK, or perhaps fully understood. All of this was, however, no fault of Supermarine.

In the Vickers-Armstrongs sales brochure of 1950, coverage was given of both the Type 510 and Type 535, the leading particulars of the two aircraft being given, as shown in the table (*above*). The Type 535 was described thus:

The Type 535 is a fighter version of the swept-back Type 510 research aircraft ... The fuselage is designed to accommodate a 'reheat' installation and the basic engine may be either a Rolls-Royce Nene or a Rolls-Royce Avon. The operational version includes a tricycle undercarriage, air brakes etc., and four 20mm guns installed in the fuselage.

This seems to suggest that in Vickers-Armstrongs' view the Type 535 had passed from the research-aircraft stage to being the basis of a fighter aircraft, which was not the view held at Supermarine by Joe Smith and his team. The Type 535 at that stage was seen at Supermarines as only a further development stage and a research tool. So did Vickers-Armstrongs' proposals override Supermarine's own view of the Type 535? If so, this could be why it attracted the interest of the Air Staff as a possible development aircraft for a future fighter; although it had a relatively low performance with the Nene engine, the possible installation of the Rolls-Royce Avon engine offered far higher performance. Further to this, why did the brochure quote four 20mm cannon in the fuselage when the Swift F.1 would only have two 30mm Aden cannon? The Type 535 was, however, of fundamental importance in the Supermarine fighter development, as it was the transition point from the tailwheel undercarriaged, centrifugal turbojet-powered Attacker to the tricycle undercarriaged, axial-turbojet-powered Swift.

The Type 535 also became the feature aircraft in the British feature film *The Sound Barrier*, which had as its basic theme the testing of a new jet-powered fighter aircraft called 'Prometheus' – this aircraft was the Type 535 in very thin disguise. The fact that Vickers-Armstrongs were prepared to allow their aircraft to be used in a film in which the aircraft supposedly crashed showed a lot of courage, especially at a time when the words 'sound barrier' were synonymous with danger in the public's mind.

The test-flying of VV119 was undertaken by Sqn Ldr Dave Morgan, who had recently joined Supermarine, and during July 1951 these tests confirmed a level speed of 622mph (1,000km/h) at 15,000ft (4,600m) and 583mph (938km/h) at 35,000ft (11,000m). Experiments were also undertaken with drag-inducing upper-surface flaps, but they caused considerable buffeting at high speed and so were

115

Supermarine Type 535 VV119 in flight, clearly showing the swept-back mainplane and tail surfaces. D. WELLS

removed. Further flight trials without these drag flaps proved that there was sufficient braking effect using the landing flaps.

Although the Type 535 suffered from some wing-dropping at high speed – to some extent caused by the limited effectiveness of the power-assisted manual controls at transonic speeds – it was less prone to this problem than was VV106. Further trials were carried out in which dummy rocket projectile loads were carried to assess the effect that these had on drag and general handling. It was found that practically no projectile configuration caused a change in handling, except that increased inertia in the roll was observed.

The Swift Emerges

At this stage in development it was considered that the Type 535 airframe was satisfactory, but that more power was required. The design having attracted RAF interest, the Air Ministry advanced funding and possible participation as a fighter with an order placed for two prototype Type 541 aircraft to Specification F.105 and Operational Requirement OR.228. The latter, issued on 9 January 1950, left a lot of detail unsaid, although it did call for a maximum speed of 547kt (1,013km/h) at 45,000ft (14,000m) and a time to that height of not more than six minutes. The contract was 6/Acft/5986 and the serial numbers issued for the Type 541 aircraft were WJ960 and WJ965. These were to be powered by Rolls-Royce Avon RA.7 engines of 7,500lb (3,400kg) thrust. The Type 541 was similar in many respects to the Type 535 but, amongst other alterations, had longer-span ailerons and increased fuel capacity. Like VV106 and VV119, the two Type 541 prototypes were hand-built at Hursley Park, near Winchester.

The contract was later extended to cover 100 production aircraft. The award of this contract was mainly due to the Korean War fiasco, where the RAF did not have a modern jet fighter to combat the North Korean MiG-15s. The MiG-15 was based on captured German aerodynamic research on swept wings and was powered by a licence-produced Rolls-Royce Nene engine (RD-45F), that the post-war Labour Government had sold to the USSR. The MiG-15 was initially tested in December 1947 and went into production in 1948. In production form it totally outclassed the United Nations fighters opposing it,

namely the P-80C Shooting Star, F-84 Thunderjet and the Gloster Meteor.

The MiG-15's excellent rate of climb and heavy armament made it a formidable fighter; even in competition with the F-86A Sabre it had a higher rate of climb, a higher ceiling and better manoeuvrability above 35,000ft (11,000m), the F-86A only being superior with a better rate of roll below 25,000ft (7,600m). However, the MiG-15 suffered from restrictive control at transonic speeds when approaching Mach 1, with poor flying control surface response.

The order for the Swift was in accordance with previous policies of ordering two different types of aircraft to meet a requirement, and also gave the Air Staff an 'insurance policy' in case the Hawker Hunter programme fell behind schedule and specification. With the award of the contract the Air Staff authorized the installation of the 7,500lb Avon engine as standard.

The first pre-production aircraft, WJ960, first flew on 1 August 1951. It was later fitted with a Tiltman Langley variable-incidence (VI) tailplane with small-chord nose-balanced elevators, operating jacks and hinged rear fuselage. As so modified it made its first flight on 4 February 1952. The second pre-production aircraft, WJ965, was generally similar to WJ960 but had an increase in fuel capacity and no VI tail. Regarding WJ960, Brian Buss of TLL:

> The VI tail designed by TLL for WJ960 was far more sophisticated than that fitted on the first swept-wing aircraft, VV106. The jetpipe was fixed and the tailplane moved through +4 to –9 degrees, again with small-chord nose balanced elevators. The design posed many problems for TLL through lack of space and non-availability of proprietary operating equipment, so special mechanical actuating jacks with several gearboxes and drive shafts had to be designed.
>
> The second pre-production aircraft, WJ965, was far nearer the true shape of an F.1 Swift, with a new more pointed nose, strengthened cockpit hood, reshaped fin with larger fillet, and repositioned wings well aft of the intakes, but yet again it did not have a VI tail. The production team at South Marsden near Swindon were no doubt wondering at this time just what the aircraft they were to produce was to look like, as an order for 100 aircraft had been placed before 1950 was out and this aircraft didn't fly until July 1952 Again an indication of the panic measures

Specification – Mikoyan-Gurevich MiG-15

Wingspan	33ft 1½in (10.10m)
Mainplane sweepback	42 degrees on leading edge
Length	36ft 5in (11.01m)
Height	11ft 2in (3.40m)
Weight	
Empty	8,333lb (3,780kg)
Loaded	11,288lb (5,120kg)
Overloaded	14,350lb (6,465kg)
Engine	RD-45a of 6,040lb (2,740kg) ST
Fuel capacity	
Normal	275gal (1,250ltr)
Overload	266gal (1,209ltr)
Armament	2 × 23mm and 1 × 37mm cannon
Maximum speed	666mph (1,072km/h)
Stalling speed	109mph (175km/h)
Initial rate of climb	10,400ft/min (3,170m/min)
Service ceiling	51,000ft (15,544m)

taken by the Air Ministry. Not only that, the Ministry were constantly changing the specification.

Supermarine's airframe construction in this period of transonic flight was not at the cutting edge of technology, for the Types 510 and 535, *circa* 1950, still employed structures using a skin riveted to ribs, stiffeners and so on, as per the Attacker. Waviness limits were hard to achieve with this type of construction, irrespective of whether a thick-gauge skin was employed or not. With transonic flight one problem is the large increase in drag, two aspects of which concern the surface finish: roughness and waviness. In regard to roughness for instance, the difference between a very good and a moderately poor paint finish can theoretically account for approximately 20 per cent of the total drag of the wing. With the laminar-flow aerofoil, waviness limits are tight and in production difficult to achieve. Stringent waviness limits must be met to avoid local shock waves and separation that causes loss of lift. Tests on model aerofoils showed significant reductions in drag, but this was not borne out on full-size wings, without the use of boundary-layer control as well as laminar flow, both of which were investigated at RAE Farnborough.

Waviness limits were difficult to achieve with the structures of the period. In the USA integral supported light-alloy skin had already been developed in which, when machining a thick skin or billet, stiffeners were machined in. This was put into production and it was claimed that this method made a saving in cost and weight, and had the advantage in regard to waviness that a simple supporting structure was feasible, with stiffeners more widely spaced. Waviness was also reduced by the elimination of the stringer–skin attachment rivets. In the same period in Britain, de Havilland was developing in conjunction with CIBA the Redux bonded structure to eliminate the riveted joint and stringer attachment, so reducing cost, waviness and drag.

Transonic flight brought one further problem, for there were rapid trim changes with large stick forces for the pilot to hold, so power boosting became necessary. As regards Supermarine and the Type 535 and Swift, one could in hindsight ask why the company's designers did not from the start introduce the all-flying tail for control with a small elevator for trim. In the end it was this type of empennage that would be required and would be introduced on the last mark of Swift, and this at last made the Swift a practical and satisfactory type of aircraft – but too late.

Aircraft on Ministry Fleet

E.41/46 VV106
17.3.49 damaged due to force-landing at A&AEE after engine failure;
2.1.50 to Boscombe Down for assessment trials;
10.5.50 loaned to firm for demonstration to AVM Atcherley, C-in-C Pakistan Air Force;
11.7.50 to RAE for measurement of coefficiency of maximum lift and drag at high Mach numbers;
31.10.50 at RAE for deck-landing trials;
14.11.50 on HMS *Illustrious*. Struck wingtip on port turret;
26.9.52 at RAE for high-speed research;
14.11.52 damaged at RAE, wheels-up landing due to undercarriage failure;
4.9.53 at RAE on high Mach-number research.

Conclusions

The slow change-over in Britain from the conventional structure (stressed skin riveted to ribs) to the machined skin, was without any doubt a major cause of British aircraft's failure to achieve the performance of the USA's jet fighter aircraft. This was not helped by the delayed introduction of the all-flying tail and boosted controls, although sometimes the boosted controls were introduced to eliminate deficiencies in the controls themselves.

The original Air Ministry specification that the Hawker and Supermarine aircraft were designed to was for an experimental aircraft, and as such the requirements were not the tight corset that they would have been for a specific fighter design. This may have fooled Joe Smith into thinking that the aircraft was not intended as a production fighter, with the result that the 40-degree swept surfaces of the wings, tailplane and fin were of 10 per cent t/c ratio. Brian Buss comments:

A strong rumour existed within the Supermarine design team around this time which said Joe Smith had always considered the Swift work to be of an experimental nature only, and perhaps this may have been one reason why he adopted a conservative 10 per cent t/c ratio for his two-spar swept wing rather than a thinner section as did Hawker on their Hunter, where a constant 8.5 per cent ratio was used outboard of the intakes.

7

The Swift

In the early post-war period, British and other Allied experts were able to examine various German research and development projects and their test results, although not all the Germans' projects in aircraft or aircraft propulsion were found to be practical or usable. In the gas-turbine field Britain had a distinct lead over both the Germans and the USA, but in the rocket and rocket-motor sectors had not developed any hardware for production, apart from aircraft-borne rocket projectiles.

In the aerodynamic field much still had to be learnt about transonic and supersonic flight, although a great deal had been done at RAE Farnborough and a great deal of time and research would be expended in pursuit of breaking what was popularly known as the 'sound barrier'. As opposed to the minute sums spent on Britain's post-war research projects, most of which were cancelled due to the parsimony of the Labour Government, the USA and USSR spent millions developing aircraft based on the German research, that resulted in hardware like the North American F-86 Sabre and the MiG-15.

The formation of shock waves and changes in control characteristics as aircraft approached the speed of sound had already been experienced during tests at RAE Farnborough in 1942–5; vertical test dives on some aircraft at high Mach numbers had been described as 'similar to flying a brick'.

Along with the need to introduce swept wings to delay compressibility effects came problems as well, for there was a tendency for swept wings to become longitudinally unstable at large incidence, due to loss of lift at the wing tips. This feature occurred at a progressively lower lift coefficient as the Mach number increased, with the result that in tight turns the stick force per 'g' tended to zero, or even to a

The first Swift prototype, WJ960.

negative figure, especially at altitude. This could affect manoeuvrability, depending on controllability in the unstable condition.

To achieve high airspeeds in the transonic and supersonic regions the thrust increases required were tremendous, and in the immediate post-war period British firms and establishments initiated experiments in the new science of rocket-motor technology. These resulted in the investigation and development of bi-fuel rocket motors and fuels and various other methods of propulsion, as well as various aerodynamic devices, to allow aircraft to go supersonic. As a result of this a number of British designs eventually became hardware, even if not as production types. Hawkers re-engined their P.1040 prototype with an Armstrong-Siddeley Snarler rocket as well as its normal Nene engine, and as such it was redesignated the P.1072. Saunders-Roe produced the SR.53, which was specifically designed for rocket propulsion with a small turbojet for the return to base. The P.1072 made a number of test flights from the end of 1950 to the start of 1951, but before the first flight of the SR.53 the Air Ministry was already showing more interest in reheat (afterburning) on the turbojet and were losing interest in rocket propulsion for aircraft. As explained in Chapter 6, Supermarine had incorporated reheat on their Type 535.

A Meteor Replacement

Although a number of specifications were issued to cover replacement aircraft for the Gloster Meteor, the main requirement was the time to 45,000ft (14,000m) and a service ceiling of 50,000ft (15,000ft). Hawkers were not satisfied with the requirements of the specifications and proceeded with a private venture under the designation P.1067. The prospects of the design eventually resulted in Hawker submitting it to the Air Ministry, who accepted it and issued Specification F.3/48 to cover it in March 1948. A number of alterations were made to the original design during the project development, but the final result was a sleek, swept-wing single-seat fighter.

Parallel with the Hawker P.1067 development (which became the Hunter), Supermarine was developing their Type 541 (the Swift) to similar requirements, but it was viewed by the Air Ministry mainly as a back-up should the Hunter design fail. How widely this view was held is open to conjecture, for in August 1950 the Assistant Chief of Air Staff (Operational Requirements) suggested in an official letter that as an 'interim' fighter for the RAF the choice would be the Swift or the purchase of a US fighter (presumably the Sabre) prior to the availability of the Hunter. Whilst Hawkers were starting with a clean sheet of paper in designing the Hunter, Supermarine were being pushed along a path based on their jet experience with the Type 535 for the Swift. When OR.228 was issued in January 1951, calling for a maximum speed of 547kt (Mach 0.95) at 45,000ft, time to 45,000ft of six minutes, and a 1,000ft/min ceiling of 50,000ft, it was obvious that this was beyond the Swift's design capability as it then stood.

As regards a new aircraft for the RAF, the Ministry of Supply (MoS) would call on the A&AEE and RAE to participate in monitoring the designs submitted, the RAE carrying out any wind-tunnel tests required and both establishments evaluating the designs, mock-ups and prototypes. Once the aircraft was flying A&AEE would carry out trials, both in conjunction with the manufacturer and at Boscombe Down. Following satisfactory acceptance and the issue of a 'Controller Aircraft Release' (CA Release) the aircraft would then go on to the Air Fighting Development Squadron (AFDS) to check its operational capabilities. All these actions were a distinct and regulated procedure.

However, due to a combination of the rush to get it into service, political arm-twisting, military expediency and possibly commercial interests, the first Swift F.1s arrived at AFDS and at 56 Squadron simultaneously. Thus the Swift fighter was rushed into squadron service before the AFDS had cleared or condemned its handling, with the result that 56 Squadron pilots were being called on to fly aircraft that had not been 'wrung out' by the test establishments. This is not suggesting that this contributed to the failure of the Swift as a high-altitude fighter, for it failed in this role both at the test establishments and with 56 Squadron. (At this point the Swift F.1 was powered with an Avon RA7 (Mk 105) developing 7,200lb thrust at 7,950rpm.)

Brian Buss of Tiltman Langley Laboratories was involved with the airframe design modifications to the Types 510–535 and Swift, and gives his close-up view of the situation:

Joe Smith who did such remarkable work on the development of the Spitfire was pressurized by the Air Ministry to produce a supersonic fighter when we in this country had little if any flying experience on which to base a successful design. The launching of a few supersonic models from under Mosquitoes off Lands End was no substitute for the hands-on work undertaken by the 'X' series in the US and by MiG. With the onset of the Korean War, the design situation with the Swift became even more chaotic.

The Korean War in 1950 came almost immediately after the Berlin Airlift, which had shown the RAF inadequately equipped for its transport role. The Korean War created chaos and panic as the RAF had a dated fighter force equipped with Meteors and Vampires. The policies pursued by the post-war Labour Government had led to a period of stagnation in the design and development of new fighter aircraft, and in the end North American F-86 Sabres had to be bought from the USA. These would not be in service with the RAF until January 1953, even though early F-86s were serving with the USAF in Korea from December 1950. The F-86 was the result of North American Aviation taking advantage of the German aerodynamic research that became available at the end of the Second World War. In its production form the F-86, in spite of a few inadequacies, would prove to be a classic fighter and dominated the Allied fighter scene of the period.

With the return of a Conservative Government in October 1951 came a review of the status of the British armed forces. This resulted in March 1952 with the introduction of the 'super-priority' system for five aircraft types including the Hunter and Swift. With the Hunter still around twelve months away from production, the Swift was viewed as a possible contender, but mainly as a back-up insurance policy. For Supermarine, this meant the acquisition of more staff for their test establishment at Chilbolton, as well as more test facilities.

Difficulties

The post-war chaos in administration and the underfunding of various research establishments, followed by the accelerated procedure to get the Hunter and Swift into production may well have contributed to the technical and flight difficulties that were encountered during the development of these two types. In the quest for a viable transonic fighter aircraft a number of unpleasant problems would be experienced by the design teams and test pilots, and the unpalatable fact would become clear that they, in spite of the German experimental results, had a lot to learn about transonic flight and flying. All of the aircraft manufacturers involved in fighter design were to experience problems – indeed, at one period during the Hunter's development, it did seem that the Swift would be necessary as a back-up.

However, the first major problem that occurred was not with the aerodynamics, but with a shortage of materials. With the 'super-priority' status of both aircraft types, the demand for tools, jigs and materials showed up the failure of the previous government to maintain a modern air force: tooling and materials could not be fully supplied from British industry and some had to be bought from European suppliers.

During early flight testing of the Hunter the pilots were to find the aircraft suffering from a number of handling deficiencies that would place restrictions on its operational role. A quick résumé of these deficiencies and problems may put the picture in its correct perspective against the problems of the Swift. The second Hunter prototype, WB195, had a brief handling trial at A&AEE, but this was terminated due to severe vibration. Other trials raised criticisms regarding a number of deficiencies, such as high aileron forces at high Mach numbers, aerodynamic 'pitch-up' at high altitude and high indicated Mach numbers, 'pitch-down' when the guns were fired at altitude, and rapid 'pitch-up' in some manoeuvres at high subsonic Mach numbers, not to mention its inadequate fuel-tank capacity. The Hunter also had problems with its rate of descent and the possibility of an inadvertent spin when the aircraft was fully stalled.

One further problem with the Hunter design related to the landing flaps, which were also intended to act as air brakes. Any lowering of these resulted in a nose-down pitch, requiring quick corrective action on the elevator and trimmer. As speed increased beyond 300kt (560km/h), lowering the flaps resulted in a nose-down pitch that was severe and violent. As a result of this problem a series of trial installations of flaps and air brakes was embarked upon that only ended with the fitment of an external air brake under the rear fuselage – but this took until 1954. Release to the service was then only granted on the fitment of this external air brake. Problems did not finish there either, for the elevators were considered heavy at high speed, the engine surged when the guns were fired, and due to a shortage of prototypes it became necessary to use the first twenty production aircraft in the testing role.

121

As well as the Rolls-Royce Avon engine raising problems on both the Hunter and Swift, so did the position of the engine air intakes. Whilst the pitot-type air-intake on a single-engined fighter usually involved the use of a long intake duct and the problems related to a shock wave during supersonic flight, the divided engine air intakes of the Hunter and Swift led to a loss of ram pressure to one of the intakes when the aircraft yawed. This affected both the Hunter and, more so, the Swift.

In spite of the difficulties referred to above, the A&AEE assessment of the Hunter F.1 finally allowed its entry into service – but on restricted release.

Early Swift Development

The first prototype Swift was the pre-production Type 541 WJ960, built to specification F.105 and OR.228 and powered by the new Rolls-Royce Avon of 7,500lb (3,400kg) thrust. Two aircraft were ordered on 9 January 1950, and the major difference in this prototype to the Type 535 was in the incorporation of the axial-flow Rolls-Royce Avon RA7 engine. With the power available being around 50 per cent better than on the Type 535, no reheat equipment was fitted so as not to compromise the endurance. WJ960 made its first flight from Boscombe Down, piloted by Mike Lithgow, on 1 August 1951. The initial flights by the company's test pilots indicated an improved take-off and climb performance, but also showed up a number of its flying deficiencies and limitations, not least of which being that it could not go supersonic. Amongst the modifications then incorporated were larger-span ailerons, a small dorsal-fin fillet and flared-out wing tips. Classed as the first pre-production aircraft, WJ960 was later fitted with a TLL-designed rear fuselage with +4/–9-degree variable-incidence (VI) tailplane, small-chord nose-balanced elevators and operating jacks. In this modified condition it made its first flight on 4 February 1953.

In spite of the previous handling deficiencies it was decided to modify the second prototype, WJ965, to F.1 production standard. This modified second prototype-cum-production Swift, which like WJ960 was hand-built, was nearing completion at Hursley Park during June 1952. It differed from WJ960 mainly in the front fuselage, where the engine intakes were moved further forward and the cockpit made wider. This aircraft had an inner wing leading edge more swept forward, so as to accommodate ammunition

for the two fuselage-mounted 30mm Aden cannon, and it also had an increase in fuel capacity. The wing skin was thinner than on WJ960 and was to prove a potential source of trouble. Swift WJ965 first flew, piloted by Dave Morgan, at Boscombe Down on 18 July 1952, by which time the retractable tailwheel unit had been fitted with doors.

It was intended to publicly demonstrate the Swift at the SBAC Display at RAE Farnborough that September, but the Avon engine was still far from reliable. This was proven again on 3 August, when during a demonstration flight by WJ960 a large uncontrollable vibration occurred on opening up to full power, followed by engine failure. The pilot, Mike Lithgow, managed to carry out a dead-stick landing at Chilbolton. Following an investigation, however, the vibration was traced to aileron flutter and not the failed engine! Then on 8 September WJ960, while flown by Dave Morgan, had another engine failure, this time on the final approach to land at Chilbolton. With the aircraft at 800ft and an obstacle in the form of the 400ft valley of the local River Test, Morgan opted to land downwind with the undercarriage retracted. Although the airframe was badly damaged the Swift's strong structure withstood the accident, and the aircraft was repaired and flying again within a few months.

After the first flight of WJ960 a production order for 150 aircraft was placed with Supermarine; the prototype WJ960 flying London–Brussels for the NATO Display in a time of 18min 3.3sec, giving an average speed of 665.9mph (1,071km/h).

The first production Type 546 Swift F.1, WK194, made its maiden flight on 25 August 1952. This aircraft and the next, WK195, were hand-built at Hursley Park. The first production-line Swift, WK196, was built at Supermarine's South Marston factory.

Following the disintegration in flight of the DH.110 prototype at the 1952 SBAC display, a certain amount of concern was voiced about airframe structural integrity during transonic flight. In particular, it was feared that 'flutter' may have contributed to the structural collapse of the DH.110. With this in mind Supermarine installed additional test equipment to monitor other points of the airframe, and began another test programme. In the end the airframe was to prove structurally sound, but deficient in performance. To get a fresh assessment of the Swift, Supermarine offered A&AEE Boscombe Down's Swift project pilot, Sqn Ldr C. G. Clark DFC, a preview flight of its handling and

The first Swift prototype, WJ960.

performance. This he made on 8 November 1952, and after two flights on WK194 he made a disturbing report on the Swift. He had found a number of problems, among which were tightening-up in turns, a propensity to pre-stall instability, and severe wing drop at the stall.

Towards the end of 1952, WJ960 had been fitted with a variable incidence tail and on 4 February 1953 it made its first flight so modified. This was followed on 18 February with Dave Morgan diving the Swift beyond Mach 1.0, but the handling deficiencies persisted. In this state the aircraft was a non-runner as far as the Air Staff were concerned, even though the Hunter still had its problems.

WJ965 had been fitted with a rigidly linked gear-tab aileron to replace the spring tabs, and the first flight with these was made on 18 February 1953, followed by Dave Morgan diving the aircraft supersonically on the 22nd. The ailerons were operated by a single Lockheed Servodyne with feed-back. The highest Mach number achieved was M.1.04 at 35,000ft (11,000m) at a dive angle of 35 degrees. There was some slight elevator oscillation, but it was suspected that this may have been caused by oscillation of the elevator spring tab. Shortly after this WJ965 was modified with two aileron power units, one in each wing.

During late 1952, flights were to start on a Swift with a Mark 2 wing that had four 30mm cannon installed. To accommodate the extra ammunition for these guns the mainplane leading edge was extended forward, thus giving a small increase of sweepback in this area. The result of what had seemed to be a trivial modification was pitch-up in turns or in pull-outs

at high Mach numbers. For instance, at M.0.85, a movement of the control column sharply to the rear could result in the aircraft flicking upwards and onto its back. The trouble originated from the airflow when the outer wings were at high incidence, the inboard lift not being balanced by the more aft and outboard lift. This was obviously not acceptable for a fighter aircraft, as it would leave it in a vulnerable position during air combat – assuming that the enemy fighter did not have similar failings.

Supermarine engineering staff at Chilbolton tried many remedies to improve the Swift's handling, these varying from extending the outer-wing leading edge forward in a saw-tooth profile, and the use of wing fences. Whilst the saw-tooth modification helped to prevent the break-away of the airflow and so improved the stalling characteristics, further undesirable handling trouble was introduced, so it was decided to move the CG forward.

Therefore, on the Swift Mark 2 some of the internal equipment was moved forward with ballast to bring the CG further forward than had been originally intended – with a consequent reduction in the aircraft's high-altitude performance. This further militated against the acceptance of the Swift in the fighter role. An official decision was taken in 1953 for the Swifts to participate in that year's Coronation Review at RAF Odiham, even though it was known that engine reliability was low. This decision was purely for publicity purposes and detrimental to the test flying programme, as it meant that time was taken out from testing to practise formation flying. The result of the practice flying was that on 15 July 1953, WK194, WK195, WK196, WK200 and

WJ965 took part in the flypast at Odiham, each having had a new Avon engine installed prior to flight! However, there were still more problems. WK194, flown by Mike Lithgow, suffered an engine failure just after the flypast and had to make another power-off landing at Chilbolton, fortunately without damage to pilot or airframe. Supermarine, having embarked on a series of flight tests of trial inlet-duct modifications to halt the engine failure rate, were relieved following investigation into the engine failure on Lithgow's aircraft to find that the failure lay with the engine and not the duct design. The Avon Mark 105 fitted to the Swift had turbine discs produced by a subcontractor who had deviated from the manufacturer's drawings, and the subcontractor's unofficial modification was the cause of the engine failure.

The Rolls-Royce Avon

During the late 1940s a development of the centrifugal-flow Rolls-Royce Nene was studied, called the Tay. Further development of this engine was cancelled in November 1950, as a Rolls-Royce axial-flow jet was giving better power figures on the test beds for a smaller cross-sectional frontal area. This was the Avon, the company's first production axial-flow gas turbine – its designation AJ.65 stood for axial jet, 6,500lb thrust. While the axial-flow gas turbine design gave higher efficiency, higher-pressure ratios and considerably improved specific fuel consumption against the centrifugal-flow gas turbine, it also suffered from blade stalling and compressor surge, and the matching of the compressor to turbine was harder.

Design work began at Rolls-Royce Barnoldswick on 19 September 1945 with a design pressure ratio of 6.2 and an airflow of 108lb/sec (49kg/sec). The first RA.1 engine was on the test beds on 25 March 1947, but was immediately in serious trouble, with the compressor being in deep stall and surging at low engine speeds. The engine could not be made to accelerate and the turbine efficiency was only 76 per cent. It was found during investigation that the first four compressor stages were restricted due to premature stalling of the blading, with a sharp reduction in pressure across the surge line of the twelve stages.

Tests were then initiated in which the first five compressor stages of stator vanes were set at progressively increasing stagger angles from stages 1 to 5.

Further testing determined that with variable inlet guide vanes for the compressor, combined with an inter-stage bleed, there was surge-free operation. This simple method and a modest pressure ratio of 6.2 were then adopted as standard.

Two Avon RA.2 engines were installed in Lancaster VM732, one in each outer engine nacelle to replace the Merlin engines. Ground running began at the start of August 1948 with the Avon-Lancaster getting airborne on 15 August, following which the aircraft-engine combination was demonstrated at the 1948 SBAC Display. The flight test programme ran for more than 350 flying hours and ended in September 1949. Another Lancaster, VL970, then joined the Rolls-Royce test team at Hucknall and was likewise converted to accept two Avon RA.2s in the outer nacelles.

After rig testing of a scale-model two-stage turbine, a full-size version of this turbine was built and showed increased engine thrust, reduced SFC, and improved engine acceleration and handling. The modified AJ.65 engine with the original-size twelve-stage compressor that incorporated the variable inlet guide vanes, inter-stage bleed valve and two-stage turbine was designated the RA.3 (100 series) Avon. This was further developed to give a dry thrust of around 8,000lb (3,600kg). Following these developments, over 660 hours' test flying of the Avon RA.3 and the further-developed RA.7 took place on VL970, as well as de-icing trials. This work with VL970 came to an end on 29 March 1955 when, on carrying out an overshoot, one of the Avons failed to spool up to full power, the aircraft departed from its flight path and dived into the ground, killing the four crew.

An Avro Ashton high-altitude flight testbed, WE670, had joined the Avon development programme at Hucknall on 23 July 1953. It was modified by Napiers at Luton Airfield by the fitting of an engine pod on the aircraft centre-line under the wing centre-section with a water spray rig ahead for icing trials. The first Avon tested was a 9,500lb (4,300kg)-thrust RA.14, followed by the 10,000lb (4,500kg) RA.28. Canberra B.2 WD930 was also operated by Rolls-Royce Hucknall to flight-test the RA.3, RA.7, RA.14 and later Avons. The RA.14 and 28 were much re-designed engines with annular combustion chambers and improved blading, but these were not fitted to the Swift. The RA.7 family of engines installed on the Swift were the Marks 105, 108, 114 and 116; basic data of the Mark 105 is shown in the table (*see* p.125).

Rolls-Royce Avon RA.7 Mk 105

Compressor type	axial 12 stage
Turbine type	axial 2 stage
Combustion chambers	eight
Engine diameter	42.2in (107.2cm)
Maximum static thrust at sea level	7,200lb (3,300kg) at 7,950rpm

At this time, around 1952–3, as well as the Hunter and Swift fighters, rocket-propelled interceptors were still under consideration as a form of target-defence fighter. Amongst these were the Saunders-Roe SR.53 and two delta-winged rocket-propelled projects from Westland, designed to specification F.124T: the Type A and the Type B; though they differed in aerodynamic configuration, both were powered by two DH Spectre rocket motors. Yet none of these rocket-propelled fighters would in the end gain overall approval from the Air Staff.

Swift F.1

The Swift F.1 was powered by one Avon RA.7 engine with no provision for reheat. Its armament was two 30mm Aden cannon individually disposed under the nose, as opposed to the Hunter's quickly detachable four-cannon pack. It had a fixed tailplane, although there were trial installations afoot covering changes to the elevators and ailerons. The thinner wing skin on WJ965, combined with the flexibility of the aileron spring tab system, was causing wing-aileron flutter at about 560kt (1,040km/h) IAS, and in the less dense air at higher altitudes the aircraft was even more prone to aileron flutter at high Mach numbers than had been experienced on WJ960. Furthermore, cameras mounted on the fuselage and fin of WJ965 also gave evidence of wing flutter.

As a result of an Air Council decision on 22 October 1953 to have 56 Squadron flying Swifts before the end of 1954, pressure was placed on getting an early release. This meant that the Controller Aircraft would need to vigorously pursue the testing and entry into service of the Swift, which was hardly the best way to get good results, and may in the end have added to the problems.

In compliance with this on-going development order, WJ965 was instrumented for an aileron and elevator vibration investigation at A&AEE Boscombe Down. The pilot, Sqn Ldr N.E. Lewis, was briefed to carry out low-speed handling trials, with power-on and -off stalls in 'clean' condition and power-on stalls with 'all-down' at heights above 15,000ft (4,600m). On 11 November 1953, twenty-five minutes after take-off at 0730hr, the aircraft was seen flying slowly at approximately 5,000ft (1,500m). Then the engine noise diminished and the Swift was seen to enter a flat spin into the ground, killing the pilot, who made no attempt to eject.

Investigation of the wreckage found that all the controls and systems worked correctly and the pilot was medically fit at the time of the accident. Evidence and an analysis of past flight-test reports appeared to indicate that the Swift F.1 had a marked reluctance to recover from a developed stall without the use of power at an early stage, but the test figures did not indicate why WJ965 was flying so slowly and below its briefed height.

The main weapon of the Swift was the Aden cannon, an automatic gas-operated gun developed by BSA Enfield, based on the principles of the German Second World War Mauser cannon. It had a cylinder (revolving drum type) with five cartridge chambers, into which the cartridges were automatically loaded as indexed by a gas-operated slide. Firing took place when a round was in line with the barrel and the whole mechanism safely locked at the time of firing. Its particulars are detailed in the table (*below*).

30mm Aden Mark IV cannon

Calibre	30mm
Length of gun	62.6in (1,590mm)
Maximum width of main body	9.45in (240mm)
Length of barrel	42.52in (1,080mm)
Rifling	right-hand, 16 grooves
Rate of fire	1,200–1,400rpm
Muzzle velocity	2,590ft/sec (790m/sec)
Total weight of cannon	192lb (87kg)
Firing method	electric, 26V DC

Mike Corner was an RAF pilot with extensive flying experience covering the period that saw the Vampire, Meteor, Hunter and Swift in service:

For reasons that were never made clear to us, the muzzle velocity of the Aden ammunition was stated as being either 1,950 or 2,800ft/sec. The high-velocity ammunition would not be available for some considerable time, so we were lumbered with the low-velocity rounds for some years to come.

Because it takes time for a round to reach a target, it must be aimed well ahead of the target, along its flight path and above it to allow for gravity drop, which at extreme ranges can be considerable. Gyro gunsights (the Mark 5 in this case) present the pilot with a sighting graticule which he places over the target and the sight automatically provides the correct deflection to allow for angle-off and compensates for range (gravity drop) and altitude (ballistics hence time of flight and hence gravity drop). This assumes that the sight is continually supplied with accurate target range information, which would normally be supplied by the nose-mounted radar ranging unit.

The old 20mm Hispanos were quite high-velocity guns and consequently the sighting solutions at both low and high altitudes were quite easily contained and within the ability of average pilots to manage. The introduction of this low-velocity Aden ammunition seriously affected the pilot's ability to engage successfully targets flying at high Mach numbers, say M.0.8 or faster, at all altitudes, but particularly at low altitudes.

While the Swift was experiencing problems, the Hunter team was also having their share. Engine problems concerned the matching of air intake to compressor intake, and surging and flame-out at heights around 45,000ft (14,000m). With the aircraft at around M.0.90–0.92 in a maximum-rate turn, a severe nose-up pitch took place and engine surge occurred. Live firing of the Aden guns had to be terminated for three reasons: the cracking of nose formers; damage caused to the underside of the aircraft by the ejected ammunition links; and the ingestion of exhaust gases from firing at high altitude and high rpm, which caused compressor surge.

This last problem was later overcome on both the Hunter and the Swift by fitting a fuel-dipping device that reduced the engine rpm milliseconds before the surge commenced. (This device had originally been developed by Folland Aircraft for the Gnat fighter.)

1953 was to prove disappointing for the Supermarine team, for with the introduction of the US off-shore arms procurement programme for NATO, a number of British aircraft were considered for possible purchase. The final choice for a fighter lay between the Hunter and Swift, and although both aircraft were criticized by the USAF test pilots, in particular over the Hunter's short flight duration, the Swift was rejected in favour of the Hunter due to its inferior high-altitude characteristics, namely its lack of longitudinal and lateral control at high indicated Mach numbers.

Although the table (*right*) gives a data comparison between the Swift F.1 and the Hunter F.1, it does not indicate their handling characteristics, and is not intended to. The Swift was faulted for its already-catalogued deficiencies, amongst which were its lack of stability at altitude and the pitch-up that occurred when 'g' was applied at Mach 0.85 and above. These problems were not acceptable on a fighter operating at high altitude in combat. To rectify this, Supermarine added a 'notched' forward extension on the outer wing. Provision was then made for the fitting of the Avon Mark 7R (Mark 108) with reheat. This was for the Swift F.4, which was intended at the time to be the main production version. However, the Avon Mark 7R had a problem in that reheat could only be applied or relit below 20,000ft (6,000m), and if switched off above 20,000ft it could not be relit. The engine at this stage was far from having the reliability achieved with the later marks that had an annular combustion chamber, such as the Mark 524-5. Although these were engine problems, to the Air Ministry officials they seemed to reflect on the Swift.

With reheat (8,950lb/4,060kg at 7,950rpm) the Swift could climb to 40,000ft (12,000m) in about four minutes, whereas the normal time without reheat (6,675lb/3,030kg at 7,950rpm) was 7½ minutes. It was found from analysis of the test reports that the fuel consumption between either type of climb was little different, due to the time difference. The first Swift F.4 (a converted F.1), WK198, made its first flight on 2 May 1953. Another problem that now raised its head was a spate of engine compressor failures, which were cynically regarded by both the Ministry people and Rolls-Royce as a further Supermarine problem. However, thanks to an unscheduled engine change the defect was traced to weak compressor-blade root fixing in the mark of Avon engine assigned to the Swift and not to the airframe intake design, as had been considered previously.

Data comparison of Swift F.1 and Hunter F.1

	Swift F.1	Hunter F.1
Wingspan	32ft 4in (9.86m)	33ft 8in (10.26m)
Wing area	306.2sq ft (28.45sq m)	340sq ft (31.59sq m)
Aerofoil section	HSA 1	Hawker high-speed
Incidence	2.5 degrees	1 degree 30 minutes
Dihedral	2.0 degrees	−1.0 degree
Sweepback angle, 25% chord	40 degrees	39.9 degrees
Flap area, total	35.4sq ft (3.29sq m)	31.9sq ft (2.96sq m)
Tailplane		
span	12ft 10.9in (3.93m)	11ft 10in (3.61m)
area total	62.48sq ft (5.80sq m)	52.9sq ft (4.91sq m)
incidence	nil	variable
dihedral	10 degrees	nil
Elevator area, total	15.4sq ft (1.43sq m)	16.3sq ft (1.51sq m)
Fin and rudder area	44.03sq ft (4.09sq m)	35sq ft (3.25sq m)
Rudder area	8.0sq ft (0.74sq m)	6.1sq ft (0.57sq m)
Aircraft length	41ft 6in (12.68m)	45ft 10.5in (13.98m)
Undercarriage track	15ft 2.5in (4.64m)	14ft 9in (4.5m)
Engine	Avon 105	Avon 107
Maximum thrust	7,500lb (3,400kg)	7,600lb (3,450kg)
Fuel capacity, internal	466gal (2,118ltr)	334gal (1,518ltr)
Armament	2 × 30mm Aden	4 × 30mm Aden
Rounds per gun	200	150
Ejection seat type	MB Mk 2G	MB Mk 2H
Aircraft weight		
tare	11,892lb (5,393kg)	12,128lb (5,500kg)
normal loaded	15,800lb (7,200kg)	16,200lb (7,350kg)
Initial rate of climb	6,300ft/min (1,900m/min)	5,800ft/min (1,800m/min)
Maximum speed at sea level	660mph (1,060km/h)	693mph (1,115km/h)
Service ceiling	45,500ft (13,900m)	48,800ft (14,900m)
Range	730 miles (1,175km)	490 miles (790km)

Displays and a Record

In September 1953 at the SBAC Show at Farnborough, WK195 and WE198 carried out supersonic dives. These were becoming 'old hat' to the professional audience, but the Swifts were renowned and enjoyed by the general public for their high-speed fly-past with reheat going, which gave a truly ear-shattering experience to the spectators. Following the SBAC Show, WK198 was prepared for an attempt on the World Air Speed Record; this was carried out in Libya where the OAT gave a speed of sound approximately 30mph (50km/h) more than in the UK. The Swift was fitted with Avon RA7 Mark 108 serial number 254, which was specially rated for the attempt using 8,225rpm, and with a large reheat nozzle of 24in (61cm) diameter fitted, so as to obtain the maximum thrust possible. With the engine on the test bed and using reheat a thrust of 10,680lb (4,844kg) at 8,225rpm was obtained, though the target figure was 10,800lb (4,900kg).

From the practice run at Tripoli Mike Lithgow reported that there was aileron hammering, so modifications were incorporated to rectify this as well as an attempt being made to improve rear fuselage ventilation. The first attempt returned a figure of 737.3mph (1,186km/h or Mach 0.931) at an OAT of 102°F (39°C). After a number of attempts, adjustments to the reheat controller, and an increase of the governed speed, an average speed of 735.7mph (1,184km/h) was finally achieved by Mike Lithgow on 26 September 1953. However, the exultant feeling was dampened when just over week later the Douglas Skyray took the record back to the USA with a speed of 753mph (1,212km/h).

Due to the need to release the Swift into unrestricted service use as soon a possible, in January 1954 two Swift F.1s, WK201 and WK202, both fitted with 7,500lb thrust Avon RA7-105 engines, were sent to A&AEE Boscombe Down for assessment. Handling trials indicated a number of persistent deficiencies, that resulted in the A&AEE test pilot writing a very critical report that May 1954 on the flight handling of the Swift and the inability of Supermarine to attack the problem.

However, it would appear that the company had already taken action, as Swift F.2 WE218 had been test flown with a much modified mainplane with a 10 per cent leading-edge extension, vortex generators on the bottom and top surfaces of the tailplane, and a modified elevator system. The results of the various defects on the Swift meant that only a conditional service release was given during January, meaning that neither the Hunter nor the Swift were fit for unconditional use on their entry into service! The Swift's maximum limited speed was 550kt (1,019km/h) IAS between sea level and 5,000ft (1,500m) and Mach 0.90 up to 25,000ft (7,600m), which was also the type's height limitation.

Into Service

The Swift F.1 joined 56 Squadron on 13 February 1954 with the restrictions as above, and thus preceded the Hunter into service by five months (July 1954), the latter aircraft also on restricted release. The unit did not, however, receive its full complement of Swifts, operating just nine Mark 1s, WK205 to WK213. One aircraft was lost on 7 May 1954 when the unit's CO, Sqn Ldr (later Group Captain) G. Storey, was investigating the low-speed handling of WK209. He was forced to eject at just below 10,000ft (3,000m), when in spite of his numerous corrective actions the aircraft continued to spin. Group Captain Storey recalls:

> The Swift was a failure as an air defence fighter although it subsequently proved to be useful in the tactical reconnaissance role in Germany. This was not surprising as it was a stable aircraft which was not easily disturbed from its flight path by the rough air experienced at low level near the earth's surface.
>
> The arrival of the Swift in February 1954 had been eagerly anticipated by the groundcrew. Although new equipment with associated problems was naturally a little daunting in the early days, it was not long before the groundcrew realized they had a monster to deal with: hydraulic leaks and failure, control problems, random and obscure electrical faults et al., and the design failure to provide for a rapid aircraft turnround did nothing to inspire groundcrew confidence in the aircraft as an operational fighter. They had an extremely frustrating and trying time in providing the few serviceable aircraft which they did achieve. It was their determination, resilience and loyalty which enabled the pilots to enjoy those very limiting hours when the aircraft were available for flying.

The deficiencies on the Swift centred around a number of points, which were: severe 'pitch-up' at high Mach numbers above 25,000ft at low 'g', thus restricting the usable turning performance; a severe loss of elevator control above Mach 0.91; heavy elevator control forces at high Mach numbers; severe wing drop between Mach 0.92–0.94; and a marked 'nose-down' trim change with the extension of the air brakes above Mach 0.94. The engine surged with or without firing the guns – this was only found out later to be due to the early type of Avon engine design and not to the airframe air-intake design.

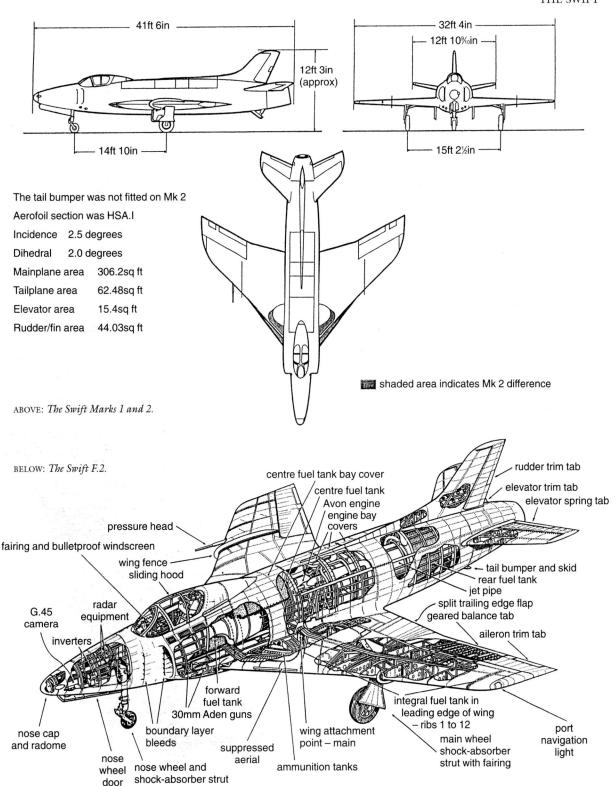

41ft 6in

12ft 3in (approx)

14ft 10in

32ft 4in

12ft 10⅝in

15ft 2½in

The tail bumper was not fitted on Mk 2

Aerofoil section was HSA.I

Incidence   2.5 degrees

Dihedral   2.0 degrees

Mainplane area   306.2sq ft

Tailplane area   62.48sq ft

Elevator area   15.4sq ft

Rudder/fin area   44.03sq ft

shaded area indicates Mk 2 difference

ABOVE: *The Swift Marks 1 and 2.*

BELOW: *The Swift F.2.*

centre fuel tank bay cover
centre fuel tank
Avon engine
engine bay covers
rudder trim tab
elevator trim tab
elevator spring tab
pressure head
fairing and bulletproof windscreen
wing fence
sliding hood
tail bumper and skid
rear fuel tank
jet pipe
split trailing edge flap
geared balance tab
aileron trim tab
G.45 camera
radar equipment
inverters
forward fuel tank
30mm Aden guns
integral fuel tank in leading edge of wing – ribs 1 to 12
port navigation light
nose cap and radome
boundary layer bleeds
wing attachment point – main
main wheel shock-absorber strut with fairing
nose wheel door
nose wheel and shock-absorber strut
suppressed aerial
ammunition tanks

Before the Swift arrived it had been decided at 56 Squadron that 'A' Flight would be converted first so that pilots could consolidate their initial flying on type, then 'B Flight would convert. However, due to the poor serviceability it was realized that 'B' Flight could not be converted if safety standards were to be maintained with 'A' Flight flying. Group Captain Storey comments:

Perhaps a measure of the difficulties we had faced were exemplified by the hours achieved during the period of fourteen months' squadron service. In the first six months there were only five Swift Mark 1 aircraft and during that time the aircraft were grounded for some two months; with aircraft strength increasing to eleven aircraft, both Mark 1 and Mark 2, in the last six months. Also, one must allow for the fact that flying times were recorded from wheels rolling to touch down. Nonetheless, a total of 720 hours was not exactly outstanding with the highest individual flying time being a mere sixty-seven hours. However, overall we did convert thirty-four squadron pilots and provide flights for nearly as many 'outside' pilots, including the CAS.

Happily, aircrew morale remained high throughout the Swift era. The loss of Neil Thornton, a popular and enthusiastic young pilot, was a sad but temporary 'blip' only, and was something which occurred elsewhere in the fighter world; fortuitously, it was the only fatality. However, that is not to overlook two ejections and the frequency of incidents, many of them serious, which the pilots experienced all too often in the air. Of course, as with the groundcrew, the pilots had many disappointments and frustrations, but their keenness to get into the cockpit never abated. The aircraft had handling problems but it was, nevertheless, exciting to fly as it provided speed, rate of roll, powerful airbrakes etc., far superior to its predecessors. It should be remembered that, at that time in particular, there was great kudos to be on 56 Squadron. It was exhilarating, and pride and enthusiasm in those circumstances would be felt by any keen young fighter pilot – and was.

At Vickers' South Marston factory, test runs of the Swift's Avon being done in the open into standard mufflers had caused a noise problem. This affected factory and office workers within a quarter-mile radius, and complaints were even received from Swindon, 5 to 6 miles away! Vickers-Armstrongs finished up installing a sound-proofed pen for the Swifts to carry out their engine runs.

The Mark 2

Steady improvement was being made on the Swift, and on 30 October 1954 Swift WK195 was despatched to Rolls-Royce Hucknall to help with development of the reheat system for the Marks 3 and 4, as the Swifts from the Mark 3s onwards were to have reheat as standard. That the reheat system of the time required a descent to 20,000ft (6,000m) for relight was obviously not acceptable to a fighter force operating at 30–40,000ft (9–12,000m). Although after test at A&AEE WK195 received a report of marked improvement in reheat operation at altitude and pitch-up instability, it was rejected as not acceptable in respect of its longitudinal handling.

Swift Mark 3 WK247. MAP

Following this, Swift Mark 1 WK198, the World Air Speed record breaker mentioned previously, was converted into the prototype Mark 4 and brought up to full production standard, still under the designation Type 546. This aircraft had a Tiltman Langley Laboratories-designed rear fuselage with a +4/−9-degree VI tailplane, operating jacks and small-chord nose-balanced elevators, with vortex generators fitted above and below the tailplane, which gave improved elevator control at high Mach numbers. It was also fitted with a saw-tooth mainplane leading edge and four Aden guns. Pre-production F.4 WK272, fitted with an Avon 114 with reheat, went to A&AEE for test in late in 1954. The trial was intended to investigate longitudinal control, the influence of the VI tail, low-speed handling and manual control. However, shortly after the trials commenced the aircraft was returned to Supermarine for modifications to the elevator control system. Further trials indicated that the VI tail gave a vast improvement with no problems in the transonic speed zone.

The end of the Korean War saw a change in priorities, so in the interest of economy the Air Council decided to cut back the fighter force and standardize on the Hawker Hunter. This resulted in reduced orders for the Hunter and cancellation of the Swift orders.

56 Squadron had received Swift Mark 2s WE221, WE239, WE240, WE242 and WE245, with delivery commencing on 30 August 1954. However, due to their inferior handling qualities and poor turning radius at altitude, all Swifts were withdrawn from squadron service during March 1955, though they were still being employed on test and development. Three Swift F.1s were flown from 56 Squadron at RAF Waterbeach to the MU at RAF Lyneham on 28 March 1955, followed by five F.2s on 3 April. Group Captain Storey again:

The Swift had been put into squadron service far too early under the political pressure to have a British swept-wing fighter in the front line. It was a significant advance on the Meteor/Vampire, both technically and in performance; unfortunately, it had been introduced into the squadron at the same time as the Swift flight trials were taking place at Boscombe Down. There is no doubt that the squadron missed the benefit of those extensive trials which a new aircraft normally undergoes before being released for squadron service. Moreover, there was not the support of the highly efficient Flight Safety organization

as exists today. Reports on incidents occurring at A&AEE, the Central Fighter Establishment and on the squadron were often not disseminated or were not circulated with the promptness which was required. Hence incidents occurred which might have been avoided and problems arose which could have been identified earlier.

However, throughout the period of the Swift, in spite of the lack of serviceable aircraft and its disappointment as a fighter, there was never a lack of confidence with the pilots. They were not glad to see the aircraft go (reverting to Meteors was retrograde) but it was realized that the aircraft was a complete failure in the air defence role.

Swift testing continued at the various establishments and at A&AEE WE220 was involved in an accident on 16 March 1955 when being flown from there. Flt Lt T.M. Crowley had an engine fail with a loud noise at 27,000ft (8,200m) at 340kt (630km/h) during a relight test, and it refused to restart during numerous relight procedures. A forced landing with wheels retracted was carried out at Boscombe Down airfield. Repair of the damaged parts was followed by engine relight checks, all of which were proven satisfactorily.

Mike Corner who flew the Swift and Hunter:

The Swift got off to a bad start with 56 Squadron and only became acceptable to the Service in the FR.5 variant where its limitations at high altitude would not find it out. As a low-level, high-speed tactical recce aircraft it would score well since it was built like a tank and the skin-rippling problems associated with low-altitude flying would affect it less than most. I imagine it was much like a Buccaneer. Tac-pilots don't mind about lack of turning power, they want only to get in fast and get out as low as possible.

The Swift also carried quite a bit of fuel and we routinely managed fifty-minute sorties, and sometimes one hour or sixty-five minutes at high altitude. Low down it was about forty minutes. In those days this was quite good and compared very closely with the Meteor (on which I had over 1,000 hours). It was a bit of a shock to find that the Hunter F.1 could only manage between thirty-five and fifty minutes maximum.

The Marks 3 and 4

Twenty-five Swift Mark 3s, serial numbers WK247–271 were built but did not see squadron service.

These aircraft were basically Mark 2s fitted with four Aden guns, reheat and tailplane vortex generators. Whilst WK248 was sold to the College of Aeronautics on 10 December 1957, the remainder were allocated as ground instruction airframes at RAF training schools.

Only six Swift Mark 4s were built. Two aircraft were delivered to 2 Squadron and two to 79 Squadron for assessment. The pre-production Swift F.4, WK272, was lost on 17 August 1955, when during intentional spinning trials it failed to recover from a spin. The test pilot, G.J. Horne of Vickers-Armstrongs, unable to get the aircraft to recover, was forced to eject. Another Mark 4, WE275, which had been retained for test flying, was powered by an Avon 114 and had been modified with a slab flying tail and datum trimming. With these modifications it was reported that the aircraft flew extremely well, so one may question why these alterations were not embodied earlier. Was this due to Supermarine being pressurized to get the Swift into service or failure on the design side to recognize the advantages to be gained? WK275 joined the Air Ministry Fleet in March 1955 and was involved in test flying from Chilbolton. Then, on 26 August 1957, it was transferred to A&AEE Boscombe Down for further testing. WE275 was later bought privately and as late as 1999 could be seen outside a large general market at Upper Hill, near Leominster, Herefordshire.

Mike J. Corner:

As a gun platform, the Swift suffered directional instability at high altitudes – let's say above 20,000ft. This manifested itself in a very annoying yaw from side to side at a rate of about one cycle per second. Clearly this made tracking a target within our requirements impossible; consequently, the makers fitted auto-stabilization, which improved matters a good deal. This device was linked to a tab on the rudder and vibrated at a very high frequency and could be felt trembling through the rudder bar. It had an on/off switch and could be turned off if required – aerobatics, for example.

It was a matter of total disbelief in the Air Force that the specification/operational requirements of the Swift/Hunter allowed these aircraft to be produced without effective air brakes (speed brakes). Belatedly, the Hunter had a ventral barn-door contraption fitted that was only just acceptable. The Swift was made to make do with strengthened flaps which were a joke. At high indicated air speeds, the air brake would not operate at all! When it did, there was a significant nose-down change of trim, which you don't want when you are letting down from high altitude in a close formation pair. Another irritation to the pilot was the strong lateral yawing that occurred when you selected undercarriage 'down'. This was caused by the nose-wheel fairing.

A number of fighter pilots confirmed that neither the Hunter nor the Swift measured up to the fighter requirements of the time, due to lack of radar-ranging gun sights, the cannon's low muzzle velocity and engine flame-outs.

Swift F.4 WK275 used for 'flying tail' trials. It eventually retired to Upper Hill Stores, Hereford.

8

Further Swift Development

Development of the FR.5

As flight trials with previous marks of Swift had found the aircraft only effective as a fighter up to around 40,000ft (12,000m), the Hawker Hunter had been accepted by the Air Staff for the fighter role in the RAF. The Swift having failed to become the RAF's new interceptor, Supermarine then began to develop its airframe in the fighter-reconnaissance role as the FR.5. This requirement came about because in the mid-1950s NATO forces were facing numerically superior Warsaw Pact forces in Europe, and there was a need for a modern, fast, low-level fighter-reconnaissance aircraft to replace the tired and obsolescent Meteor FR.9. For this role the Swift's robust construction was highly suitable. Although the FR.5 was considered an interim type by the Air Staff, prior to the introduction of the Hunter FR.10, it set a standard for low-level, high-speed reconnaissance that the Hunter was unable to replicate. While the Hunter was to have a better serviceability in service,

it was not as happy or as smooth at the low levels that the Swift was regularly flown at.

The Type 549 Swift FR.5 was basically an improved F.4 powered by a reheated Avon 114. It had a lengthened nose housing three F.95 cameras: one in the extreme nose and the other two positioned one each side of the fuselage, forward of the air intakes, for oblique photography. It also had an enlarged fin, a clear-view canopy, a VI tail and a sawtooth mainplane leading edge. To extend its range a 220gal (1,000ltr) ventral fuel tank was fitted as standard, and it carried two 30mm Aden cannon (four 30mm cannon was considered by some experts to be 'over-kill'), which could be augmented by bombs and rocket projectiles (RPs).

The airframe redesign work was initially undertaken by Tiltman Langley Laboratories on behalf of Supermarine. Brian Buss of TLL:

> Due to the Swift's inability to perform as required at high altitude, work was undertaken to convert the

A Swift Mark 5 with full load of rocket projectiles at RAE Farnborough.

type into a low-level fighter-reconnaissance aircraft and this became the FR.5 Type 549. In order to do so, the fuselage had to be strengthened and TLL undertook much of the preliminary layout work before Supermarine took over. The nose was lengthened to house three F.24 cameras and an initial order for thirty-four aircraft was followed by another for eighty-one, but later reduced to fifty-eight off.

Swift Mark 1 WK200 was converted into the prototype FR.5 and went to A&AEE Boscombe Down as such in July 1953 to undertake service trials; it was eventually scrapped at Bicester in 1956. Powered by the Rolls-Royce Avon 114 of 7,175lb (3,254kg) static thrust and at an all-up-weight of 21,000lb (9,500kg), the FR.5 had a maximum speed of 685mph (1,100km/h). The first production FR.5, XD903, made its maiden flight on 27 May 1955 with Les Colquhoun at the controls. The following two production Mark 5s were further modified to improve their suitability for their role, being fitted with the 220gal drop tank to raise the fuel capacity to 998gal (4,537ltr) and a clear-vision cockpit canopy.

A&AEE Boscombe Down carried out an initial assessment of the FR.5 on a converted F.4, WK272, during May 1955, the conclusions of which were fairly satisfactory. Taking off using reheat, it was found that the elevator became effective at about 100kt (186km/h), with the nose rising at 115kt (214km/h) with a best lift-off at 150kt (279km/h). The ailerons and elevators remained light and effective at cruising speeds between 400–500kt (745–930km/h), but rudder response and effectiveness was poor and deteriorated with increasing speed, and airframe buffet increased as the maximum speed was approached. The maximum speeds at sea level were recorded as 590kt (1,100km/h) with ventral fuel tank fitted and reheat used, and 600kt (1,120km/h) 'clean' with reheat. The normal approach speed was made at 140–145kt (260–270km/h) with a touchdown speed of 130kt (240km/h).

Following this an AFDS trial on a Swift FR.5 was carried out and its assessment was more or less in line with the previous A&AEE report, although the AFDS considered that visibility in the rain would be a problem. Four Swift FR.5s were released to the RAF before the end of 1955, eight months after the withdrawal of the Swift F.1/F.2 fighter at RAF Waterbeach.

Following the handling and performance trials, and the acceptance of the Swift FR.5 into service, flight handling notes were issued. These emphasized that the handling of the aircraft in the low-level fighter-reconnaissance role presented no problems, provided it was flown (as with other aircraft) in accordance with the instructions. On take-off the aircraft accelerated rapidly with no tendency to swing, the rudder becoming effective at 60–70kt (110–130km/h). As there was a high degree of elevator boosting (15 to 1), care needed to be taken to avoid over-controlling during the take-off. The elevator became effective at 110–115kt (200–214km/h), so slight backward pressure was all that was required to raise the nose wheel at 115–120kt (214–224km/h), the aircraft flying off at 145–150kt (270–280km/h). Pilot's Notes stated that the aircraft was not to be pulled off the ground, and if a belly-tank was fitted, then the fly-off speed was 155–160kt (290–300km/h). The take-off run with a full ventral tank and using reheat was 1,310yd (1,200m).

The aircraft was stable throughout the speed range up to Mach 0.86, when a nose-down trim change took place. Throughout the lower and medium speed range the elevator was very light, the ailerons light and powerful, with the rudder light and effective. At speeds up to 300kt (560km/h), care needed to be exercised with the ailerons, as full movement could cause slight yaw in the opposite direction to that applied. As the Mach number increased up to Mach 0.91 the nose-down trim continued, then little further change occurred up to Mach 0.955, when a slight nose-up trim change occurred. Above this speed the aircraft was stable.

The ailerons gave a high rate of roll up to Mach 0.935, when wing heaviness occurred, from then on and up to about Mach 0.945 the rate of roll was reduced. As the aircraft became supersonic the elevator became heavy with reduced effectiveness, and it was then that the variable-incidence tail needed to be used. The rudder became progressively heavier as speed increased with the rudder-tab effectiveness becoming less above Mach 0.9. It was recommended that excessive amounts of rudder should not be applied due to high foot force. At speeds below 250kt (470km/h) there was a gradual lightening off of the foot load, which was more pronounced with the undercarriage 'down'. The flaps could be used as air brakes at any speed or Mach number, and up to Mach 0.9 there was very little trim change, but at high Mach numbers there was a nose-down trim change, which could however be held on the elevator.

Swift FR.5 WK277, which was modified from F.4 standard. It is seen here at Newark Air Museum.

Technical Features

The hydraulic system of the Swift was of the Lockheed 'LiveLine' type and operated the retraction/extension of the wheels, wheel brakes, trailing-edge flaps, gun-bay scavenge flap, and elevator and aileron hydro-booster units. Power was supplied by two engine-driven two-stage pumps, with two accumulators providing a reserve of power for the gun-bay scavenge flap, main flaps, hydro-booster units and wheel brake over-ride, with a smaller accumulator connected to the normal wheel-brake circuit. In an emergency the alighting gear and flaps could be operated by compressed air to blow them down.

The Avon 114 engine of the Swift FR.5 had a thrust without reheat of 6,815lb (3,090kg), but with reheat this was increased to 8,970lb (4,070kg)

at 7,900rpm. The Swift's rate of climb with reheat was exceptional, more so when compared with the Hunter, which was not equipped with reheat. The Swift's time to height from wheels rolling was as detailed in the table (*below*).

The engine was supplied with fuel from an internal tank system with a capacity of 506gal (2,300ltr), that could be supplemented by a belly tank holding 220gal (1,000ltr). The internal fuel system was comprised of five tanks, a forward fuselage tank of 112gal (510ltr), centre fuselage tank of 98gal (445ltr), rear fuselage tank of 104gal (473ltr) and two wing leading-edge tanks, one in each wing, each of 96gal (436ltr) capacity.

The Vinten F.95 camera installed on the operational Swift FR.5 had followed the F.24 camera into service and proved a great success: at the time and

Climb rate of Swift FR.5 aircraft (minutes)

Height to attain	Clean aircraft	With belly tank	Reheat, aircraft clean	Reheat, belly tank
5,000ft (1,524m)	2.0	2.25	1.4	1.5
10,000ft (3,048m)	3.25	3.5	1.8	2.1
20,000ft (6,096m)	5.75	6.75	2.7	3.2
30,000ft (9,144m)	8.75	11.0	3.9	4.6
40,000ft (12,192m)	13.75	20.5	5.7	6.5

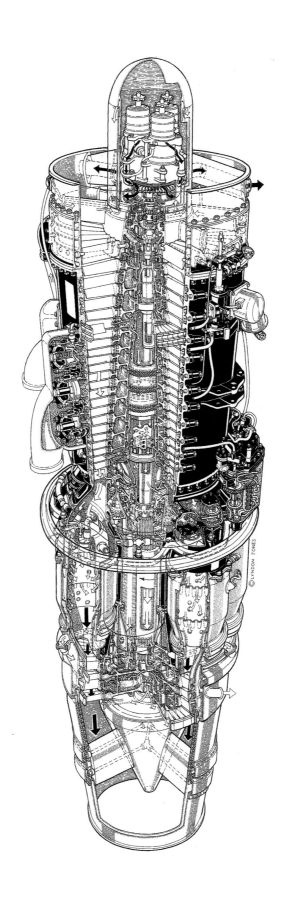

The Rolls-Royce Avon R.A.7.

Data and Performance Figures – Swift FR.5

Wingspan	32ft 4in (9.86m)	Armament, cannon	two 30 mm ADEN
Wing area	320.7sq ft (29.79sq m)	Ejection seat type	Martin-Baker
Aerofoil section	HSA 1	Engine type	RA.7R/Avon 114 with reheat
Incidence	2.5 degree		
Dihedral	2.0 degree	Thrust rating	
Flap area (total)	31.5sq ft (2.93sq m)	with re-heat	8,970lb (4,070kg) at 7,900rpm
Tailplane			
span	12ft 8.5in (3.7m)	without reheat	6,815lb (3,090kg) at 7,900rpm
area	62.06sq ft (5.77sq m)	Maximum speed	713mph (1,150km/h) at sea level
dihedral	10 degrees		
incidence (variable)	+4 to –9 degree	Maximum initial rate of climb	4,660ft/min (1,420m/min)
Elevator area	12.48sq ft (1.16sq m)		
Fin and rudder area	53.10sq ft (4.93sq m)	Climb to 40,000ft	5.7min (12,000m)
Rudder area	8.0sq ft (0.74sq m)		
Length	42ft 3in (12.88m)	Service ceiling	45,800ft (14,000m)
Undercarriage track	15ft 2in (4.62m)	Range, with full fuel	
Weight		best range	445 nautical miles (825km)
tare	13,435lb (6,093kg)	typical FR sortie	336 nautical miles (626km)
maximum all up	21,500lb (9,750kg)	Take-off run (full fuel)	
maximum landing	17,000lb (7,700kg)	without reheat	1900yd (1,740m)
Fuel capacity		with reheat	1310yd (1,120m)
maximum internal	506gal (2,300ltr)		
plus external tanks	726gal (3,300ltr)		

for a number of years later they were the best cameras for low-level, high-speed photography. So they complemented the Swift FR.5, with its excellent performance in the rough-air conditions at low altitudes over difficult routes and terrain, and in poor weather conditions. Obviously, as any Tac-R or FR pilot will confirm, weather conditions would determine the effectiveness of visual reconnaissance.

Operational Service

The arrival of the Swift FR.5 at 2 Squadron in early 1956 also saw the arrival of Jeffrey Quill, Les Colquhoun and technical representatives from Supermarine, as well as Mr Sparrow of Rolls-Royce, on the squadron as a trouble-shooting team. This mass of expertise, in conjunction with the RAF technical groundcrews, started to show an upturn in serviceability, all to be spoilt in late 1957 with a spate of hydraulic failures due to the type of hydraulic pump employed.

Phil Crawshaw flew the Swift FR.5 with 2 Squadron 2nd TAF and remembers a maintenance problem:

A major drawback from the servicing side was the hydraulic system. The pipes tended to leak and they were routed under the engine which, as it incorporated a good reheat system, could lead to excitement. I did not experience any problems, but some did, and the groundcrew became very proficient at removing engines to rectify hydraulic leaks and then putting the aircraft together again.

As stated previously, the ailerons and elevators were power-operated, with the aileron circuit including three boosters. The centre booster was connected to two aileron control rods; the other two were positioned one adjacent to each control circuit and connected through the respective control rods. The elevator circuit used a single booster that operated in a similar manner to the aileron booster, the main difference being that the control valve and piston-rod locking pawl was attached to the control circuit.

The integrity of the Swift's structure was borne out by the fact that, in the most demanding role of high-speed, low-level reconnaissance, it operated for four years with Nos 2 and 79 Squadrons of 2nd TAF in Germany without a structural failure. No. 2 Squadron's first Swift FR.5 arrived at Geilenkirchen on 23 February, but due to poor winter weather and poor serviceability the pilots' conversion onto the Swift progressed slowly. Delivery began to 79 Squadron during June 1956, with delivery being completed by 1 September 1956.

Apart from its flight characteristic of tightening-up in turns, it was one of the best, if not the best, of the fighter-reconnaissance aircraft in use in that period. Its robust construction was a major factor in making it possible to fly punishing high-speed, low-level operations under enemy radar surveillance in steady flight, whilst its handling control at low level gave it a distinct advantage when crossing the varying and difficult terrain of Eastern Europe on reconnaissance missions.

The post-1945 period of retrenchment and lack of spending on the British Services and operational research, as had happened post-1918, resulted in 1951–2 with an attempt to relieve the situation by speeding up the aircraft development programmes to catch up with American hardware. However, as regards the Swift, its acceptance into squadron service as a replacement for the Meteor FR.9 appears to have shown the Air Ministry short of ideas or cash – or both, as the following shows. Geoff Marlow of 2 Squadron:

When it was decided by the powers that be that the Swift would be the replacement for the Meteor

FR.9 my squadron commander selected me to go to a meeting at the Air Ministry, along with Dave Moffat of 79 Squadron, to discuss the specifications we would like to have on the Swift FR.5.

The aeroplane was based on the Swift Mark 4, modified to take three F95 cameras in the nose. One of the things we requested was more fuel capacity because the range of the aeroplane was too short. We were told that in order to get more fuel we would have to reduce some weight, so after much discussion we agreed that we would sacrifice two of the four 30mm cannon. As it happened, when we received the Swift on the squadron we couldn't fire the guns anyway, because it was feared that the smoke would enter the engine intake and put out the fire. This problem was solved only after the aeroplane had been in service for about two years.

We then asked for a navigation aid such as a Radio Compass. We were told that it was against Air Ministry policy to fit such aids because in wartime they could be jammed and if we were to get used to relying on them we wouldn't be able to find our way around in a war.

Another item we requested was a mirror giving 180 degrees' rear view. A civil servant told us that such mirrors were not normally fitted because they gave a distorted image. I replied that our role was low-level reconnaissance, which involved flying at low level to and from the target. As they were not prepared to give us any navigational aids at all, that meant we would be navigating at 420kt at about 100ft with only a map, a compass and a wristwatch. I explained that that required a fair degree of concentration leaving little time to watch your six o'clock. I only wanted a mirror to let me know if there was something behind me and I would soon find out what it was. They gave us the mirror we wanted.

After the meeting at Air Ministry about the Swift FR.5s equipment, Geoff Marlow found another problem on arrival on 2 Squadron: as there was no two-seat version for training purposes, training was carried out from the first solo, learning all the way. This alone kills off some of the ill-founded remarks about the operational Swifts, as well as giving credit to their pilots:

Eventually, in 1956 we received our first Swift. The Swift was to be the first aeroplane in which my first flight was to be my first solo and it contained many new features and capabilities.

On my first flight I taxied out. That was fine, the ride was a bit harder because the tyres had a very high pressure. I lined up on the runway and stopped. I applied the parking brake which involved flicking down something that resembled an old fashioned domestic light switch. I then pushed the throttle fully forward up to maximum rpm, checked everything was OK, then selected reheat. The aeroplane gave an almighty lurch and the nose went down about a foot, depressing the nose-wheel leg, but the brakes held. I checked everything was OK again, and then flicked off the brake switch and we were away, much faster than in a Meteor. After leaving the runway the wheels quickly retracted and the aeroplane crossed the airfield fence with the nose twitching up and down madly as I was trying to get used to the powered controls.

At about 500ft I switched off the reheat and continued climbing up to about 10,000ft. Then I started getting used to the feel of it. I was wearing an anti-G suit for the first time, so I tried some tight turns to get used to that. Then I tried accelerating using the reheat and slowing down using the air brakes, and then some aerobatics. The powered ailerons were fantastic, giving a very fast rate of roll. All the instruments and controls were well positioned. Visibility was excellent. It was as comfortable as you could get for a fighter. You could control cockpit temperature to any degree, and you could even produce snow in the cockpit, which you only did once, for obvious reasons.

The aeroplane was great. Man and machine were getting along fine together and I was impressed. So I returned to the airfield for my first landing. The nose-wheel door was hinged fore-and-aft, so when the wheels were lowered it acted like a rudder and a bit of right rudder trim was required. The landing was straightforward but you crossed the fence at about 140kt, which was about 35kt faster than in a Meteor. The brakes had a non-skid capability and were very effective, and this was about thirty years before ABS brakes were fitted to cars.

For my second trip I was to do a reheated climb to 40,000ft and then do a supersonic dive. The Swift could climb to 40,000ft in four minutes from a standing start. It was the only aeroplane in the world in squadron service that could climb at anything like that rate, and ironically we had it for a low-flying role.

On the day I did it there was fairly solid cloud from about 5,000ft to just over 25,000ft. So half my climb was on instruments. By the time I entered cloud I still hadn't got accustomed to the angle at which I was sitting and the aeroplane was climbing. On entering cloud my climbing angle wasn't steep enough and my speed built up rapidly in the cloud. I then over-corrected and had the aeroplane climbing almost vertically, then the speed started to fall off rapidly. So I had to push the stick forward hard and I suffered what seemed ages of negative 'g' before the speed started building up again, and then before I had regained my breath we flew out of the cloud top. I had come very close to stalling and possibly losing control, and it might have been very difficult to recover with my lack of experience in type. I continued climbing to 40,000ft in the clear.

I didn't tell anyone about my reheat climb, but months later in the bar we were talking about our early experiences on the Swift, and it emerged that several of us had had a hairy time on this exercise, but after the first time there were no repetitions of the problem.

Next came the supersonic dive. This was an anticlimax. I dived fairly steeply and the speed built up quickly and as the needle passed Mach 1 there was a very slight twitch on the stick. I kept the aeroplane pointing downwards and the speed built up to Mach 1.15 and it would not go any faster. Throughout the dive the aeroplane was under control.

The F.5 Assessed

Contrary to critics and unofficial accounts that degrade the Swift's performance and handling, as well as the bad press given to the aircraft in general, the FR.5 version on 2 and 79 Squadrons in Germany received pilots' plaudits. In fact, Group Captain Nigel Walpole, one of the most experienced Swift pilots, wrote a book called *Swift Justice* to describe what went wrong and what went right with the Swift, the aircraft's re-emergence as the FR.5 and its success story in squadron use.

As opposed to this, a magazine article by an aviation writer about a simulated combat between a Hunter F.4 and a Swift FR.5 at 20,000ft (6,000m), in which the Hunter won, completely misses the point that the Swift FR.5 was a low-level aircraft and out of its working environment at 20,000ft, whilst the Hunter F.4 would be, and was, found wanting at the low heights at which the Swift FR.5 normally flew. The Swift FR.5 was also far more manoeuvrable at low level than its US contemporaries in the tactical reconnaissance role, such as the RF-84 and RF-101, and the pilots of 2 and 79 Squadrons exploited the

Swift's low-level capabilities and best turning speed by judicious use of reheat combined with its large flap-cum-air-brake.

The two Swift squadrons routinely carried out training in competition with the NATO Hunter F.4s on 'rat and terrier' interception exercises, so as to hone the capabilities of both types of aircraft operations. In air-to-ground gunnery exercises the Swift pilots racked up scores of around 60–80 per cent with their two 30mm Aden cannon. These exercises indicated that a Swift FR.5 at low level, using reheat and evasive action, could survive against the MiG-15 in the hostile airspace over East Germany, should the Warsaw Pact countries declare war. The MiG-15 was most effective at greater heights than those in which the Swift FR.5 operated, while the MiG-17, although improved in its handling, would have found the Swift hard to handle low down and using reheat.

Geoff Marlow of 2 Squadron describes his first low-level cross-country flying a FR.5:

My third trip was a low-level cross-country and during it I took a few pictures to see if there would be any difficulties in aiming the cameras. I would now be flying in the second Swift to be received by the squadron and this was to be my designated aeroplane with the letter E for Easy painted on the fin. We were told that it had been painted with a new kind of camouflage paint which enabled it to fly faster.

The low flying was excellent. The Swift was steady as a rock both in the lateral and vertical planes but would respond very quickly when you wanted it to. It kept its course well and if there were any bumps around I didn't feel them. On a trip several months later my 'g' meter recorded a bump of 25g, but I only noticed that it had been a slightly bumpy ride. When it came to using the camera I didn't know how I was going to aim it. On the Meteor we had used an imaginary line extending forward from the wingtip, but on the Swift the wingtip was too far back. So I just guessed at the line using a mark on my cockpit canopy and it worked. Taking pictures in the Swift was easy, but you had to remember to open the camera doors first, just like ordinary photographers have to remember to remove the lens cover.

After finishing my cross-country I climbed out of the low flying area to return home and I flew at about 2,000ft. On the way home I flew through a hailstorm. As I was taxying in I noticed everyone staring, more than usual, at my aeroplane. When I got out I could see why. The new type of camouflage paint had

all been stripped off by the hailstorm. So my next trip in this aeroplane was to fly back to England to Supermarine's airfield at South Marston to have it repainted with the old type of camouflage paint.

The total production of the Swift FR.5 totalled ninety-four aircraft. This included thirty-five modified F.4s and fifty-nine newly built airframes. The conversions were serial numbers WK274, WK276–WK278 and WK280–WK315; the new-build airframes were WN124, XD903–XD930 and XD948–XD977.

The Swift FR.5 brought to the fighter-reconnaissance scene high-speed, low-level sorties under the enemy radar surveillance, and in this role the Swift's effectiveness was proven in May 1957 when two Swifts of 79 Squadron came first and second in the annual NATO Reconnaissance Competition 'Royal Flush', held at Laarbruch. This competition was a low-level 260 nautical mile (480km) visual reconnaissance at below 500ft (150m) with photographic confirmation.

That same month 2 Squadron would demonstrate the structural integrity of the Swift when Flt Lt L. Cockerill had an engine 'flame-out' in XD930 when over-flying RAF Wildenrath at 2,000ft (600m). The engine refused to relight, so a quick emergency landing was required. At that height with no thrust there was too little time to lower the undercarriage and flaps, so a powerless and clean landing was made on the Swift's drop tank! After that, all that was required was to lower the undercarriage and tow it into the hangar, the aircraft requiring slight attention to the fuselage underskin, another drop tank and a replacement engine.

The Swift's success in the NATO Reconnaissance Competition was repeated two years later against strong competition from other NATO air forces equipped with US-designed aircraft, such as the RF-84 and RF-101. By this time remedies to various technical defects had improved the Swift's serviceability, and there had been an improved downward trend in incidents and accidents. However, technical problems stayed with the Swift FR.5 to the end of its service, hydraulic system snags being the worst. Geoff Marlow:

You soon became used to the new capabilities and features of the Swift. It was great to fly and great for our role except for its shortage of range. It had one enormous problem, though, and this is why it got a bad reputation. The problem was serviceability. Out of sixteen aeroplanes on the squadron the average number serviceable was around four.

Phil Crawshaw was another pilot who flew the Swift Mark 5 in the fighter-reconnaissance role from RAF Jever until the Swift was replaced with the Hunter Mark 10:

There is no doubt that as a high-level fighter it left much to be desired. It was heavy and the wing loading precluded rapid changes in direction desirable in an agile fighter. However, this shortcoming became a positive advantage in the low-level recce role. The aircraft was extremely stable and reluctant to change direction – up or down or from side to side.

From a pilot's viewpoint, in the role we operated the aeroplane, I am not aware of anyone who disliked the Swift and I was sorry to see her go. It was solid, as Flt Lt Pat King found out when he flew through the top of a forest – or as he put it, the cloud turned green! My only incident was a two-wheel landing when the starboard wheel decided to have a rest. In the excitement I overlooked the airbrake/full flap over-ride and consequently the landing was hot and long, ending up on the Station golf course! However, apart from a ventral tank replacement the aircraft was ready to fly again within the week.

The aircraft was also a very good air-to-ground firing platform. The Swift lacked navigation aids but this did not bother us unduly since if one could not see the ground, reconnaissance was somewhat pointless. We did however develop a respect for the GCA controllers who sorted us out when the weather necessitated the rare IFR landing.

In the Swift the RAF had acquired a fighter-reconnaissance aircraft whose airframe was well suited for the low-level role – some would say low-low level role – as the Swift FR5's was so steady that only extremely strong turbulence affected it. The Swift FR.5s remained in 2nd TAF in Germany until December 1960, by which time the airframes were tired, both from normal service life and from some unorthodox handlings – and mishandlings!

The Swift FR.5s of 2nd TAF were eventually replaced by the Hunter FR.10. 2 Squadron started re-equipment in March 1961, whilst 79 Squadron's last Swift flew out of RAF Gutersloh on 7 February 1961. Although the Hunter FR.10 had a better serviceability record than the Swift, it was neither as steady nor as smooth at Tac-R sortie heights, nor as good in the air-to-ground attack role, and in early sorties the FR.10 suffered nose deformation and skin cracks.

Opinions on the Swift FR.5's handling varied slightly; naturally this depended on the pilot's previous aircraft types, but was in general favourable to the Swift in its low-level role. The Swift could not be called beautiful, but like the Beaufighter it looked like an aggressive and strong beast. This is described by Peter J. Adair of No.2 Squadron, who flew the Swift FR.5 as well as the Hunter FR.10, and flew the unit's last operational Swift from Jever to Manston upon re-equipment with Hunter Mark 10s:

My first sight of a Swift was on arrival on my squadron in Germany. I thought it looked bulky but not pretty. The old adage of if it looks good on the ground it flies well.

There was no dual aircraft, but this didn't bother me having converted to the Vampire and Hunter with no dual. Having read the Pilot's Notes I was advised, if I wanted to survive, to add 20kt to the circuit speeds.

Settling in the cockpit the first thing that I was impressed with was the spaciousness. Superb layout and elbow room. Taxiing was a pleasure with the low-pressure tyres. Line up on the runway, full power against the brakes. Brake boost on and select reheat. Nose oleo depresses to the stops. Brake boost off, nose rears and away we go. First impressions was that this is not a Hunter. Conversion consists of general handling and height climbs. Up to 40,000ft, level off then turn. In the turn we felt we were falling out of the sky. This aircraft was never a high-altitude interceptor.

After conversion we then went on to low level, when this aircraft came into its own. Even at low level its turning was abysmal, but you could fly it in the tops of the trees, in severe turbulence, at 620kt, and it was steady as a rock. Whoever made the decision to make it low-level FR was a genius. All-round visibility was great as was rearward with the mirror. You would be cruising at 200ft, 360kt when espying a Hunter curving in to attack. At 900yd bring in the reheat and see him disappear from the mirror.

Air-to-air firing was a problem, as we maximized the low aircraft to 6,000ft. Even then it was difficult to attain the angle-off required. Air-to-ground was a delight, she was as steady as a rock. No one had not experienced a hydraulic failure, and in manual control she was a pig.

It sounds as if I am degrading this aircraft, but there you are wrong. I loved it, it was made for the role.

When the time came to re-equip we wanted the Scimitar, a twin-engined Swift with longer range. We were denied this and given the Hunter with overload tanks. I have seen chaps throw up after a two-hour sortie in those, as they were affected by the turbulence.

As stated by Mike Corner, who had extensive experience on a wide range of fighter aircraft as well as being on the flying staff of the Fighter Weapons School, the system of aircraft development took too long. This, plus poor political decision-making in the early post-war years, ensured that the Swift and Hunter only entered service four years after the prototypes first flew. However, in early 1957 the British aircraft industry and the Royal Air Force were both emasculated by politicians, this time by a Conservative Government. The Prime Minister, Harold MacMillan, entrusted his Defence Minister, Duncan Sandys, with reducing costs in the British Armed Services. The result of this was a bombshell dropped in the British Parliament on Monday 1 April when Sandys, having been misled by the missile experts' promises, ruled out any further manned fighter aircraft for the Royal Air Force after the English Electric Lightning. That this policy in the end had to be changed due to failed missile projects is of little interest, as by then design and development time – and export markets – had been lost to foreign designs.

Type 552 Swift F.7

As can be seen from the previous section, the Swift FR.5 was an entirely different animal to the Swift Marks 1–4, and it was further improved on with the introduction of the Mark 7. This originated when Supermarine developed their Type 550 Swift PR.6 to replace the Meteor PR.10. The first PR.6 was XD143, which was partly constructed when in 1956 it was cancelled as part of the cutbacks to the Swift and Hunter programmes following the end of the Korean War.

The Type 550 design was a developed, unarmed F.4 that brought in long-span wings and a slab tailplane, the lengthened fuselage housing a more powerful engine, and the guns and ammunition replaced by extra fuel tanks, with one F49 and two F52 cameras mounted behind the cockpit. Tiltman

Langley Laboratories were again subcontracted in the design. Brian Buss:

In 1952, the Air Ministry placed an order for a prototype unarmed photographic reconnaissance Swift to become a long-range PR.6, Type 550. Supermarine at this time was still overextended in trying to develop the Swift as an acceptable fighter and looked to TLL to undertake this work. The Redhill-based company had by this time proved itself capable of undertaking complex design work and hence it was contracted to produce all the drawings to convert an F.4 into a PR.6. This entailed replacing the gun and ammunition bays with fuel tanks, providing pick-up points for a central long-range fuel tank and installing two long-focal-length F52 and one F49 cameras aft of the pilot. TLL even designed a system to allow the pilot to relieve himself on a long flight! All work was completed and the aircraft XD143 was within four days of its first flight when the Air Ministry cancelled the order.

Cancellation of the PR.6 came on 25 April 1956, another disappointment to Supermarine. However, the design team believed that its features could be exploited as a fighter. This became the Type 552 Swift F.7 that was submitted by Supermarine as a radar-guided interceptor. Armed with Fairey Fireflash air-to-air missiles, it was a very potent fighter with high kill capability; armed with four missiles, it had a maximum level speed of Mach 0.93 and could pull up into a reheat climb to intercept targets flying at Mach 0.85 at 47,000ft (14,500m). Reliability was also good and the aircraft's manoeuvrability satisfied the fighter pilots allotted to fly it.

The Avon chosen for the Swift F.7 was a reheated version of the RA.7 that featured a liquid-fuel starter, top-temperature controller and increased-area nozzle guide vanes, so was given a new rating of RA.21R and designated Avon Mark 116. Similar to the RA.7 family of engines, it did not embody a tubo-annular combustion chamber; its details are given in the table (*right*).

The F.7 was the first aircraft to incorporate the Fireflash guided missile, which had been developed under the code name *Blue Sky* by Fairey Aviation. Under the aircraft's original specification the armament was to be four Blue Sky missiles and four 30mm Aden cannon, though none of the F.7s built actually carried cannon. The nose was extended to accommodate radar guidance equipment. As an aid to development

Rolls-Royce RA.21R (Avon 116)

Type	axial-flow turbojet
Compressor stages	twelve
Turbine stages	two
Combustion chambers	eight
Thrust rating	
without reheat	7,110lb (3,224kg) at 7,900rpm
with reheat	9,745lb (4,420kg) at 7,900rpm

TOP: *Swift F.7 XF113 armed with Fairey Fireflash missiles at RAE Farnborough in 1956.*

ABOVE: *Swift F.7 XF114 used for guided-weapon trials.*

of the type, Swift F.4 WK279 was modified to the aerodynamic standard of the F.7 and equipped with detachable Blue Sky missile launch rails for firing tests during October 1955.

The Fireflash was a radar beam-riding missile comprised of a body housing a high-explosive warhead, proximity fuze and guidance, powered by a pair of jettisonable booster rockets. The latter fell away when exhausted, having accelerated the explosive body to a speed of around Mach 2 to reach the target, where its impact fuze would detonate. There were some problems with target acquisition in cloudy conditions, and although 300 were issued for operational training and firing, the missile never entered operational service.

Two Mark 7 prototypes, XF774 and XF780, were ordered during October 1953, and the first flight made in April 1956. A further order for seventy-five Swift F.7s numbered XF113–XF129, XF155–XF180, XF196–XF217 and XF244–XF253 were ordered on Contract 6/Acft/9757. However, in the end only twelve were built, XF113–XF124. These twelve were modified to carry Blue Sky missiles and were the first RAF aircraft to be equipped with guided missiles rather than cannon; they were delivered to No. 1 Guided Weapon Development Squadron (GWDS) at RAF Valley, the last Mark 7 to be delivered arriving there on 8 July 1957. The remainder were cancelled in two batches, on 19 March 1954 and 20 March 1956.

Initial trials with the Swift F.7 and Fairey Blue Sky/Fireflash were carried out at A&AEE Boscombe Down, followed by guided-weapons tests at No. 1 GWDS, which had been established in 1957 at RAF Valley and was a detached section of the Central Fighter Establishment at RAF West Raynham. The purpose of the unit was primarily to develop handling, testing and storage techniques and systems for the Fireflash missile. Secondly, the unit was charged with producing tactical-attack procedures if ever the missile, or developments of it, were accepted into service. Aberporth in Wales was the range head for the firing of missiles, with batteries of cameras, radars and telemetry around the harbour and surrounding countryside to record all aspects of firing.

The Commanding Officer of No. 1 GWDS was Wg Cdr J. Dalley, the Flight Commander was Sqn Ldr Bob Price, and the pilots were Flt Lts Bob Marirez, Bill Hester, Les Davies, Toby Stobart and Mike Corner. The unit was housed in a couple of hangars on a remote side of RAF Valley: visitors were discouraged by RAF Regiment guards. The unit received its first Swift in March 1957, and Fairey Aviation personnel were at hand to deal with any missile malfunction/analysis. Mike Corner records his impressions of the trials squadron:

Whilst there I logged 300 hours on the Swift F.7 and another twenty-five hours on the dear old Meteor. Until December 1958, our unit carried out trials on the beam-riding Fairey Fireflash air-to-air missile, which was the first missile handled by the Air Force. The Swift F.7 was a rebuilt F.5 with a longer nose housing Plessey/Ekco radar and wider-span wings with 'saw-tooth' leading edges. The four-gun Aden pack was removed. During our time there, housed in a couple of hangars on a corner of the airfield remote from everyone else, we carried out a lot of firing in Cardigan Bay controlled from Aberporth. We also developed a wide range of tactical exercises all the way up to 50,000ft!

However, we knew at the time that the RAF would not use Fireflash in squadron service. Our efforts were, thus, largely a waste of time, but at least highly capable, highly qualified technical experts in the fields of electronics, avionics and advanced armaments were brought together and produced an immensely valuable pool of knowledge which benefited the Service in years to come.

The major part of our flying was taken up by practising in pairs at all heights from 15,000ft to 45,000ft. We simulated a missile firing by tracking for ten seconds, booting left or right rudder and dropping a wing to simulate the firing, recovering and tracking the target Swift (at 3,000yd) for twelve seconds. All this, naturally, recorded by the camera gun. This is not as easy as it sounds, particularly if atmospheric conditions were less than perfect.

Expendable, radio-controlled target aircraft were then, as always, in very short supply; consequently we used Meteor 7s as out-of-range targets on the Aberporth range. The target Meteor flew a race-track pattern and the attacking Swift would be vectored onto the target and carry out firing at about 4 miles (at 15,000ft). The Fireflash would stall out long before it got anywhere near the Meteor, but our cameras would record everything and our stats people would tell us a few hours later if we would have had a kill. The Fireflash, incidentally, carried a flare to make it photographically visible.

Very occasionally we did fire Fireflash at radio-controlled targets on the range. Believe it or not, we had to use radio-controlled Firefly piston-engined ex-Navy aircraft which were based at Brawdy (I think – but I might be wrong). These relics flew at all of 150kt, but these were the days before the Jindivik. The Fireflash carried a fairly hefty explosive charge detonated by a direct hit or a very good Doppler/acoustic transmitter/receiver housed in the dart that would set off the warhead if the missile passed within 50ft or thereabouts.

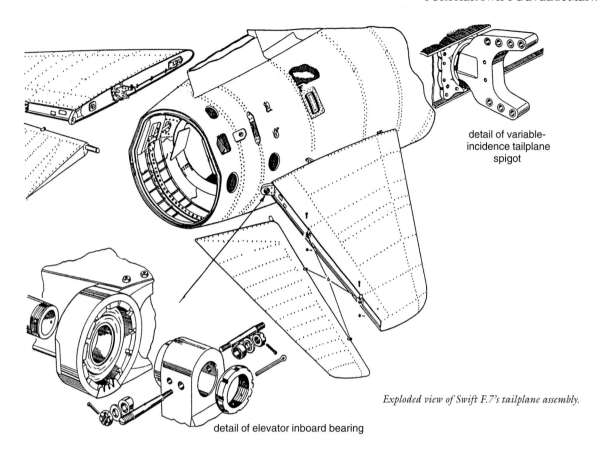

detail of variable-incidence tailplane spigot

Exploded view of Swift F.7's tailplane assembly.

detail of elevator inboard bearing

Although for its time (1957) the Fairey Fireflash proved quite effective in the air during its testing, it was not accepted for operational service due to a number of faults. It was difficult to maintain, had an unreliable proximity fuze, and it was not a 'fire and forget' weapon, the pilot having to target-track the missile with his aircraft sight.

It must be remembered that, although the Germans had been experimenting with the idea of guided air-to-air missiles (AAMs) during the final stages of the Second World War, even in the late 1950s the technology was still in its infancy. The first successful Allied AAM was the US AAM-N-7 Sidewinder, which used passive homing on infrared (IR) emissions, based on a photo-voltaic cell that reacted to a heat source. In rain and cloud, or near the ground, IR-guided missiles could go astray, and of course the attack had to be from the rear of the enemy aircraft so as to home on the heat of its exhaust. It was not until the late 1960s, with the introduction of the Sidewinder AIM-9H model,

that it had a successful fire-and-forget capability against fighter aircraft. Yet even in the Vietnam conflict in 1968, Sidewinder successes were only just above one 'kill' for every ten fired, proving that the aircraft cannon was still a necessary part of aircraft armament.

Of the Swift Mark 7 itself, its cockpit was pressurized and fitted with a fully automatic ejection seat. The controls had full-power ailerons and power-assisted elevators, with both having manual reversion facilities. A variable-incidence tailplane was provided to trim out changes of stick force with speed and was operated by twin electric motors. These were mounted as a single unit on the upper forward face of frame 31, and operated by means of a drive shaft and bevel gears and two actuators of the screw-jack type. The tailplane had a range of movement for normal flight of –6/+2 degrees, but in an emergency it could be operated from –11/+2 degrees. This was controlled by a lever on the control box for manual selection of either range.

145

After selecting by feel the tailplane angle to give zero stick force for a given flight condition, the elevator was then in a trailing position without any airload imposed on it. The tailplane control had a two-speed control on the control column handgrip for FAST or SLOW operation. The flying control system was quite conventional with the control run employing push-pull rods, cables and chains, with tension compensators in the rudder and elevator control runs in the fuselage.

The fuel was housed in six tanks, four in the fuselage and one in each wing, with a fuel recuperator incorporated in the fuselage centre tank. The front fuselage tank was flexible with a capacity of 112gal (509ltr) and was installed aft of the cockpit between frames 12 and 15. The centre tank was a rigid type housing 104gal (473ltr) and was installed in the bay between frames 15 and 19, whilst a flexible 101gal (459ltr) tank was fitted immediately aft of frame 28 and around the centrally mounted jetpipe. The port gun bay held a tank with a capacity of 35gal (159ltr) with each wing tank holding 98gal (446ltr), the whole giving an internal fuel capacity of 548gal (2,491ltr), giving the Swift F.7 a long-range capability even without external fuel tanks.

One of the annoying features of the Swift was the operation of the reheat, as described by Mike Corner:

Although Pilot's Notes for the Swift state that engine rpm could be varied to a limited degree in reheat, let me assure you that they could not! It was SOP to line up on the runway in pairs. The leader would signal 'engage reheat' and both aircraft would go through the reheat gate at the same time whilst on the brakes at full rpm. There was a delay of three seconds whilst the reheat petals opened in the tailpipe and then you were off if you released the brakes or not. I was amused to see in the Pilot's Notes that it says 'release the brakes and then go'. You really don't have a choice.

If as number two, you moved ahead of your leader, you certainly wouldn't touch the throttle. If you did, you would almost certainly cancel reheat and it would be a further three seconds before you could re-engage it – by which time your leader has disappeared and the end of the runway is rushing towards you at an alarming rate! So if you moved ahead of your leader, you gave him a little wave and got airborne some way ahead of him. Generally, reheat was cancelled upon becoming airborne and would be used to gain speed more rapidly at high altitude.

The End for the Swift

At the end of production of the Swift Mark 7 only two prototypes and twelve production aircraft had been built. Most were used by the Guided Weapons Development Squadron at RAF Valley to test-fly early guided weapons such as Fireflash. The last Swift F.7s were retired from RAF Valley to RAF Aldergrove in December 1958.

Whilst some pilots on test duties have reported that the earlier Swifts had 'solid' controls in a dive from altitude until the Mach number decreased at lower altitudes, the Mark 7 has been described by some of the pilots who flew them to be outstanding with superb longitudinal handling. Of the Swift/Fireflash combination flying, Mike Corner comments:

The Swift would transport the Fireflash missile up to 45,000ft and up around Mach 0.93. Whether we would have ever hit anything at those heights I have no idea, since to the best of my knowledge few missiles were ever fired above 15,000ft and none by the RAF. We were tasked with firings at 15,000ft against out-of-range targets (Meteor 7s) flying at Mach 0.6, or at Firefly radio-controlled targets at 150kt. Compare this to the then threat of Soviet bombers able to fly at 40–45,000ft at Mach 0.8–0.85.

With the termination of Swift production in any form, and the standardization on the Hunter in the fighter and fighter-reconnaissance roles, Supermarine were outside any RAF contract in the ever-reducing British aviation industry, which was being allowed to wither due to the action, or inaction, of inept politicians and senior members of the Royal Air Force and Air Ministry.

Brian Buss of Tiltman Langley Laboratories commenting on the termination of the Swift:

So some nine years of Swift development came to an end, as the Hunter, which had its own share of early development difficulties, was starting to overcome them. I look back and in hindsight consider that to a large extent, Supermarine was plunged into the Swift debacle through no fault of its own. The politicians in 1945 were not interested in high-speed flight, but by 1950 a new government certainly was, particularly with a new war on their hands in Korea. It pressurized Supermarine and Hawkers with lucrative incentives in the way of

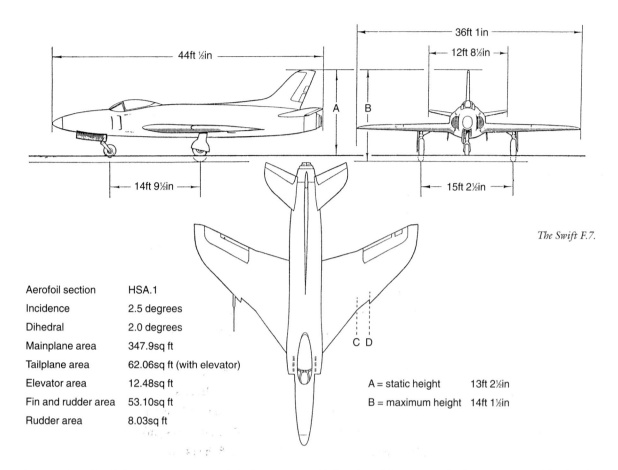

Aerofoil section	HSA.1
Incidence	2.5 degrees
Dihedral	2.0 degrees
Mainplane area	347.9sq ft
Tailplane area	62.06sq ft (with elevator)
Elevator area	12.48sq ft
Fin and rudder area	53.10sq ft
Rudder area	8.03sq ft

A = static height   13ft 2½in
B = maximum height   14ft 1½in

The Swift F.7.

large orders for fighters, to compete with those already in production in the USA and Russia. Supermarine did its utmost to make up for those lost years by using existing Attackers rather than starting from scratch as Hawkers did with the Hunter. Once Supermarine had two swept [wing] Attackers flying, there was no way it would be allowed to turn back and research just what was involved in creating a high-speed aircraft that could fly safely through the transonic region. Whether it liked it or not, it was forced to press on with the disastrous consequences we all know about.

I wonder how much longer it would have taken the UK and perhaps Hawkers, to understand how to overcome the difficulties of transonic and then supersonic flight if we had not had the Swift?

The Swift's problems stemmed back to failures in the form of a post-war socialist government not interested in RAF re-equipment with modern fighters and failure to carry out further high-speed research at RAE Farnborough and the A&AEE.

Following this, too much time was wasted in developing the Swift's true potential with an all-flying tail, datum-shift trimming, machined skins and an increased wingspan. All this should have been foreseen years before, but too many vital years had been wasted, mainly before the Korean War.

Of the total number of 499 Supermarine Types 510–552 ordered, only 177 were actually built. Swift production figures were: two prototypes, two pre-production F.1s, eighteen production F.1s, sixteen production F.2s, twenty-five production F.3s, ten production F.4s, ninety-five production FR.5s and fourteen production F.7s. (Some aircraft originally built as one Mark were later upgraded to a higher Mark, which is why the Mark-by-Mark breakdown comes to more than 177 aircraft.)

Conclusion

The main use of the Swift F.7 was its employment at the Guided Weapons Development Squadron, which in hindsight appears a total waste of an

147

Data comparison – Swift F.7 and Hunter F.6

	Swift F.7	*Hunter F.6*
Wingspan	36ft 1in (11m)	33ft 8in (10.26m)
Wing area	347.9sq ft (32.32sq m)	340sq ft (31.59sq m)
Aerofoil section	HSA.1	Hawker H.S
Sweepback angle	40 degrees	39.9 degrees
Incidence	2.5 degrees	1.5 degrees
Dihedral	2.0 degrees	–1.0 degrees
Flap area	31.2sq ft (2.9sq m)	31.2sq ft (2.9sq m)
Length	44ft ½in (13.42m)	45ft 10½in (13.98m)
Tailplane		
aerofoil	HSA.1	Hawker symmetric
span	12ft 8½in (3.87m)	N/A
area with elevator	62.06sq ft (5.77sq m)	53.9sq ft (5.01sq m)
dihedral	10 degrees	nil
incidence	variable +2 to –11	variable
sweepback angle	40 degrees	41.9 degrees
Fin and rudder area	53.10sq ft (4.93sq m)	35sq ft (3.25sq m)
Rudder area	8.03sq ft (0.75sq m)	6.1sq ft (0.57sq m)
Undercarriage track	15ft 2½in (4.64m)	14ft 9in (4.5m)
Weights		
empty	N/K	12,760lb (5,790kg)
tare	13,735lb (6.229kg)	14,122lb (6,405kg)
loaded	21,400lb (9,700kg)	17,760lb (8,050kg)
Engine	Avon RA.7/116	Avon 200
Internal fuel capacity	548gal (2,491ltr)	392gal (1,782ltr)
Maximum speed		
at sea level	700mph (1,130km/h)	710mph (1,140km/h)
at 36,000ft (11,000m)	N/K	630mph (1,010km/h)
Initial rate of climb	14,000ft/min (4,300m/min)	8,400ft/min (2,560m/min)
Service ceiling	49,600ft (15,100m)	51,500ft (15,700m)

aircraft with potential as an air-defence fighter with high rate of climb to altitude. As opposed to that, it was not designed for maintenance, and aircraft like the F-86 Sabre were already in service with better flight characteristics and handling.

The Fireflash had a number of perceived faults and further development was cancelled, but its handling and trials did help in the assessment and information for future missile systems.

9

Final Developments

Designs and Development

The Swift was Supermarine's final true fighter design to go into squadron service but, as related in previous chapters, it was replaced by the Hawker Hunter, and the last marks of Swifts were used in the low-level fighter-reconnaissance role, where their strong structure made them superb. The Swift was followed by a number of experimental and development aircraft that ended with the Type 544 Scimitar.

One of the aircraft that followed the Swift was the Type 545, which was the ultimate development using the experience gained with the Swifts. It was designed against specification F.105D2 and competed against the Hawker P.1083. The Type 545 was of more advanced design than the Swift and used an area-ruled ('Coke bottle') fuselage shape. It had a nose intake with a centre-body that fed a 9,500lb (4,300kg) thrust Rolls-Royce Avon RA.14, which with reheat could give 14,500lb (6,600kg). The mainplane was of crescent shape in planform, employing compound sweepback on the thicker inboard wing section and 30-degree sweepback on the outer section. The tail unit was similar to the Swift's, though the fin had a gently curved leading edge. Supermarine secured a contract in February 1952 with two prototypes ordered, XA181 and XA186. However, the Hawker P.1083 was cancelled in July 1953 and, with the first prototype well under construction, the Type 545 project was also cancelled in early 1955. The reason for the cancellations was the appearance of the twin-engined English Electric P.1, which was offering a much higher performance in its development into the Lightning.

The development of what was to become the Type 544 Scimitar started with the Type 505. Obviously, in the correct sequence the Type 505 would have been covered earlier in the text, but it was a purely experimental design that evolved in 1945 not as a fighter aircraft but as a project for an aircraft without an undercarriage, intended to be catapulted off aircraft carriers, landing back on using a flexible 'carpet' in conjunction with arrester wires. This had originated in a proposal put forward in 1943, and was followed up in 1945 by developments at the Naval Aircraft Department of RAE Farnborough. With this, the first landings were carried out at RAE Farnborough using a Vampire fighter without an undercarriage, flown on test by Lt Cdr E. Brown of the Fleet Air Arm.

Swept wings were considered for the Type 505, but as the Supermarine design team, like others, knew little about swept wings and their problems, it was decided to design the Type 505 with tapered wings, having a symmetrical section that was constant over the whole wingspan.

Without the need to accommodate an undercarriage the Type 505 was given a relatively thin wing of 7 per cent thickness/chord ratio and a wing area of 270sq ft (25.08sq m), and to reduce tail drag and interference an all-flying butterfly tail was incorporated that used differential elevator movement to give both directional control and pitch control. The experiment was hardly a success and wasted two years getting nowhere until the Admiralty changed track and abandoned the Type 505 project, so the design was modified by Supermarine to emerge as the Type 508 with a conventional nose-wheel undercarriage. As with the Type 505, the Type 508 was designed with a view to naval procurement, and was in response to Admiralty specification N.9/47, which called for a high-speed fighter aircraft powered by twin Avons and suitable for aircraft carrier operation. Supermarine's response to this was an experimental aircraft with thin-section mainplanes without sweepback, and with a butterfly tail.

Resulting from what can only be termed as a lack of knowledge by Supermarine of swept wings, this decision to stay with the straight, tapered wing was a negative factor in the type's development and certainly inhibited the design. On the Type 508 the wing thickness/chord ratio was increased to 9 per cent to reduce landing speed and to accommodate the undercarriage, with the wing area increased to 370sq ft (34.37sq m).

The major difference from the Type 505 were the main wing spars, which were now run under the engines to provide undercarriage anchorage points, which in practice meant the engines were installed on the floor. To improve the type's flight handling during carrier landings, leading edge droop was incorporated. This operated automatically with the lowering of a certain amount of landing flap, and the ailerons also moved to the droop position.

Three prototypes were ordered, the first being VX133 which made its maiden flight on 31 August 1951 from Boscombe Down, after being transported there by road. The first two prototypes were each powered by a pair of Rolls-Royce Avon RA.7 engines, each delivering 6,500lb (2,950kg) thrust. As VX133 was able to fly off the necessary qualifying hours early enough, it made its appearance at the 1951 SBAC Farnborough Air Display. There, its configuration raised interest, but not its flying display, which had to be restrained due to its prototype status. Initially the controls were not power-operated, but after a number of incidents (as opposed to accidents!) it was ascertained that the cause of violent airframe vibration was aileron flutter, and this was solved by powered controls being incorporated in the design.

To follow the Type 508 came the Type 529 with serial number VX136. This was based on the Type 508, but sufficiently modified that it was allocated the new type number; it made its first flight on 29 August 1952. It differed very little, both technically and in appearance, from the Type 508, but it had certain cleaned-up features and extended strakes forward at the tailplane root to fuselage join-line; four 30mm Aden cannon were also installed. VX136 was sent on carrier trials, but not in operational condition, and it was not planned to put the type into production, although its take-off from the aircraft carrier was excellent. The Type 529 was despatched to the Royal Navy test unit at Bedford for Fleet Air Arm type testing on 15 April 1953, but during the trials there it suffered a forced landing that required repairs being carried out. Following this it started catapulting trials before being returned to Supermarine at Chilbolton for further test flying. The test flying showed that the 529, like the 508, suffered the usual jet fighter bugbear – snaking – and both aircraft had a low Mach number limit.

The final outcome of the test flying with the Types 508 and 529 was the first flight of the Type 525 on 28 April 1954. This new aircraft was serial numbered VX138 and was again an experimental twin-Avon, carrier-borne fighter design, but this time with sweepback on the mainplanes, and conventional cruciform tail surfaces. The Type 525 was the final development aircraft produced to draft specification N.113D, and would be developed through the Type 544 to the Scimitar.

Supermarine Type 508 VX133 with undercarriage and flaps down, carrying out a deck landing.

ABOVE: *Supermarine Type 529 VX136 at RAE Farnborough in 1952.*

RIGHT: *Supermarine Type 529 VX136 with wings folded at RAE Farnborough (note flying control in background).*

Experimental work at RAE Farnborough and other establishments into aerofoil design determined that the mainplane boundary layer could be controlled, by either suction or blowing of air through slots or orifices in the mainplane surface, thus maintaining the flow energy and delaying the airflow breakaway. In the case of the Type 525, flap blowing was introduced to help the control of the boundary layer and so improve control and stability. This was basically an arrangement that projected a thin, high-pressure jet of air, bled from the engine compressor, along the trailing edge of the wing just ahead of the flap hinge. The basis of this flap blowing was the Coanda effect, which on the Types 525 and 544 bent the thin jet of high-pressure air from a narrow slot along the wing trailing edge, to follow the contour of the flap and so prevent the breakaway of the boundary layer. This reduced the approach speed by a reported 18mph (29km/h) as well as lowering the stalling speed. With the smoother airflow wake, there was stable air over the trailing edges, which resulted in better control and stability at low approach speeds. Unfortunately, VX138 was lost in a fatal crash on 5 July following an uncontrolled spin.

Development into the Scimitar

The follow-on to the Type 525 was the Type 544 Scimitar, which was originally visualized and designed as a single-seat naval fighter, but due to changing operational requirements was then required as a supersonic interceptor fighter, tactical nuclear bomber and reconnaissance fighter – jack of all trades and master of none!

With the redesign of the airframe into the Type 544, specification N.113P had been issued, which resulted in the airframe nose being lengthened and 'area rule' applied to the fuselage cross-section, with a slim dorsal spine that ran half the fuselage length and blended into the fin. The appearance of a rather bulky mid-section fuselage, housing two Rolls-Royce Avon engines, was offset by the beautifully blended contours. Blown flaps, having been proven satisfactory by the Type 525, were incorporated as standard on the Type 544 design, the system being operated by high pressure air bled from the Avons' compressors. This was very effective, for it delayed the onset of turbulence over the mainplane at low speeds and high angles of attack, as occurs on the landing approach to the carrier and during catapult launches.

The first Type 544 was WT854, which made its maiden flight on 20 January 1956 from Boscombe Down flown by Mike Lithgow. This aircraft had a number of novel features for the time: the blown flaps, Fairey power-operated flying controls, double slotted flaps, lift spoilers and air brakes (the latter similar to the Attacker's), as well as a dive-recovery flap and leading edge slats. The use of power-operated

Type 544 Scimitar XD212 in climbing flight. D. WELLS

controls on the Scimitar brought with it a number of further problems, for stability at the high speeds being flown at the time had become a problem for pilots worldwide, and 'pitch-up' and 'pitch-down' were familiar words in test pilot's reports. In the case of WT854, the rate of roll was very high at moderate Mach numbers, and with the original Fairey powered controls it was found that the ailerons were over-sensitive and required fine tuning to achieve acceptable handling. Modifications were then made to the control system by introducing supplementary hydraulic jacks along with differential gearing to produce a fine control accuracy.

After a series of simulated deck landings at RAE Bedford, initial deck landing trials were flown from HMS *Ark Royal* during April 1956, followed by more comprehensive trials later with the third prototype. This resulted in a presentation of the Scimitar to senior Naval and Ministry personnel at Lee-on-Solent in November 1957 when, among other technical details, it was stated that the Scimitar had carried out 148 deck landings and catapult launches. At this point the recommended approach speed was 124kt (231km/h) at a landing weight of 28,000lb (12,700kg) using 'flap blowing', but with flap blowing the aircraft's attitude on the approach was nose high, so this was reduced to improve the pilot's line of sight.

Unfortunately, in spite of its swept aerofoil surfaces and high power (at that time it was the most powerful swept-wing fighter) the Scimitar could not go supersonic in straight and level flight, and could only just exceed the speed of sound in a dive. Like many other aircraft of this period it initially experienced 'pitch-up' at high altitude and high Mach numbers, and effective control at high speeds were problems that Supermarine (as well as other designers) were having to investigate, along with similar research at RAE Farnborough. Eventually the Scimitar's wing was re-designed with a notched leading edge, boundary-layer fences and Kuchemann-type wing tips. The greatest improvement, however, came with the inverting of the whole tail unit, with the 10-degree dihedral being changed to 10-degree anhedral – shades of the McDonnell-Douglas Phantom!

The armament included four 30mm Aden cannon installed below the engine air intakes, plus Sidewinder air-to-air missiles and the possible carriage of a nuclear bomb. To emphasize its strike ability, the Type 544 was equipped with a nose probe for in-flight refuelling.

The initial contract was expected to be for well over 100 aircraft, but in fact only 100 were ordered, thanks to the previously mentioned Duncan Sandys edict, and later on twenty-four of these were cancelled. The role of multi-mission naval fighter was later assumed by the Rolls-Royce Spey-powered version of the McDonnell-Douglas Phantom, which was introduced in 1968 and was really supersonic, with a top speed of Mach 2.1. However, at the date of the Scimitar's introduction into service, it was certainly faster than any Fleet Air Arm aircraft in service or any that had preceded it. The production run covered the airframe serial numbers XD212–XD250, XD264–XD282, and XD316–XD333.

The Scimitar was a huge advance on the aircraft then in use, in weight, speed and complexity. The first production example was XD212 and made its maiden flight on 11 January 1957, following which it carried out its acceptance trials at A&AEE Boscombe

Specification – Supermarine Scimitar Mark 1

Wingspan	37ft 2in (11.43m)
Wing area	484.9sq ft (45.05sq m)
Length	55ft 3in (16.85m)
Height	17ft 4in (5.28m)
Mainplane sweepback	45 degrees at 25 per cent chord
Weights	
Empty	23,962lb (10,869kg)
AUW at take-off	34,200lb (15,500kg)
Maximum speed	
At sea level	Mach 0.968
At 30,000ft (9,000m)	587kt (1,088km/h)
Rate of climb	6.65min to 45,000ft (13,700m)
Service ceiling	46,000ft (14,000m)
Range	1,422 miles at 35,000ft (2,288km at 11,000m)
Engines	two 11,250lb (5,100kg) s.t. Rolls-Royce Avon 202
Armament	four 30mm Aden cannon plus missiles or bombs

Scimitar XD219 of FAA 617 Flight. The pilot's head and the hood proportions give an idea of the size of the aircraft. MAP

Down and on HMS *Ark Royal*. It later shared development flying with a number of other Scimitars, the development of which now angled the aircraft's operational role as a missile- or bomb-carrier. In production form the Scimitar, with its substantial fuel tankage, could also act as a buddy-buddy refueller with a good radius of action, or as a tactical bomber with a speed on the 'deck' of about 630kt (1,170km/h), with a reported speed of 622kt (1,160km/h) at 10,000ft (3,000m). However, the fact that the Scimitar could not go supersonic did raise gibes about an 'over-powered brick', and other such comments.

The first Scimitars were designated for intensive flying trials and arrived at No.700X Trials Flight at Ford in August 1957, after which, following certain recommendations and modifications to the aircraft, a number of FAA pilots were trained at Boscombe Down. The Scimitar then joined its first operational Fleet Air Arm unit, No.803 Squadron at Lossiemouth, which had been formed in June 1958. Following this the Scimitar formed the equipment of three more operational units, Nos 800, 804 and 897 Squadrons, with aircraft also in use at Nos 764B and 771 Training Squadrons, and at 776 FRU at Hurn. Scimitar squadrons operated from the aircraft carriers *Ark Royal*, *Centaur*, *Eagle* and *Hermes*.

In service use the Scimitar showed no outstanding ability nor any major failures, but what tasks it carried out it carried out successfully – and noisily! The acoustic waves set up by the engine noise initially caused cracking of panels in the rear fuselage structure that required modification. Apart from these cracking panels it certainly operated efficiently, and furthermore was not in the 'dangerous to fly' category, though it was already obsolescent in comparison with aircraft entering service with the US Navy.

The Scimitar was used in the low-level strike role with bombs and/or rockets, and as such it performed successfully, no doubt mainly due to the fact that its wing technology made it a comfortable aircraft to fly, with full control of speed, manoeuvre and rate of descent on landing, thus giving its pilots confidence in its handling. Whether the design could have been re-engined with more powerful engines such as the Spey, is open to debate, for Royal Navy/FAA policy had changed, and so had the government, with a change of emphasis toward two-seat naval fighters and bombers. The Scimitar was replaced later in the 1960s by the Buccaneer, though it remained in service for a few more years as an in-flight refuelling tanker. It also found use as a weapons trials aircraft.

The Scimitar, although not strictly in the fighter line, has been included in this work for it was to be the last of Supermarine's production designs. Soon after the Scimitar appeared, Supermarine was one of the companies and groups that were amalgamated, under government pressure, into two major companies and then into British Aerospace (BAe). The end of an era and the end of a famous company name.

Abbreviations

A&AEE	Armament & Aeroplane Experimental Establishment		IFF	Identification Friend or Foe (interrogation radio)
AC	alternating current (electricity)		IMN	indicated Mach number
ADDL	airfield dummy deck landings		ITP	instruction to proceed (Ministry to manufacturer)
AFDU	Air Fighting Development Unit		JPT	jet pipe temperature
'all down'	flaps and undercarriage in down positions		LF	fighter with low altitude capability
AOC	Air Officer Commanding		LH	left-hand
AUW	all up weight		LOX	liquid oxygen
BAe	British Aerospace		Lt	Lieutenant
'beading'	application of bias on control surfaces		Lt Cdr	Lieutenant Commander
			Mach number	air speed in relation to speed of sound
BER	beyond economic repair			
bhp	brake horse power		MAP	Ministry of Aircraft Production
blower	general name for supercharger		MS	medium-speed supercharger gear
bmep	brake mean effective pressure		NAA	North American Aviation
boost	pressure leaving the supercharger in psi		NACA	National Advisory Committee for Aeronautics
CA Release	Control Aircraft Release		NASA	National Aeronautics and Space Agency
CG	centre of gravity (CofG)			
CO	commanding officer		NATO	North Atlantic Treaty Organization
DC	direct current (electricity)			
DH	de Havilland		nm	nautical miles
DOR	Directorate of Operational Requirements		NPL	National Physics Laboratory
			OAT	outside air temperature
dor	direction of rotation		OC	Officer Commanding
DTD	Director (or Directorate) of Technical Development		PR	photographic reconnaissance
			psi	pounds per square inch (pressure)
FAA	Fleet Air Arm			
Flt Lt	Flight Lieutenant		PV	private venture design
fps	feet per second		RAE	Royal Aircraft Establishment
FS	full speed supercharger		RATO	rocket assisted take off
FTH	full throttle height		reheat	burning neat fuel in the exhaust (after-burner)
Fw	Focke Wulf			
HE igniter	high energy igniter		RH	right-hand
HF	fighter with high altitude capability		RN	Royal Navy
hp	horsepower		RNAS	Royal Naval Air Station
HT	high tension		RP	rocket projectile
HTP	High Test peroxide (H_2O_2) (rocket fuel)		rpm	revolutions per minute
			RSA	Royal Small Arms (Royal Ordnance, Enfield)
IAS	indicated air speed			

ABBREVIATIONS

SBAC	Society of British Aircraft Constructors	TAS	true air speed
		t/c	thickness/chord ratio
Sqn Ldr	Squadron Leader	u/s	unserviceable
SIS	Secret Intelligence Service	USAF	United States Air Force
SOP	standard operating procedure	VI	variable incidence
ST	static thrust	Wg Cdr	Wing Commander
TAF	Tactical Air Force	w/m	weak mixture (air-fuel ratio)

Bibliography

This book is mainly based on reports from A&AEE, RAE Farnborough, the Public Record Office and HMSO Air Publications. For readers wishing to further their knowledge or reading about Supermarine aircraft and Rolls-Royce engines, the following books and articles are recommended.

The Aeroplane, 'Developing a Naval Jet Fighter', 12 June 1953

Banks, F.R., *I Kept no Diary* (Airlife, 1978)

Bingham, V., *Merlin Power* (Airlife, 1998)

Bingham, V., *Major Piston Aero Engines of World War II* (Airlife, 1999)

Birtles, P., *Supermarine Attacker, Swift & Scimitar* (Ian Allan, 1992)

Brown, D., *The Seafire* (Greenhill, 1989)

Goulding, J., *Interceptor: Royal Air Force Multi-gun Single-seat Fighters* (Ian Allen, 1986)

Harker, R., *Rolls-Royce from the Wings* (Oxford Press, 1976)

Harvey-Bailey, A., *The Merlin in perspective. The Combat years* (Rolls-Royce Heritage Trust, 1981)

Henshaw, A., *Sigh for a Merlin* (John Murray, 2003)

Hooker, Sir H., *Not much of an Engineer* (Airlife, 1984)

Lloyd, I., *Rolls-Royce, Merlin at War* (MacMillan, 1978)

Mason, F.K., *The British Fighter Since 1912* (Putnam, 1992)

Moyes, P.J., *Supermarine Spitfire I & II* (Profile, 1971)

Price, A., *The Spitfire Story* (Arms & Armour, 1982)

Price, A., *Spitfire, a Documentary History* (Jane's, 1979)

Price, A., *The Spitfire at War* (Ian Allan, 1985)

Quill, J., *Spitfire, A Test Pilot's Story* (Crecy, 1998)

Quill, J., *Birth of a Legend, the Spitfire* (Quiller Press, 1986)

Rendall, I., *Splash One* (Weidenfeld & Nicolson, 1998)

Rubbra, A., *Rolls-Royce Piston Aero Engines* (Rolls-Royce Heritage Trust, 1990)

Schlaifer, R. and Heron, S., *Development of Aircraft Engines* (Harvard Press, 1950)

Vickers-Armstrongs, *High Performance Aircraft* (Vickers-Armstrongs)

Walpole, Group Captain N., *Swift Justice* (Astonbridge Publishing, 2000)

White, G., *Allied Aircraft Piston Engines of World War II* (Airlife, 1995)

Wilkinson, P.H., *Aircraft Engines of the World 1946–51* (Wilkinson)

Reports

R&M 1683 Matthews, F., 'Cooling of aircraft engines', HMSO

R&M 2222 'Research on high-speed aerodynamics at RAE during 1942–45', HMSO

Air Publications

AP 1565A to R, 'Spitfire Mk I to XIII', HMSO

AP 2816A to C, 'Spitfire Mk 22 and 24', HMSO

AP 4302A to B, 'Attacker', HMSO

AP 4348A to G, 'Swift Mk I to 7', HMSO

Index